The Life Of A Soldier

Euell White

© Euell White 2008
All Rights Reserved

Cover © Euell White 2008

ISBN 978-0-615-26146-1

Acknowledgements

To my wife, whom I love with all my heart, and who has been my companion for more than fifty years, I owe my gratitude for being the stability in our home during my frequent absences during my army career. No matter what hard times I had to endure, knowing that she was faithfully awaiting my return brought me immeasurable comfort.

I owe my thanks to Dr. Hollis Todd, my classmate in elementary and junior high school several decades ago, who gave me invaluable encouragement and assistance in organizing this book after reading the draft.

To my dear friend, Dr. David Keyser whom I met in Kenya over twenty years ago, I also owe my thanks. With his expertise in Publishing On Demand and on the computer, he worked with me for many hours, preparing the book for publishing.

Foreword

Euell White is a remarkable man--with a deep spiritual faith--who cares deeply for his family and his country: That care and devotion never waned throughout his years of service. He was an impressive soldier and an incredible warrior in Vietnam while serving his country in the United States Army.

He got his start in rural Lauderdale County, in north Alabama, near Rogersville. I became acquainted with him, in the Rogersville Elementary School, in the early 1940s. Almost immediately, I recognized that he was one of the best and brightest students in my class. But I lost track of him when he left Junior high school and didn't become reacquainted with him until a high school reunion at Rogersville High School in 2002—our 50th reunion. We have corresponded—either by mail or e-mail--for much of the time since that reunion.

I wasn't surprised by Euell's successful climb in the Army from private to Sergeant First Class and then to be given a direct appointment to second lieutenant; Subsequently rising in the ranks to become a major more than three years before his retirement with 21 years service, half of it as an enlisted man.

The narrative, in this book, will give the reader a "look" at a remarkable man as the Army trains him and you'll get some pretty good glimpses of him with his family and his church family at various locations over time.

Much of the narrative logs his battles. It also relates his battle wounds; especially the one that almost led to his demise. His subsequent rescue on the battlefield, hospitalization, and recovery can only be seen as miraculous. He relates some other poignant accounts of fellow soldiers and good friends that didn't survive as well.

For those who served in Vietnam and were acquainted with NCOs and officers there and other locations--as you trained--in route to Vietnam, you'll find a connection with this soldier and maybe you have actually crossed paths on an occasion.

You'll also find some of his frustrations and "his trials" with some fellow soldiers and officers, but his service was that of a consummate professional even under some adverse circumstances at times.

Euell became proficient in the Vietnamese language that served him well in "working" together with the Vietnamese officers and troops in relating to the them and their culture as he often directed/coordinated battle plans and attacks on the enemy or led the companies or battalions against enemy assaults.

His being conversant with the Vietnamese and understanding their culture made Euell respect and appreciate them—and led them to appreciate and respect him. This respect precluded him from engaging in the rather typical racial language of bigotry so common both in Korea and Vietnam. He had the heart of a soldier who was endeavoring to serve his country and was also in Vietnam to help them defeat the enemy—Viet Cong and the North Vietnamese army to preserve their country.

He and his comrades in arms were so disappointed and discouraged by the enemies of the war back in the states who led to defeat in the halls of congress as the funding for the war was cut-off. He could have come out of Vietnam a very embittered man, but he didn't. He and all responsible Americans were "heart-sick" at the slaughter of millions of people in Vietnam and Cambodia after the congress surrendered to the enemy. The American soldiers and their families felt "heartbreak" too because of the egregious action by the congress that made all the sacrifices in Vietnam futile, and that must not be repeated.

Euell White, the warrior, was awarded many medals for his superb army service on the battlefield—including the Purple Heart Medal with one oak leaf cluster; The Bronze Star Medal with "V" device and three oak leaf clusters. He was also awarded The Combat Infantryman's Badge; The Master Parachutist Badge; and the Parachutist Badges of the Republics of China, Korea and Vietnam.

In "The Life of a Soldier" Euell captures--up close and personal--the essence of what a combat soldier is all about that will be an interesting read for combatants or non-combatants who have served. It is also a good read, for those who were never in an armed service, because the narrative and logs offer one some keen insights in one soldier's life--to borrow an apt phrase--who's "been there and done that."

Hollis E. Todd, Ph.D.
Retired, Professor of Sociology,
Lipscomb University
Specialist 3, US Army, Korea, 1956-57

A Leader is a *Person* that people will follow to a "*Place*" they wouldn't have gone to otherwise! Throughout his entire life, Euell has proven to be a true Leader whether in times of war or peace, but especially by serving as an exemplary role model for the many lives he has touched.

As a very young boy, my parents took my brothers and me to visit my Uncle Euell and Aunt Euna at Fort Campbell, Kentucky. Little did I know what a life altering experience that trip would have on a *floundering* High School student many years later. My decision to follow in Euell's footsteps by joining the Army is the single most pivotal event in my life which took me to "*Places*" I wouldn't have gone to otherwise.

Randy L White
President and CEO of PGT Industries (Retired)
Former Member of the 20th Special Forces Group Airborne

Contents

Chapter   Page

1.   Introduction..11

2.   First Enlistment- July 1951-June 1954..............15

3.   Second Enlistment-August 1954-May 1960.......51

4.   Third Enlistment- May 1960-April 1962...........87

5.   First Infantry Division-April 1962-April 1964.....99

6.   First Special Forces Okinawa 1964-967.............115

7.   Stateside 1967..131

8.   Vietnam 1967-68..137

9.   Stateside 1969-70...215

10.   Vietnam 1971 (101st Airmobile)....................227

11.   Final Assignment, Retirement and Afterward...269

Contents

Appendix	Page
A. Tragic Accidents	276
B. Unforgettable Characters	284
C. Unusual and Interesting Assignments	302
D. Guerilla Warfare Exercises	317
E. Vietnam 1965	358
F. Significant Battles, Vietnam 1967-68	390

Euell White

Sources

The sources for the information, incidents, characters and events in this book are my journals, letters and memory. The journals and letters are accurate. The memory is not always perfect.

I want to stress that what is written here from my memories is as accurate as I could make it. Others involved may remember incidents differently. Any misrepresentation is unintentional.

Euell White

The Life Of A Soldier

1.
Introduction

I was born during the great depression, to Thomas Thornton White and Sarah Nannie (Jackson) White, the youngest of ten children born by my mother, five boys and five girls, but one of each gender died in infancy.

Keith Nolan published a book in 1988 titled *Into Laos*, based on an operation in 1971 in which my battalion participated. Nolan described me in the book as "a mustang, the eighth child of a poor Alabama family." The term "mustang" is used mostly by the navy to describe an officer who was commissioned from the ranks. When I read the part about being from a poor family, however, I was momentarily shocked. I knew that I didn't use the word "poor" during our interviews, but Nolan came to that conclusion from my description of my childhood.

I never thought of my family as poor, although our living conditions were primitive by today's standards. I was born the day after Christmas in 1933, during the depression at the "bend of the river" West of Florence, Alabama. I was about five years old when the lines for electricity came to our neighborhood on a rural route of Rogersville, Alabama. A few years later my dad bought a refrigerator, which for a time became a curiosity for the neighborhood. Before the refrigerator, we cooled our milk by letting it down into the well in the bucket we used to draw water. And, of course, our source for the milk was the cows.

Euell White

We always had food and shelter, and most important, parents that were present and who loved us— and taught us according to Biblical principles how to live our lives. The concept of breaking up a home through divorce was unheard of and unimaginable.

Both at home and in school we were taught to love our country. Contrary to what many from other regions of the nation believe, we were not taught to honor the confederate flag over the United States flag. In fact, I don't remember ever seeing a confederate flag during my childhood. At school we were taught that George Washington, the father of our country, and Abraham Lincoln, the emancipator of the slaves, were both great men. At school, we regularly pledged our allegiance to the flag of the United States of America and to the Republic for which it stands. We also had Bible reading and prayers at school during the weekly assemblies.

My Dad was a carpenter during the years I remember, though he had worked as a blacksmith and farmer. One of his older brothers who died in 1952 was a blacksmith all his life and as far as I know his was the last shop in East Lauderdale County.

Although Dad made his living as a carpenter, he knew a lot about farming and owned land to keep us kids busy. He worked for the Tennessee Valley Authority for most of my years at home. Dad worked on all of the Tennessee River dams from Watts Bar Tennessee to Picwic Tennessee, including Guntersville, Wheeler and Wilson dams in Alabama.

My mother died less than two months after my 13th birthday and her 52nd after suffering a stroke. The pain that I experienced at her death is indescribable. At that time I

The Life Of A Soldier

felt that the only person in the world that I knew for sure loved me unconditionally was taken from me.

A few days before my 15th birthday, My dad married a woman who had never been married before and had no desire to be bothered with children. I lived with them for awhile, but she made it clear I Was not welcome. I left home and lived with my sisters some of the time and in boarding houses some of the time until I enlisted in the army at age 17.

When I look back on it, my displacement from home at such an early age, although painful at the time, had a positive result. I was forced to grow up early and learned to take responsibility for myself. This was also a benefit to me when I became a soldier. In my 21 years of military service I didn't have one blot on my records. I was never punished , and never missed a day of duty except when injured in the line of duty or wounded in combat.

Euell White

The Life Of A Soldier

2.
First Enlistment
July 1951-June 1954

I enlisted in the army at age 17 on 17 July 1951, during the so-called Korean conflict. I had decided that I wanted to be a paratrooper and enlisted specifically for Airborne. I had a shallow understanding of the role of paratroopers in the Army. I had seen movies and comic books that portrayed paratroopers descending from the sky with sub-machine guns blazing.

The recruiting office in Florence was in the post office. The Recruiting Sergeant put me on a bus for the main recruiting station at Gadsden, Alabama early on 16 July. Before we left the post office for the bus station my brother Almon, a World War II veteran, arrived. He gave me some money and he had tears in his eyes

In Gadsden, they put me in a hotel that had army cots stacked two high. The next day, 17 July, we were sworn in and given our aptitude tests. I had no idea at the time just how significant were these tests. Although I hadn't completed the 9th grade, my scores were high enough to give me an advantage as an enlisted soldier, and contributed to my qualifying for a direct commission ten years later

There were a lot of 17-year-olds in that hotel, and some of them cried for their mothers that night. I am sure that had they realized they were not yet in the army and they could turn back and go home to their mothers, some of them would have.

Euell White

In the late afternoon of 17 July, a Sergeant took a van load of us to the train depot. He told us we were going to Fort Jackson, South Carolina. I objected because I knew that the Airborne (Jump) School was at Fort Benning, Georgia. I was skeptical when the Sergeant explained that one had to be trained in some branch of the Army (in my case, the Infantry) before becoming a paratrooper.

At Fort Jackson I was assigned to Company "F" 61st Infantry Regiment of the 8th Infantry division for sixteen weeks of infantry training. The training was physically demanding but I had no problems. Back then we didn't have "Drill Sergeants" with the Smokey Bear hats. This tradition was later copied from the Marine Corps. I am not critical of this. I have a list of other things the Army would do well to copy from the Marines, one of them being separate training for women.

Instead of Drill Sergeants we had what was called "Cadre." They were noncommissioned officers and they wore helmet liners with the division insignia painted on them. The Cadre Platoon Sergeant for my platoon was Sergeant Davis. He was a combat veteran of the Korean War that was in progress at that time. I never once heard Sergeant Davis curse and never saw him do anything to humiliate or degrade a trainee. I don't know if Sergeant Davis was the rule or the exception to the rule, but I have always respected him. I don't agree with using humiliation and degradation as training tools. Training can be made tough and demanding without humiliation and degradation. It is contradictory to say we lead by example then set an example of degrading and humiliating subordinates.

The Life Of A Soldier

Racial integration was a settled fact at Fort Jackson in 1951. As I grew up in Alabama, racial segregation was a fact of life. It was not an "issue" that we discussed, but simply a fact of life. I can't remember any direct teaching that the "Colored People," which was considered the respectful term in those days, were inferior, but it was taught by example and by answering questions. We had no close neighbors that were black out in the country where we lived, therefore I was not often confronted with any requirement to practice discrimination.

The use of the "N" word was not uncommon. My Dad used it as though it were acceptable, yet we were cautioned that the respectful term was "colored." It was a confusing message that it would be disrespectful to use the "N" word in the presence of a black person, but it was all right to refer to them that way out of their hearing.

One day when I was five years old, I was riding with my dad in our old Model A Ford, returning from Elgin Crossroads to our home on what we called the Red Lane. An elderly black man they called "Uncle Mack Ingram" was walking and my dad offered him a ride. At this time I had never ridden a bus and didn't know what the rules were. I had been taught to be respectful of older people and that included giving them the front seat. As I started to get out for "Uncle Mack" to get in the front, he laughed and told me he was supposed to sit on the back seat. Then as we rode along, he talked to me, and laughingly told me that he and I were kinfolks. I was puzzled by this and he mentioned that some of his ancestors worked for some of mine. I don't remember whether he used the word "slave" but I think now that is what he meant. A family history that I recently read tells that one of my Great Grandfathers owned slaves.

After we let Uncle Mack out at his destination I asked my dad why he wouldn't ride in the front seat, and his reply was, in effect, that it was appropriate for "Colored Folks" to ride in the back. Years later when I rode the city buses in Florence, I saw black people standing in the back with plenty of empty seats forward of the line that distinguished the front from the back.

When I was 16 I had an accident one night on Highway 72 with a black man. It was entirely my fault because I started to turn and didn't see him. I sideswiped his car. The car had a New York plate. I told him that if he would send me a bill I would pay for the damage to his car. I gave him my name and address and he gave me his business card. He worked for one of the soft drink bottling companies. Later I told some family members about the incident and one family member scolded me, saying that I should never admit to a colored person that I was wrong. I had been taught that I should be honest and truthful and pay everything that I owed. This contradiction simply didn't make sense. I never did hear from the man. I suppose his company paid for the damage.

In vacation Bible School and Sunday School we sang, "Jesus loves the little children; all the children of the world. Red or yellow, black or white, they are precious in his sight." I am still amazed that the same people who taught their children that Jesus loves everyone, no matter what color, could also teach their children that black people were inferior.

The Life Of A Soldier

When I took my first leave from Fort Jackson, South Carolina, I boarded a bus in Columbia. A black soldier who had been in my basic training company was riding the same bus, and we sat down together in about the middle of the bus. Neither of us was consciously defying the law or tradition. We had lived in an integrated society for about 5 months with no contact with the outside world and we simply forgot the reality of segregation momentarily. The bus driver came back to where we were and demanded that my friend go to the back of the bus. He moved and I moved with him, then the bus driver ordered me to move forward.

A few weeks before the end of our sixteen weeks training cycle, a personnel team came to our training site one day and called out three of us for interview. Their purpose was to recruit us to attend the Third Army Leadership School at Fort Jackson upon completion of basic training. This eight week school was basically the prep school for the Infantry Officer Candidate School at Fort Benning, Georgia.

The others who were called out were George Lane from Lake City Florida, and Thomas Wallace from West Memphis, Arkansas. The three of us had several things in common. We were all seventeen, high school dropouts, Airborne volunteers, and had high enough aptitude scores to qualify for Officer Candidate School. The age requirement for Officer Candidate School was nineteen, so we were not qualified for that.

The bait they used was that we would be promoted to Private First Class (PFC), pay grade E-3, when we started and if we graduated from the leadership course in the top one-third of the class, we would be promoted to Corporal, pay grade E-4. By statute we were to be promoted to Private 2 upon completion of four months in the Army. We were not enthusiastic at first about this offer. We all had our focus on being paratroopers and we saw this as a threat to our goals. The personnel team promised us, however, that if we would volunteer for the leadership school we would be sent to jump school immediately after graduation. We accepted and we were transferred to the school and promoted to PFC the day following completion of basic training, having only about two weeks in grade as Private 2.

      The leadership school at Fort Jackson was 8 weeks in three phases. The first three weeks (Phase one), we lived in the barracks and had classes in the classroom and on the drill field. The subjects that made the greatest impressions on me were Leadership and Methods of Instruction. The Leadership because it was so interesting and the Methods of Instruction because it was both interesting and frightening. We had to prepare lesson plans and give presentations while being graded, not only by the instructors, but also by our fellow students. This was terrifying to me and as I repeated this experience several times during my career, I still dreaded it. When I took Homiletics in Bible College, it was not a pleasant experience because of this same system.

      We learned to teach Dismounted Drill and Physical Training. One of the subjects we had was Judo. My instructor for Judo was a man named Sharp from Florence, Alabama. I didn't try to become acquainted with him because I didn't want to draw any extra attention to myself.

The Life Of A Soldier

I learned where he was from by a remark he made to the class. In 1976 I was invited to speak to a group of men at Forrest Hills Baptist Church and he was there. After 25 years I recognized him.

The second phase was two weeks in the field where we were tested in our leadership potential. I remember being on the march all night one night and at daybreak lining up at the mess tent for breakfast. When we went through the line with our canteen cups as we were ordered to do, we were served a half-cup of black coffee. That was it, the only breakfast we received. Then we went out in small groups for patrolling. Each group had a grader in charge. He would change leaders suddenly by declaring that the leader was a casualty. He would create different situations to require the leader to make decisions and get the other patrol members to do whatever the task was.

The grader would call a break once in awhile, but we were not allowed to sit down. We were on our feet for the entire day and had nothing to eat. When the grader called a break, he would sit down and lean up against a tree, eat a candy bar then smoke a cigarette, but we were not allowed to do either. This went on for 24 hours and by the time we were through there were some that were near hysterics. I admit that I was hungry for food, but the worst thing was not being able to smoke. In all we went about 36 hours without food and 24 hours without smoking.

The third phase of the leadership school was three weeks of practical application. I was the cadre platoon Sergeant for a platoon of recruits. I taught them how to march and how to do the manual of arms with their rifles. I also taught them how to take care of their bodies, personal equipment and the barracks.

My entire platoon was from one county in Illinois. They were draftees, but it was sort of like a national guard unit because they all knew each other. Another thing that most of them had in common was that they had the flu, and they passed that on to me. I didn't feel like getting up in the morning, much less spending about 16 hours trying to make soldiers of these men who all seemed to have two left feet. I stuck it out, however, because my final grade in the school would be greatly influenced by the evaluation the company commander of the training unit gave me. By this time I had come to appreciate the significance of being a corporal rather than a private.

My brother, J.G. (John), who is fifteen months my senior, was in the Air Force. He returned from Johnston Island and got married during that time. He and his wife Billie Faye came by to see me one evening, but I was so sick I couldn't enjoy visiting with them.

On 15 February 1952, Lane, Wallace, and I graduated from the leadership course high enough in the class and were promoted to Corporal. They kept their word. We were on a train the following day for Fort Benning. Lane, Wallace and I were roommates at jump school, and all were assigned to the 82nd Airborne Division upon graduation. I was assigned to the 504th Airborne Infantry Regiment, Wallace was assigned to another Airborne Infantry Regiment, and Lane was assigned to a Field Artillery Battalion. I never saw or heard from George Lane again, and saw Thomas Wallace only once.

Jump school was only three weeks, but very intense. The attitude there was that they had just as soon see you

The Life Of A Soldier

fail as succeed. Obviously they had no quota as to how many they were expected to graduate. It was very easy to get thrown out. Any disobedience of the rules was cause for dismissal and there was no appeal. We ran about five miles every day, and if you lagged behind, that was it.

During our daily exercises in the sawdust pit, if any instructor ruled that you weren't doing the exercises correctly, you received a demerit. In the first week if you received two demerits you had to take the Army physical fitness test and if you failed, you were out. If you received three demerits, you were out. In the second week the standards were raised. One demerit got you the test and two got you dismissed.

One of the rules was that you couldn't use any of the various elastic devices to blouse your boots. Instead, you were required to tuck your pants legs into your boots. The first day that we had training on what was called the suspended harness, where we learned to guide the parachute, we lost several students. When they were hooked up to the harness their pants legs were pulled up to reveal that they had blousing devices. Up to this point, none of the instructors had inspected us to see if we were in compliance with this rule. The violators were immediately dismissed. I felt sorry for them in a way, but the lesson that a soldier should develop the self-discipline to obey whether anyone checks him regularly or not was well taken. A civilian that has never been subjected to such discipline might ask, "What did it matter how they bloused their boots?" But that was not the issue. The issue was obedience and self-discipline.

During the jump training we were required to do pushups continually. For any reason or no reason, any of the instructors could command, "Give me ten" and we were required immediately to do ten pushups. If the instructor didn't like the way you did them or thought you were too slow in getting into the position, he would require you to repeat them.

One day, probably about the second day of jump school, one of the instructors somehow found out that I had only been in the army seven months and was a corporal already. He was a P.F.C., one grade lower than me, and he had been in the army six years. Every day from then on I did hundreds of pushups to pay for this. The instructor would say, "How long have you been in the army, corporal?" I would reply, "Seven months." Then he would ask, "Do you know how long I have been in the army?" I would reply, "Six Years." Then he would say, "Give me ten." He never let me off with just the ten, but would require me to repeat them because I was too slow or something . It was a game but he was the one having all the fun.

I was tested during the last week of jump training on having the courage to take a stand in the face of injustice. The last week is called "Jump Week" and each class makes the five jumps to quality during that week. Because of inclement weather we were unable to jump before Wednesday of that week, and it turned out that we made two jumps on Friday and graduated that same day.

The last jump was to be a tactical jump, requiring us to jump with weapons and have a tactical assembly. We were to leave our parachutes on the drop zone and assemble according to a plan. I was designated a squad leader for that

The Life Of A Soldier

jump. It turned out that while we were "chuting up" the word was passed that the tactical exercise was canceled due to time because we had the graduation ceremony. The problem was that the first lieutenant that was my platoon leader failed to pass the word. The assembly point for our platoon was in a woods on the far side of the drop zone from the administrative assembly point. The terrain was such that you couldn't see the administrative assembly point from the woods.

When I landed, I did what I was supposed to do. I gathered up my squad in the woods and started trying to coordinate with the squads on my flanks. I found the squad on one flank but couldn't find the other one. After a time, we knew that something was amiss. I walked back to the drop zone where I could see the administrative assembly point. The last truck was pulling out. I took charge of the two squads and had them secure their parachutes and move to the administrative assembly point. There was a sergeant from the army engineers plowing up the drop zone and he had a phone. He called in and told them about us. Soon a vehicle came to pick us up.

When we went to turn in our parachutes, we were told that the Operations Officer wanted to see the other squad leader and myself. When we went into his office, the lieutenant platoon leader was there looking scared. He had failed to account for two of his four squads

The operations officer, a major, made a lot of noise then threatened to make us go through the whole course again to get our wings. Then he asked what we would do if he did that. The other squad leader didn't say anything but I spoke up and told him that I wouldn't go through it again–that I had already earned my wings and that none of this was my fault. I told him that if I hadn't taken the initiative we would still have been in the woods when they came looking for us causing further delay. That ended it. He dismissed us and told the lieutenant to stay. When we finished shaking out our parachutes and boarded transportation to return to the barracks, the lieutenant joined us and apologized, acknowledging it was all his fault. I appreciated that, but would have appreciated it more if he had spoken up earlier in the major's office when we were threatened.

After graduating from Jump School on 28 March 1952, our class was held at Fort Benning for several days. We heard they were waiting to see if we were needed as replacements in Korea. A class ahead of us was sent to Korea as replacements. Ultimately, most of us were assigned to either the 82nd or 11th Airborne Divisions. My roommates and I were all assigned to the 82nd.

On the last day of March, which was for us payday, I went into Columbus. Thomas Wallace also went to town but separate from me. George Lane stayed in the barracks. I returned around midnight and George was asleep. Thomas Wallace was still out. The next morning before we got out of bed Wallace said he heard someone in the room near my bunk after he went to bed. I knew immediately that he was lying. After a few minutes I checked my footlocker and found that the money was gone from my billfold. I didn't say anything about it. I knew Wallace had taken it.

After breakfast I had a chance to talk with George Lane alone and the first thing he said was, "He took your money, didn't he?" I said yes, but I asked George not to say

The Life Of A Soldier

anything to anyone about it until I had time to decide what to do. I really can't explain my reaction to this. Instead of anger, I felt pity for Wallace. We knew that he was capable of something like this and more. He had been a part of a street gang in West Memphis Arkansas where he grew up. Wallace stayed out of our sight for most of the day then in the late afternoon came to the room and started packing his gear. When we asked where he was going he said he was moving to another building. He then said everyone in the company was looking at him funny because I had told them that he had stolen my money. We told him that neither of us had said anything to anyone about it, and asked how he knew the money was stolen if he didn't steal it himself.

I never did report Wallace for stealing the money. A few months later at Fort Bragg while at the marshalling area waiting to make a parachute jump, I saw Wallace with a big "P" stenciled on his shirt and an armed guard following him as he picked up trash. I spoke to him briefly and asked what he was in prison for. He said he punched out his First Sergeant, but I knew he was lying. I could always tell when he was lying. I imagined that he was caught stealing. That was the last time I saw Wallace and I never saw George Lane again.

I spent eleven of my 21 years on parachute status and made 72 jumps. I was awarded the Senior Parachutist Badge while serving with the 101st Airborne Division at Fort Campbell in 1959, and the Master Parachutist Badge while serving as advisor to the 20th Special Forces Group (Airborne), Alabama National Guard in 1969. I was also awarded the parachutist badges of the Republics of China, Korea and Vietnam.

I was fortunate in that I never really had a parachute malfunction. The only time my reserve parachute was opened was on my 43rd jump on 10 January 1957 at Munich, Germany when another jumper bumped into me and tangled up with me. The reserve chute was opened by tangling with his equipment. We did what we were trained to do--held together until we reached the ground and fell away from each other. Neither of us was hurt. On my 45th jump at Breckenridge, Kentucky on 18 March 1959 I landed in a very tall tree and had to let out my reserve chute, get out of the harness and climb down as far as I could, then fall free. I managed this with no injuries. On my 7th jump at Fort Benning Georgia on 25 September, 1952, my first night jump, I fractured my ankle.

After the jump training I was assigned to Company F, 504th Airborne Infantry Regiment (A.I.R.), 82nd Airborne Division at Fort Bragg, North Carolina. I was assigned as a squad leader in the third platoon and from that time until my retirement from the army I was always in some leadership position except when I was a student, and a brief stint in Panama. I led infantry squads, both infantry and tank platoons, and commanded a rifle company. I commanded an airmobile infantry battalion briefly in Vietnam and served as advisor to a Vietnamese airborne ranger battalion and an infantry battalion in combat. I also served as executive officer of a rifle company and two infantry battalions.

The 504th A.I.R. was named "The Devils in Baggy Pants" by the Germans in World War II, and had some interesting traditions and characters. During the first jumps

The Life Of A Soldier

in jump school, an instructor would tap you on the backside when it was time to jump. The Sergeant Major of the Second Battalion of the 504th A.I.R., whose name I cannot recall, served with the regiment in World War II. Even after jumping in combat, he could not jump out of an airplane without someone tapping him on his backside.

The platoon sergeant of the Third Platoon of Company F, to which I was assigned, was Master Sergeant Blue who was also a World War II veteran with the regiment. The troops called him "Mother Blue" (behind his back of course) because he was always trying to grow grass in the sand around the barracks, and worked us at that task when we weren't training during the spring and summer. He made us "sprig" grass, but it never caught on. The grass never did prosper, but I don't think anyone but Master Sergeant Blue cared.

Another interesting WW II veteran was a Sergeant First Class Tillison from Gadsden, Alabama. He was our Platoon Guide, or Assistant Platoon Sergeant. There was a regimental tradition that no one could use the regimental parade field as a shortcut. The only person in the entire regiment that was allowed to walk on it except in formation was the junior second lieutenant in the regiment. It was his duty to police it and anyone else caught walking on it was fined. The officers and noncommissioned officers clubs were across the parade field from the barracks. Sergeant Tillison would drink at the N.C.O. club every payday and after enough drinks he would decide to walk on the parade field. He always got caught and had to pay a fine, but he never gave up trying.

Euell White

My first assignment as a squad leader was not easy. Some of the men in my squad who were Privates first class, had, like the instructor in jump school, been in the army for several years. Promotions had been frozen for awhile except for Korea and special situations like the school I attended. When these men found out how young I was (18 by then), they made it hard for me. In reality, however, they were unwittingly helping me to develop as a leader. I learned a lot from them about how to lead men that helped me in later years as a noncommissioned officer and as a commissioned officer.

The only time in my army career that I ever thought that maybe I had made a mistake by enlisting, was when I first joined Company F. On the first Saturday I was there my Platoon Sergeant assigned me the task of teaching on the assembly, disassembly and functioning of the Browning Automatic Rifle (B.A.R.) on the Monday following during the annual qualification firing. I didn't realize at the time that I was being set up. They wouldn't let me keep one of the rifles out to study and practice with over the weekend, and I didn't know enough about it from basic training to do it.

When I realized that weekend as I vainly tried to assimilate what I needed to know from a manual, that I was going to be humiliated on Monday, I doubted my decision to join the army. I spent the weekend poring over the manual with a knot in my stomach. Monday came and I stood before the men and started to try to teach. The B.A.R. gunner from my squad started asking me questions I didn't know the answer to. Finally, the platoon sergeant rescued me and taught the class. I was being punished, or put in my place, because they resented my being promoted to

The Life Of A Soldier

corporal in such a short time. After that the platoon Sergeant was always kind to me. In retrospect I believe he expected me to beg off and appreciated the fact that I at least made an attempt. Ironically, when I attended the Light and Heavy Weapons Noncommissioned Officers course at Fort Benning later on, I fired a perfect score with the B.A.R.

My first experience with racial integration was in basic training. It was a fact, already established and I never questioned it. I honestly had never embraced the idea of racial superiority in the first place so it was not a big adjustment for me. I read recently that the whole army was integrated in 1948 but this is not true. The 82nd Airborne Division was integrated after I joined it in 1952. Prior to the integration there was one Battalion of the 505th Regiment that was all black. Some of their officers may have been white, I am not sure. When the division was integrated, those black troopers were scattered throughout the other regiments and white troopers were assigned to the formerly all black battalion. A Black lieutenant named Coffee became our platoon leader. He was a good officer.

There were classes in preparation for the integration, and some classes after the integration was effected. As with most changes in a bureaucracy, the army overdid the indoctrination phase, and it became a pain for both blacks and whites to sit and listen to historical facts that we already knew. I am sure there were some who resented the integration but the indoctrination didn't change their minds.

Euell White

Later in 1952, I returned to Fort Benning Georgia to attend a 14-week Noncommissioned Officers School. I fractured my ankle on a parachute jump on 25 September. It was my first night jump. I was about half way through the course, and after being hospitalized for six weeks had to start over with a new class. Consequently, the 14 weeks stretched into about seven months. My sister, Rose Nell who was in the army and stationed at Camp Picket, Virginia, came to visit me one weekend while I was in the reconditioning ward. We called it the slave-labor ward because they required us to paint the hospital corridors. I sneaked out of the hospital to spend time with her.

On Monday after my weekend away, I was called before an evaluation board of doctors and nurses to determine whether I was ready to be discharged. I had a cast on my leg and the fracture had not completely healed. The cast was removed before I went before the board, and although it was painful, I walked in like there was nothing wrong so that they would release me. I was needing another parachute jump by then so I wrapped up my ankle so tight with an ace bandage it couldn't move and made a jump with it.

While I was at Fort Benning, I became engaged to the lady who has been my wife now for more than 55 years. The memories of our first years of marriage are so vivid at times that it is difficult to believe it has now been fifty-five years. I suppose there is nothing unique in the fact that there are many times and events that I would like to re-live. Some, simply because of the joy in them, and others because I would like to make better decisions, and have different priorities.

The Life Of A Soldier

Euna and I became engaged on George Washington's birthday, Monday, February 22, 1953. We had known each other for about three years and had dated some before I enlisted in the army. Leading up to the day that I proposed marriage to Euna was a time of reflecting on my life and what I wanted to do with it. Every time I thought of having my own family, Euna came to mind. Finally there was a time when I knew that I loved her and that she was the one I wanted to be my lifetime companion if she would have me.

I had not communicated with her for some time and didn't know her status. For all I knew she might be engaged or dating someone steady, but I wrote to her and asked her if she would see me on the long weekend of George Washington's birthday. I received what seemed to me a cool response. She wrote that she would be glad to see an old friend again. I thought there was an implied emphasis on the word "friend" to tell me that was all I was to her.

Nevertheless.I drove home to Florence that weekend with a determination to propose to her and spent as much time as possible with her. On Monday, 22 February I proposed to her and she sad "yes" making me a very happy young soldier. We set a date for sometime in May.

In late March 1953, I returned to Fort Bragg and found that my unit was in Nevada where they participated in a nuclear bomb test. They jumped in near ground zero shortly after the blast. I have always been thankful for the fractured ankle that caused me to miss that trip. I have read that many of those who participated in those tests contracted cancer and died at an early age.

When my unit returned to Fort Bragg I learned that I was the senior corporal in my company. Promotions had opened up during my seven months absence and I missed out because I was away. Later when I was promoted to Sergeant, it was a bitter-sweet experience. Going from senior corporal to junior sergeant had some disadvantages in addition to the obvious advantages. As the senior corporal I was the last corporal to be put in charge of work details that called for a corporal. But as the junior sergeant I was the first to go when they called for a sergeant.

The Life Of A Soldier

My last Photo as a Corporal, April 1953

On 20 April 1953 I participated in the first test parachute jump from a C-124 Globemaster. The C-124 was

Euell White

a 4-engine propeller cargo aircraft capable of transporting heavy equipment such as vehicles and weapons systems. We thought we were going to jump on 17 April which was a Friday. We spent the whole day on Friday chuting up, lining up, boarding the plane, then getting off the plane, with Edward R. Murrow's cameras in helicopters flying around filming us. Finally at the end of the day we were told to leave our parachutes on the seats and come back on Monday. They were making such a big deal out of this that I became worried about it, but I learned a lesson. I worried all day Friday about a jump that didn't even happen that day. I decided that I was not going to start sweating over a jump again until the plane was at least heading down the runway. The jump went off without a hitch. Nobody was injured.

Sometime in April 1953, the First Sergeant of Company F, William ("Bull") Markham, called me in to tell me that I was going to Panama for jungle training with the First Battalion during April and May. When I told him that I was scheduled to be married in May, he replied: "Aw Hell you can get married anytime but you might never get another chance to go to Panama." He was right. We rescheduled the wedding for 16 June and I never again went to Panama.

Although I wasn't excited about going to Panama it was valuable to me in more ways than one. First of all, it was valuable because of the survival training. I learned how to survive in the jungle and this helped me tremendously later on. It was also good for my physical conditioning. I carried a packboard with a five gallon can of water through

The Life Of A Soldier

the jungle and much of that time was running rather than walking.

Another way that it benefited me was to humble me. I didn't realize that I needed to be humbled, but apparently I did. I was a corporal and had never been anything less than a squad leader in a unit. I was assigned to the 2nd battalion of the 504th and I went to Panama with the 1st Battalion. They were low on strength and had to be full strength for the jungle Training. I was attached to Company A, and assigned as a senior rifleman. This was a comedown for me from squad leader to senior rifleman and the squad leader who was a Sergeant First Class, named Holly, really enjoyed reminding me that I was only a rifleman.

I got off to a bad start with Holly. One day while we were preparing to go to Panama, he told us that we were to write a letter to our family telling them where we were going and how long we would be gone, and leave the letters unsealed in his office for the platoon leader to read. I ignored this and when confronted about it told him that no one had a right to read my mail, and I had already notified my fiancée by telephone.

When I returned from Panama, on the last day of May, the First Sergeant was waiting for me as I deplaned, with my Sergeant stripes in his hand. I had been promoted on 26 May. I had no idea at that time how important was that promotion to me in view of the fact that I was soon to be married.

Euell White

Euna and I were married in the home of the minister at Hopewell Cumberland Presbyterian Church on Bailey Springs Road in Florence.

After a honeymoon trip to 'Lookout Mountain and a few days visiting our folks, we headed out to Fort Bragg in my 1941 Chevrolet. On the way we lost two piston rods and by the time we arrived, our funds were critically low.

Our first breakdown was in Lexington, South Carolina. They didn't have a motel or hotel, but a Bed and Breakfast. I will never forget that night because it was the first of my many failures as a romantic. We were on the second floor and walked out on the veranda. There was a full moon and Euna was feeling romantic, humming or singing "Carolina Moon," but I was so concerned about the car that I couldn't get into the romantic mood.

The Life Of A Soldier

We did have enough to pay a deposit and a month's rent for an apartment in Fayetteville. It was an upstairs apartment in the house of a woman who hated all soldiers and their families. She constantly complained that we were making too much noise and let us know how low life she thought army people were. Immediately after I returned to duty after my wedding leave, I attended the 82nd Airborne Division Jumpmaster School.

Left to Right: CPL Evans, CPL Guilemette, SFC Dyke, Sergeant White, Lt Potts

I made four jumps during the course. On the night of 6 July, I bruised my tail bone on the jump and didn't dare tell the medics for fear I would be disqualified for failure to make a proper parachute landing fall and also because I had one more jump to make the following day to complete the course.

My car had been wrecked in a crash with a drunk driver in Fayetteville and I was having to ride the bus to and from work. We were still living in the apartment we rented from the wicked witch. I had to stand up on the bus because it hurt so much to sit down. When I arrived home, Euna had fallen asleep and I couldn't get in the upstairs apartment by the outside door. I had to awaken the wicked witch to let me in. She ranted and raved about it and reminded me how much she despised all soldiers and their families.

This made us more determined to get out of there and not long afterward I was notified that post housing was available for me. This was good news to us. I would not have been eligible for this as a corporal. The quarters they assigned us were like heaven to us after living in the house of the witch. The post quarters had a coal furnace and was not at all attractive but we spent the first year of our marriage there and loved it.

Our Quarters at 3 Devers Street
The quarters we were assigned was in an apartment complex in the city of Fayetteville, remote from the post but it belonged to Fort Bragg.

Euell White

Over the twenty plus years I was in the army, we lived in North Carolina, Georgia, Kentucky, Tennessee, Kansas Alabama, Okinawa-Japan, Germany, (where our daughter Sherry was born), and Hawaii (where I was commissioned a Second Lieutenant and Sherry was naturalized). Apart from my family, I served in Vietnam (three times), Korea, Taiwan, Panama, Germany and Okinawa.

It is not possible for anyone who has not experienced it to fully appreciate the role of the military wife. Often the husband and father is away when his presence with the family is most critically needed, and the wife simply has to fill the gap. Our daughter Sherry who was raised as an "army brat" is a testimony to the excellent job that Euna did as an army wife.

Shortly after we settled into our new home at Fort Bragg, Euna started to work at First Citizens Bank and Trust Company in Fayetteville. She had resigned her job at First National in Florence to marry me. At the bank we met some Fayetteville citizens who were opposite of the witch landlady. The people at the bank treated Euna as someone special and they were very kind to me.

In the summer of 1953 our Regiment underwent a test of the Table of Organization and Equipment, called the TO&E. We had a field exercise and everything had to be exactly as authorized by the TO&E, both in personnel and equipment. Actually there were two regiments involved in the exercise, one organized and equipped according to the existing TO&E and the other according to the proposed new TO&E. Our regiment was using the old one, and I can't remember which regiment was using the new.

The Life Of A Soldier

To fill the personnel shortages they gave us men from recently deleted units who were not parachutists. We were supposed to convince them to become parachutists, but the effort was largely unsuccessful.

I was the weapons squad leader for the 1st Platoon of Company F. To fill up my squad I received three privates. Two of them were from an engineer battalion, one named Cole and the other named Dunn. The third man was from an intelligence unit and he was a Lithuanian whose name I can't recall.

The Lithuanian, and Cole were fairly good soldiers and didn't cause me any grief, but Private Dunn was something else. Euna and I had been married only a few weeks when Dunn came into our lives and, although she never met him, she came to despise him because I was spending more of my off duty time with him than I was with her.

For this exercise, the machine gun ammunition bearers had to carry ammunition containers containing sand with the equivalent weight of the ammunition. Dunn continuously poured out the sand from his containers, and made sure that one of the evaluators saw him do it. He would not do anything right if he could find a wrong way to do it. He was continually sending us a message that he wanted no part of being a paratrooper.

After the exercise was over, Dunn's behavior didn't improve. In fact, being back at the barracks provided him even more opportunities to cause trouble. I could inspect him thoroughly in the morning and make sure his uniform was proper, then he would meet an officer on the company street, and deliberately mess himself up to get the officer's attention--unbutton his shirt, turn his cap around backwards—anything to get in trouble. He would fail to salute the officer and talk disrespectfully to him. I would wind up before the Company Commander, Captain Sam Muse, getting chewed out for Dunn's sloppiness and disrespect. The captain's solution was to not courts-martial Dunn, but to give him extra duty under the non-judicial punishment article. This meant someone had to supervise Dunn after duty hours and guess who that was.

This was one of those testing times. Although I felt that I was being treated unfairly, and being punished for the misdeeds of a man who didn't want to be a soldier, I did learn some things about leadership. I understood that a leader is always responsible as an abstract principle, but my company commander, Captain Sam Muse made it real for me.

One weekend Private Dunn went home for a weekend pass and brought a car back with him. There was a requirement to register your automobile on post within a certain time period. Dunn didn't do that and I had no knowledge of him having a car. When the Military Police discovered the car, I ended up on the captain's carpet again. I offered the excuse that I didn't know about the car and I couldn't control what my men did while they were on pass away from the post. This caused a reaction from Captain Muse explaining to me in very convincing language that a leader is always responsible for his men no matter where they are. Although I was technically correct, the principle was valid, that a leader cannot deny his responsibility.

Private Dunn finally pushed too far and I was finally rid of him. The company drew post guard duty and

The Life Of A Soldier

Dunn was assigned a post at the Stockade (military confinement facility) on a tower. He laid down his rifle, left his post and went AWOL. Finally, Captain Muse decided he had done something too serious to be corrected by extra duty.

The TO&E test was tough. It was the hottest part of the summer and the North Carolina sand reflected the sun, making it that much hotter. I can empathize with those men in the extreme heat in Iraq. We were allowed only one quart canteen of water per day except for the beverages we had with our occasional hot meals, and we had to use some of that quart to shave and brush our teeth. This water discipline training proved invaluable to me later on, especially in combat.

On 17 November 1953, there was an accident during a parachute drop involving the battalion I was assigned to, the 2nd Battalion, 504th A.I.R. For the details of this tragedy see Appendix A: Tragic Accidents (Air Tragedy at Fort Bragg, Page 277).

During my career I served in the 11th, 82nd and 101st Airborne Divisions as well as the 1st, 5th and 20th Airborne Special Forces Groups. I made 72 jumps and earned the Master Parachutist Badge. I have jumped in Alabama, Tennessee, Kentucky, Louisiana, North and South Carolina, Germany, Korea, Okinawa-Japan, Taiwan and Vietnam. I was also awarded the parachutist badges of the Republics of Korea, China and Vietnam. The Republic of China was Taiwan at that time. I also served in the 1st, 8th, 24th and 25th Infantry Divisions.

Euell White

In the fall of 1953, a new commander, Colonel Dodd, was assigned to the 504th Airborne Infantry Regiment. He was a fanatic for tradition and for sports competitions and made support for the regimental football team--which was named the "Blue Devils"-- a requirement. The regiment formed on the parade field every weekday morning at 0430 year round for our daily physical exercises. We would do what we called the daily dozens, then we would run for about five miles.

The new Colonel added something to this daily routine during football season. After we did our daily dozens, we had to practice our cheers for the Saturday football game before our run. In response to signals given by flags like the Navy uses on their ships, the entire regiment would chant, "Yea devils, Go devils" until the volume was sufficient to please the Colonel.

Then on Saturday afternoons we were required to attend the football games. Before the game started the regiment formed on the football field in uniform and did the cheers we had practiced. I was a newlywed and didn't get to spend much time with my bride. I hated this, and have never cared much since for attending ball games nor watching them on television.

On Friday evening before the big division championship game for the 1953 football season in which the 504th team was a contender, the regimental commander, Colonel Dodd, decided to have a celebration. He put out the word that there would be free beer at the regimental football practice field. Very few of the troops showed up. There were good reasons. Two of the reasons they didn't attend is that it was cold out there and they had free beer at the enlisted men's club where it was warm, every Friday

The Life Of A Soldier

evening. Probably another reason is that they were tired of being forced to support the football team.

The Colonel was displeased and on Saturday morning called for a formation of the regiment on the parade field. There he ordered all company commanders to march their troops back to the barracks and have them pick up their canteen cups then march them to the football field. Then they were told to march the troops through the line to receive the free beer they didn't accept the evening before.

One of the platoon sergeants in Company F was a Sergeant First Class Simpson who was from the hills of Kentucky. Simpson was a good platoon sergeant but he had a drinking problem. The company commander, Captain Sam Muse, was helping him and had managed to keep him sober for several months, until that day when he was ordered to march through the free beer line.

Simpson had courtesy patrol duty at the football game that afternoon, to help maintain order. He showed up in his class "A" uniform with the arm band designating him as part of the courtesy patrol. He was, however, very drunk and when Simpson, who was a small man, got drunk he always found something to stand on and preached the Gospel. He could quote the appropriate Scriptures and preach repentance as good as any preacher I ever heard. The "anointing" came on Simpson and he stood up on the front row of the bleachers facing the spectators and started preaching. The Colonel was furious and wanted to punish Sergeant Simpson, but Captain Sam Muse said no, we are not going to punish him. He told the Colonel that Simpson had admitted his problem and sought his help and had been sober for several months until ordered to get in a beer line.

Captain Muse grew taller in my eyes that day. Here was a real leader. I thought it a waste when he gave up commanding infantry units to fly a single engine aircraft. Later while assigned to the 502nd in the 101st at Fort Campbell, I was given the assignment one day to drop some propaganda leaflets to a unit on a field exercise. When I reported to the airfield, the pilot was Captain Sam Muse. I have never experienced air sickness but I thought I was going to that day. He made the plane roll, and did all kinds of crazy things that had nothing to do with dropping the leaflets. I don't know whether he did this all the time or was just trying to impress me.

I served in the 504th A.I.R. honor guard and drill team as a squad leader for a time after I was promoted to Sergeant. The honor guard drill teams of each of the three Airborne Infantry Regiments comprised the 82nd Airborne Division honor guard. To be on the drill team you had to be at least 5 feet 10 inches tall, slim and have good reflexes. I can still do the Queen Anne salute, although I might need some help getting up, as it requires you to assume a kneeling position.

The army decided on an early release in the summer of 1954. I was told one day in June to report to the out-processing center for discharge, although my enlistment wouldn't end until 16 July. I was discharged on 16 June, our first wedding anniversary. We celebrated our first wedding anniversary by having our quarters inspected so that we could clear the post. I wanted to stay in the army but I had promised Euna when we married that if she didn't

The Life Of A Soldier

like it I would get out. She didn't dislike it but she wanted me to go to college.

Euell White

The Life Of A Soldier

3.
Second Enlistment
August 1954-May 1960

We were out of the Army for 48 days and I became so unhappy that Euna agreed that I should re-enlist. When we decided that I would reenlist, we decided that I would reenlist for the 11th Airborne Division at Fort Campbell, Kentucky so that we wouldn't be too far away. Euna's mother had a stroke in the Spring of 1954, and she felt responsible for helping care for her.

I drove up to Fort Campbell to reenlist. Fort Campbell is about fifty miles northwest of Nashville, and is in Kentucky and Tennessee. The Post headquarters is in Kentucky. The nearest town is Clarksville, Tennessee. I arrived at Fort Campbell on a very hot afternoon. The heat was so intense that the work day was from early in the morning until noon.

I went to the Re-enlistment office where I was told that if I wanted to reenlist specifically for Fort Campbell I needed to decide which unit and secure a letter of acceptance. I drove around the post and as I drove by the 76th Tank battalion I saw a softball game in progress. Apparently, although it was too hot in the afternoon for training, it was not too hot for softball. I parked and joined the spectators for awhile, then went to the battalion headquarters and found the Sergeant Major.

I introduced myself to the Sergeant Major and showed him my DD form 214, which is a summary of your service. He told me they had an opening for an Infantry

Euell White

Sergeant in their Recon Platoon, and he would get me the letter of acceptance. He called someone from the Headquarters and Service Company and they gave me a bed for the night.

The following day I took the letter of acceptance to the Re-enlistment Sergeant and he sent me to the hospital for my physical. They told me to return in one week, at which time I reenlisted, keeping my rank of Sergeant.

One of my concerns at that time was` to find us a place to live. I learned an important lesson in this process. Housing there was in short supply, but I found a basement apartment that seemed to be reasonable. The man required three months rent in advance and I was dumb enough to do it. That wasn't the dumbest, however. When I went back home to get Euna she asked me how many closets the apartment had. Then it occurred to me that I didn't look for closets. I replied that I was sure there were plenty of closets. She correctly predicted that there were no closets. After that, anytime I looked at a house or apartment that was my first concern.

I was promoted to Sergeant First Class in 1955, and attended the Armor School's 16-week noncommissioned officers course at Fort Knox, Kentucky that same year. In February 1956, the entire division deployed to Germany. Euna traveled with me, by train, to Brooklyn then by ship to Bremerhaven Germany. We traveled separately by train from Bremerhaven to Munich. We really enjoyed our three years in Germany and made some lifelong friends while we were there.

In preparation for this move to Germany, the 11th Airborne Division went through some tough exercises at the hands of the commanding general, Major General

The Life Of A Soldier

Wayne C. Smith. For details see Appendix B: Unforgettable Characters (General Wayne C. Smith, Page 285)

The 11th Airborne Division was scheduled to replace the 5th Infantry division in Germany and the 5th Infantry was to come to Fort Campbell. The local politicians protested, however, that they wanted an Airborne Division at Fort Campbell. So, in the name of national security I suppose, the 101st Airborne Division which was at Fort Jackson, South Carolina was moved to Fort Campbell. I don't know what happened to the 5th Infantry Division, but judging from the condition of the tanks and equipment we inherited from them it was a good move if they were de-activated.

We boarded the train for Brooklyn, New York at Fort Campbell, in the early evening of Saturday 28 January, 1956. Most of the NCOs and junior officers had driven their cars to Brooklyn for shipment to Germany. The Battalion Commander and his staff had some NCO's drive their cars so that they could ride the train.

Since we weren't taking a car, we rode the train and had a compartment adjacent to Claude and Freda Hager. I had never met Freda before and knew Claude only as an NCO in the same unit, Headquarters and Service Company. Euna had met neither of them, but during this trip we became lifelong friends. Claude was a Sergeant First Class and senior to me by date of rank. He was the Battalion Wheel Vehicle Maintenance Chief. We had a good time on the trip and they lived near us in Munich. We became like family.

Euell White

Claude and Freda Hager 1956

We arrived at Brooklyn in the late afternoon of Sunday, 29 January and were taken to the Saint George Hotel. There we ran into Sergeant Lyle Fuller and his wife. Sergeant Fuller was the Battalion Personnel Sergeant and they were from Brooklyn. His wife was from an Italian-American family and some of them were there to see them off. They invited us to dine with them at an Italian restaurant.

Afterwards, I decided to try to call Raymond Manners who attended the NCO school at Fort Benning with me in 1952-53. Raymond was in the New York National Guard and lived in Queens. When I looked in the

The Life Of A Soldier

phone book there were dozens of Raymond Manners listed. I picked one at random and dialed it. A woman answered and I told her my name and that I was trying to locate a Raymond Manners that I knew at Fort Benning in 1953. She said her husband was taking a bath but she would ask him. She yelled and told him there was a man named White on the phone looking for a Raymond Manners he knew at Fort Benning. I heard his reply as he yelled, "Ask him if he is from Alabama." Raymond and his wife came by and took us on an interesting sight seeing tour. I never heard from them again.

Euell White

> When I think of Raymond Manners I remember an experience we shared that demonstrated to the young New Yorker, racism, southern style. Raymond and I, along with a young man from the Texas National Guard, who was Hispanic and very dark-skinned, went to Opelika one night to a dance hall. It never occurred to me that Manuel would attract negative attention. Very soon after we entered the place, a man showed me a knife and another showed me a pistol he had in his belt under his jacket. Both men let me know that we were not going to get away in one piece. Raymond and Manuel didn't see this and were oblivious to what was going on. There was an off-duty policeman working as security, so I approached him and told them we needed his protection to get to our car. He walked to the car with us and no one bothered us. I told Raymond and Manuel what happened after we got moving in the car. I really felt bad about exposing them to this.

On Monday morning, January 30, 1956, we boarded the U.S.S. Butner. Immediately after being shown to the bunkroom that I would share with three other NCOs during the trip, a call came over the PA system for me to report to some location. Being unfamiliar with navy lingo and ships, I had no idea where to go, but I finally located it.

The Life Of A Soldier

My First Sergeant, told me that I was to be the senior color bearer for a ceremony bringing the colors on board the ship. I don't know what happened to the guys who usually had this detail, but they assigned me three others who didn't know what to do either. The senior color bearer carries the U.S. flag and gives the commands for the others, which includes the bearer of the unit colors and two color guards armed with rifles. I got hold of a drill manual and we practiced for a few minutes before the ceremony. Everything went well. There was another battalion and a regimental headquarters on the ship with us. I was stuck with the extra duty of Senior Color Bearer for two years.

Euell White

The Life Of A Soldier

On the ship, those of us who were accompanied by our families were billeted on the cabin class deck in bunkrooms. Our wives shared cabins with other wives. The First Sergeant had made many Atlantic Crossings and always remained deathly sick for the entire journey. He designated me to take his place and he reported to sick bay as soon as the ship got underway, where he remained for the trip.

The Navy had issued badges, color-coded to designate where passengers were allowed to be on the ship. The badge I was issued only allowed me on the cabin class deck. As acting First Sergeant, however, I had to go down into the troop hold to see about the men and to assign work details. The first time I started down there I was confronted by a Petty Officer First Class and learned to appreciate the old saying, "cussing like a sailor." For details see Appendix B: Unforgettable Characters (The Cussing Sailor Page287)

After we docked at Bremerhaven we boarded a train for Munich. Our families were left aboard ship for a few hours to give us a head start. The train ride was miserable, There was no heat and we weren't dressed for the below zero temperature. It was 30 below that night. We were taken to our barracks and after a briefing and getting our troops settled in to the barracks, we were introduced to our sponsors who were officers and men who had arrived earlier with the advance party.

Our sponsor was a sergeant and he accompanied me to the Bahnhoff and accompanied Euna and me to our quarters. The German bus was very comfortable and delivered us to our quarters. The sponsor had a key and had stocked the refrigerator and pantry with food. It was a two bedroom apartment, very clean and furnished with nice furniture. Everything we needed was there including silverware with all of the extra forks.

    I cannot describe how much of a blessing this was for us—to be taken to the apartment that was to be our home for 3 years and find everything done for us. I never forgot this and when I had opportunity to do this for others, I was diligent to do it. The furniture, provided by the quartermaster, was nice and if anything happened it would be replaced. I remember that our daughter Sherry decided one day to dress up like her mom. She put on some of her clothes and tried to apply lipstick, She had lipstick all over herself, and all over the sofa and window drapes. The quartermaster simply sent out a new sofa and new drapes.

    While we were at the Munich Bahnhoff waiting for our wives to arrive, our First Sergeant told the NCOs to take the following day to get our families settled in. Early the following morning while we were yet asleep, our doorbell rang. When I went to the door I found 1st Lieutenant McNatt who was with the advance party there to give me a ride to the Kaserne. In 1971, I returned from Vietnam on the same plane with McNatt who was by then a Colonel. Apparently, the First Sergeant had exceeded his authority by giving us the day off. Claude and Freda Hager's apartment was a short walk from ours in the same area, Neu Harlaching. No one came for Claude, so he and Freda found Euna and the three of them explored the area, locating the commissary, deli and movie theater at McGraw

The Life Of A Soldier

Kaserne where the Southern Area Command and Munich Sub Area headquarters were located.

We arrived in Munich on Wednesday, 8 February, and that weekend we had a practice alert. After all units were assembled at the designated wooded area, the commanders and staff moved by wheel vehicle to a wooded area near Inglestadt for a command post exercise (CPX). I was designated to supervise a work detail to erect tents and stoves for the battalion headquarters. The detail consisted of the men from my rifle squad. We were given a 2-1/2 ton truck and told to follow an officer in a jeep. I didn't know where we were going. I rode in the cab of the truck with the driver and thought I was going to freeze to death. I knew the men in the back were also miserable. When we arrived at the site, one of my men was stiff as a board. The medics worked with him for quite awhile and he was OK, I was really scared and was diligent thereafter to make sure my men exercised in situations like that.

Our quarters were just inside the city limits of Munich on one side and Henry Kaserne was just outside the city limits on the other side. The Dachau Concentration Camp was near Henry Kaserne and had been converted to a quartermaster laundry. I never met a Munich resident who would acknowledge that they knew people were being exterminated at Dachau.

When we first arrived, Claude Hager, Jerry Martelli and I were designated to drive a 2-1/2 ton truck to our housing areas for the purpose of picking up men of the battalion in those areas in the event of alert. There were three areas, New Harlaching where Claude and I lived,

Euell White

Perlacher Forest, where Jerry Martelli lived and another one south of McGraw Kaserne, whose name I can't remember. Both Neu Harlaching and Perlacher Forest were North of McGraw Kaserne. The truck was a real blessing to us at first because neither of us had brought a car. However, Claude bought a car soon afterward and Jerry started riding with him. Everything rolls down hill and I was the junior of the three, so the truck became my sole responsibility.

    I tried in vain to convince the First Sergeant that it was not necessary to have the truck in the housing area overnight. When we had a practice alert, I would have to wait for the guys to get dressed and ready and by the time that was done a driver could have driven the truck from the Kaserne. One morning it was so foggy that you couldn't see your hand in front of your face. I drove by memory and instinct and amazingly made it through the city and to the road that went by the Kaserne. I missed the turn however and instead turned into the entrance to the rifle range. I started hitting bumps and knew something was wrong. I got out of the truck and found I was on the rifle range going over the birms. When I arrived at the company I told the First Sergeant that from now on if it was foggy he shouldn't expect to see me til the fog lifted.

    I decided then I was going to find a way to get rid of the truck. I had bought a car by that time, a 49 Opel, but couldn't use it for going to work because of the truck. The following morning after the fog, I started the truck and pulled the throttle out which created a lot of noise. I went back inside and had my breakfast while the truck was warming up—not at idle speed which was my usual way---but at advanced speed. My doorbell rang and it was

The Life Of A Soldier

Sergeant First Class Steve Gelegonia who lived in the apartment above us. Steve was the Operations Sergeant for the Munich Provost Marshall and he told me that the neighbors were complaining that I was waking up their babies. It was about 4:30 A.M. I told him he should write me up. He didn't want to but I insisted.

The write up was called a DR (Delinquent Report) and commanders seemed to respond to them. As soon as the report arrived at my unit I was called in and I presented my case for discontinuing the truck driving. That ended my truck driving in Munich.

We found the equipment left us by the 5th Infantry Division in poor shape. Most of the vehicles were in deadline status, needing parts that were not in stock. When the spring thaw came we found vehicles that had been abandoned in the snow outside the Kaserne.

Claude Hager was given the responsibility to take a truck to Augsburg, where the division headquarters was located, every day to pick up parts. One day Claude stopped at a PX snack bar along the Autobahn between Munich and Augsburg for coffee. He didn't realize there was a Military Police Station over the snack bar in a position to observe traffic. When he left the snack bar, Claude made an illegal turn onto the autobahn. The MPs followed him and found he was exceeding the speed limit. There were no maximum speed limits on the autobahn for the Germans, only minimums, but the military had speed limits for all military personnel and military vehicles. Claude offered an explanation to the MPs that he was going for parts and the speedometer on the vehicle he was driving was inoperable. The MP's response to that was to add that charge to the ticket. This was the first DR for traffic in the Battalion in Germany, so Claude had to be the example. He was reduced one grade from Sergeant First Class to Sergeant. I felt it was an injustice and urged Claude to appeal it, but he wouldn't. He just continued to do his job with the same dedication and diligence. He was a real soldier in the best connotation of that word.

We didn't get any time to catch our breath when we arrived in Munich. We had to be ready to meet the Soviets if they came across the border and the equipment was in poor condition. The night we arrived, the temperature was 30 degrees below zero and there was a big snow on the ground until spring.

There was a problem with frostbite because our troops weren't accustomed to weather that cold. The 7th Army Commander, General Bruce C. Clark, had a policy that if a man got frostbite every leader in the chain of command from his squad leader or tank commander all the way up to the Corps Commander, had to report to him. The officers were so nervous about it that if they saw a soldier in Munich in civilian clothes without his ears covered, they would stop him and instruct him to cover his ears.

Another couple that we met on the ship and became friends with, was Ray and Lillian Taylor, from Kentucky. Ray was assigned to the 503rd Airborne Infantry Regiment stationed at Warner Kaserne. He and Lillian lived in the area south of McGraw Kaserne. Most of the apartments had twin beds and you were stuck with them. The only way that Quartermaster would exchange them for double beds was for medical necessity. Most of us adapted. Euna and I pushed our twin beds together and stuffed blankets in the

The Life Of A Soldier

gap. Ray and Lillian, however, could not be happy with the twin beds. To help them get the double bed, Euna did some creative writing. She wrote a letter with a lot of psychobabble about the emotional distress from the separation during the night. The quartermaster bought it and exchanged the beds.

General Bruce C. Clark was a very wise man and made a lasting impression on Me though I never met him personally. On every building in the 7th Army in compliance with General Clark's order, there was a plaque that read, "An organization does well only those things the boss checks." When I first read that it offended me, but as time went on, I came to realize that he was right.

The rules we lived by there were so much different than today it is almost unbelievable. We were not allowed to attend a movie without a coat and tie, except those on the Kasernes (posts). The National Anthem was played before the movie started and everyone stood.

While in Germany we took one vacation in Austria, (Salzburg and vicinity), and two or three to Garmisch and Bertchesgarden. We adopted our daughter Sherry Lynn in Munich. We took her into our home and started the adoption process just a few weeks after our arrival. She had been born on December 19 before we arrived in February. She was and still is a joy to us. Both of our children are adopted, and I can't imagine that it would be possible to love either of them any more than we do. We adopted our son Daniel in 1981 when he was nine months old.

Euell White

Sherry Lynn on my 1949 Opel behind our apartment building

The Life Of A Soldier

Daniel Aaron White

Euell White

The Life Of A Soldier

**Sherry at the wall of a woman's prison
Behind our apartment building**

Euell White

The Life Of A Soldier

One day a young woman showed up at our door and offered to be our maid and we hired her. She was an Austrian, and 18 years old. We paid her 65 German marks per month, which was about $18.00, plus providing her room and board, and that was more than the average. Her name was Josepha Wunder and we called her Josie.

Josie

Josie loved opera and her dream was to be a dancer. Our quarters included a room in the basement for a maid, but we had her sleep in the room with Sherry who was about four months old when Josie came. Josie was a good worker and very dependable. She was available to baby sit anytime we needed her. Her only outside interest was the opera, which she saved her money to attend.

Josie taught Sherry to walk on her toes and also taught her to speak German. After Josie had been with us about a year, a singer, Katerina Valente, came to the Munich Opera House. She was a popular singer in Europe and could sing in several languages. We heard her on the radio and had at least one of her albums.

Josie went to the opera house one night for her concert and went backstage afterward to get Katerina's autograph. She was invited to go out to eat with the cast, and met a man who was a performer. She fell in love with

The Life Of A Soldier

him and he started taking her out. We were suspicious because he wouldn't come to pick her up. She would always meet him somewhere away from the house.

Finally Josie told us they were going to be married and she was to meet him in Rome. We tried to caution her but she was so infatuated with him she couldn't accept the possibility that she was being taken for a ride. I drove her to the Bahnhoff to catch the train for Rome and felt like I was saying goodbye to my own daughter, even though she was only about five years younger than me.

We didn't hear from Josie for some time, then we received a letter from her telling us the man had deceived her. He was already married and she had been living with an Italian family in Rome, ashamed to tell us what had happened. We sent her a ticket and told her to come home. When she returned she worked for us half time and our best friends, Claude and Freda Hager half time, but she lived with us all time. When the time for our departure was getting near, we allowed her to find another job with a captain and his wife. They were very nice people and good to Josie. They brought her to the Banhoff to see us off when we left.

Later on we had a letter from her. She was in New York City. The family we left her with had arranged for some doctor in New York to sponsor her and she was working for his family while attending school to learn ballet. We heard from her once more and she was back in Germany attending Frei University in Berlin.

When we went to Germany I was the squad leader of the only rifle squad in the 76th Tank Battalion. The squad was part of the reconnaissance platoon which had, in addition to my squad, an 81mm mortar squad, a tank section with two light tanks, and a scout section with four jeeps with 30 caliber machine guns mounted on them.

Some of my Rifle Squad. I had three more not pictured

The transportation for my squad was an armored personnel carrier. Every so often, we had a maintenance competition and my vehicle won the "Best Maintained Tracked Vehicle" award every time.

The Life Of A Soldier

I had an advantage because I had nine men for one vehicle that was simpler to maintain than the medium tank with only four men. Winning this maintenance competition brought me to the attention of the Battalion Commander, Lieutenant Colonel Carleton Preer and he picked me to be the Headquarters Tank Platoon Leader, a lieutenant's position.

The Headquarters Tank Platoon consisted of four medium tanks. One for the Battalion commander, one for the Artillery Liaison Officer, one for the Air Liaison Officer and one for the Battalion Operations Officer.

Soon after arriving in Germany, our platoon sergeant, Master Sergeant John Day had some health problems. We were at a training center and one morning as we were getting ready to go out to the field for the day, our platoon leader, First Lieutenant Floyd Cox, drove up and asked me to ride with him in his jeep. On the way to the field, he told me about Sergeant Day's health problem and that he would have to be replaced as platoon sergeant. Then he told me that he wanted me to be his platoon sergeant. I told him that Sergeant First Class Jerry Martelli was promoted to Sergeant First Class the same month that I enlisted in the army and had combat experience in the Korean War. Cox said that he knew that but that all of Martelli's experience had been in Infantry and I was school trained in armor. Martelli's assignment at that time was Scout Section leader which rode in jeeps rather than tracked vehicles. I assured the lieutenant that I would help Jerry Martelli all I could. Jerry was assigned as platoon sergeant, and I never told him that the job had been offered to me. He did a good job, but didn't get promoted to master Sergeant in that assignment.

Floyd Cox was an excellent officer. He was single and always volunteered for the duty officer duty on thanksgiving and Christmas so that the married officers could be with their families. For some reason he enjoyed provoking me to argue with him. When we were out in the field he would come by my position and make some unjustified critical remark just to get an argument with me. Sometimes we would get into a yelling match with one another, out of the hearing of the soldiers, and he seemed to really enjoy it. Cox was a graduate of the New Mexico Military Institute and was commissioned as a regular Army Officer.

In 1957, the 11th Airborne Division became the 24th Infantry Division. Under the new Table of Organization and Equipment, the battalion was authorized an Assistant

The Life Of A Soldier

Operations Sergeant. The Colonel again picked me for that job which gave me invaluable experience. I soon became the editor or proof reader for the officers in the section. I corrected the writing of these officers with college degrees while I was a high school dropout and G.E.D. graduate. The greatest effect from the division designation change was that we were no longer on parachute status, a loss of $55 per month for enlisted men and $110 for officers.

Colonel Preer was one of the finest examples of an officer and gentleman I encountered during my military career. He was competent, confident and demanding, but I never heard him raise his voice. He didn't use profanity and made it known in a quiet way that he didn't appreciate it from others. The officers who did use profanity were careful to not use it in his presence and if an enlisted man did, they would quietly reprimand him.

The Colonel had a good sense of humor which was demonstrated by his reaction to Private Martin. For this story see Appendix B: Unforgettable Characters (Private Martin, Page 288).

In the summer of 1957 we had a heat wave in Germany. The temperature was higher than it had been for several decades and some of the German people died from the heat. I was attending the 7th Army Noncommissioned Officers Academy in Munich and I remember the shoe polish melting on our shoes and dripping on the floor. The tactical NCOs gave us demerits for our shoes not being shined and for the floor not being clean, on the one day a week when we changed our bed linens and displayed our shoes on the bed springs .

Euell White

As it turned out, my attendance at the academy, which I viewed at the time as a major inconvenience, was a blessing in disguise. I was in the process of applying for Officer Candidate School and one of the requirements was to have completed a leadership school or noncommissioned officers academy with a class standing in the top one-third of the class. I had accomplished this when I graduated from the Leadership School at Fort Jackson in 1952, but my records did not reflect my class standing.

The battalion had a requirement to send a NCO to the 7th Army Academy, and I volunteered with the idea that this would be faster then obtaining the information from the school at Fort Jackson. There was something going on at the time that caused the S-3, Major Biondi, to decide that he couldn't do without me during that period. Maybe the Operations Sergeant was on leave, I can't remember what it was.

I wrote for the information I needed from Fort Jackson and the same day that I received it in the mail, we had a requirement to send someone immediately for another class at the 7th Army academy. Someone in our staff section had dropped the ball and failed to task one of the companies to fill the quota.

Major Biondi's solution was to send me since I had tried to volunteer for an earlier class and the foul up was the fault of our section. My explanation that I no longer needed to attend the academy fell on unsympathetic ears.

While I was at the academy, my physical exam and my security clearance form expired. They had to have been completed within the past 90 days. This meant that I basically had to start all over again. The security form had to be perfectly typewritten and it was not easy to get that

The Life Of A Soldier

done. I was so frustrated that I decided to just drop the idea of OCS.

During the heat wave my battalion was out for field training and a polio outbreak came. Several of the officers and men of the battalion, including some on the battalion staff were stricken. The cause was never determined as far as I know. Some of the men fully recovered, but some were left with impairments. Looking back later, I realized that this inconvenience of the school protected me from exposure to the polio just as the fractured ankle back in 1952 protected me from exposure to nuclear radiation.

Sherry's first name was Angelika, and the Notar (Lawyer) who handled the adoption told us we could choose another name to change it to. Freda and Claude Hager suggested the name Sherry. We liked it and Euna added the middle name Lynn. We were unable to have children and she was God's gift to us. She had Euna's brown hair and brown eyes and my nose (until mine was changed by an automobile accident and the surgery following).

> We once visited Sherry's natural grandparents who were farmers at Neuhausen, about 30 miles from Munich. Amazingly, the grandfather looked almost identical to a portrait of Euna's paternal grandfather. We spent an enjoyable Sunday with the family but never saw them again. No one would have ever guessed Sherry wasn't born to us. We knew, however, that we could never keep that fact a secret and decided to be open with her about it.

One interesting experience I had in Germany was being in a television play. For the details of this, see Appendix C: Unusual and Interesting Duties (The Television Play, Page 303).

While I was Headquarters Tank Platoon Leader, we went to Belsen in the British Zone for tank gunnery competition firing. The competition required two gunners for each tank crew. I scored 795 points out of 800 and was awarded the Master Gunner certificate. I can't remember how our battalion as a whole came out but all of my gunners won the Master Gunner Certificate.

It was an interesting time. We were on a British post and they ran everything. It had always been a tradition in our army, whether you were firing tank guns or rifles, to get up early during range firing and try to fire the first round at first light or as soon as there was enough light. The British, however, didn't get out so early and the British commander said we couldn't start until a decent hour. Of course that pleased all of the enlisted men. Then our

The Life Of A Soldier

officers decided we would still get out to the range early and do other work such as getting the ammunition ready, but when the British commander found out, he vetoed it, saying that nobody would be on the range until a certain time. The British have breaks for "tea" and they would allow no work during that period, another frustration for our officers who wanted the ammunition details to work during that time.

    We left Munich in October and arrived at Brooklyn on 22 October. We sailed on the USNS Geiger which had been built for The United States Lines, but had been converted to use for transporting military passengers. Unlike the USS Butner which had taken us to Germany in 1956, the majority of the passengers on the Geiger were families. The Geiger was the nearest thing to a luxury liner we would ever see. There was no work, no chores. The emphasis was on comfort and entertainment and although we were eager to get the trip over with, we enjoyed it immensely.

    Our car was waiting when we arrived in New York. I had bought a German Opel in Germany, then later bought a 1954 Chevrolet from a friend and had it shipped back. We drove to Alabama to see our families and Sherry was thrilled to see her grandparents, aunts, uncles and cousins that we had told her about. She walked right into their hearts, especially Euna's Dad. She became very attached to him and it was a mutual feeling. Euna's Dad died about four months later with Leukemia. Sherry loved her other Granddaddy of course, but my Dad never paid much attention to his grandchildren. I don't mean this to be critical, everyone is not alike.

After a few days leave I reported in to the 101st Airborne Division at Fort Campbell, Kentucky. I was assigned to the 502nd Airborne Battle Group. The division had recently added to its organization an Assault Gun Platoon for each of the battle groups. The platoon consisted of three sections with 2 guns in each section . I was assigned as a section leader. The gun was called the SPAT (Self Propelled Antitank Gun). It was a full-tracked vehicle with a 90-millimeter gun. It had no armor except for a gun shield. It was a good weapon, but the vehicle was top-heavy, which we would learn from a tragedy.

The SPAT was designed to be dropped by parachute in an airborne assault. The military occupational specialty (MOS) for the SPAT crew member was infantry heavy weapons. I had been school trained in this MOS in 1952 at Fort Benning. But I had never worked in it. My experience with the 90mm tank gun served me well.

The top-heaviness of the SPAT was illustrated by a tragedy that touched me. For the details of this see Appendix A: Tragic Accidents (Vehicle accident at Fort Campbell, Page 281).

Don Walker was an outstanding NCO. He was in the Korean War with the 187th Airborne Regimental Combat Team and was involved in the breakup of a prisoner of war revolt on Koji Do Island. In the process his vocal cord was injured and he couldn't speak except in a sort of whisper. Don didn't believe in discomfort and pain. He would go out into the cold for days with what everyone thought was insufficient clothing, and when anyone commented about it he would smile and say that being cold

The Life Of A Soldier

was all in the mind. Once when we were going on an airborne assault exercise we were issued three days of "C" rations. While everyone else was packing the cans in their pack for the parachute jump, Don opened the cans and ate all he could hold then buried the remainder along with the litter.

His response to questions about that was that it is easier to carry that weight in your stomach than in your pack. As far as I know, he didn't eat anything else for the next three days. He also was very adept at keeping control of the platoon when they assigned us a lieutenant platoon leader. He knew how to make the lieutenant believe he was in control while avoiding any changes to his own efficient way of doing things.

We had some interesting experiences during the 18 months I was assigned to that platoon. The first time we dropped the SPATS by parachute we were on an airborne assault exercise. After the drop we secured the air head and while we were in the defensive position Major General William Westmoreland, the division commander, came by my position and talked with me for quite awhile. He asked questions and learned that I had last been assigned as a tanker. He wanted to know what I thought of this new anti-tank gun.

A few days later when the exercise was nearly over, my section was supporting a rifle company that was assaulting a hill, and I decided to pretend we had tanks instead of antitank guns and went charging up the hill. I knew better but we were bored. What I didn't know was that our battle group commander and General

Euell White

Westmoreland were on the hill observing the maneuvers. I learned later that General Westmoreland said "That is probably Sergeant White. He was a tanker and hasn't gotten over it." When the critique was held at the conclusion of the exercise, one of the main points was a reminder that the SPAT was not a tank but an antitank gun. Some six years later, General Westmoreland, commander of US Army Vietnam, pinned the purple heart on Captain White and remembered me from that day I charged the hill with two anti-tank guns.

In the hottest part of the summer of 1959 we flew to Fort Polk Louisiana and parachuted in. We didn't take the SPATS on that exercise. We conducted patrols all night, then the next day we walked about 20 miles to the main post. We had walked all night the night before and had no sleep. The heat was so intense that men were falling out along the way. Ambulances would pick them up and take them a few miles and dump them again. Some would recover enough to rejoin their units as they passed by, but some had to be transported all the way. All of our platoon was together when we arrived, but Don Walker and I were the only ones who had not taken at least a short ambulance ride. We were the two oldest men in the platoon.

We flew to Puerto Rico in the winter of 1959 as an air mobility test. I had a C-124 Globemaster for my two SPATS and crews. We flew down there, unloaded and drove about a half-mile to a campsite where we pitched pup tents. Then 48 hours later we returned. We were at Roosevelt Roads Naval Station. We didn't do anything while we were there except some of the men went to a club and picked a fight with the Navy.

The Life Of A Soldier

We also went to Fort Stewart Georgia to the tank training center to fire our 90mm guns. We rode a chartered bus and our SPATS were transported on lowboys. I had been there before when I was in the 76th Tank battalion.

We had found a house in Clarksville, Tennessee when we returned from Germany and the nearest church was Grace Baptist Church. Soon after the death of Euna's Dad, we attended Grace Baptist Church. Neither of us had ever been inside a Baptist church before. Euna was raised in the Methodist Church and I was raised in the Cumberland Presbyterian Church.

Euna responded to the invitation that morning. The pastor and a deacon came to visit that afternoon. While the pastor talked to Euna about baptism, the deacon talked to me about committing my life to God. We were both baptized that evening and joined the church, but we never set foot in that church again. That week, the army suddenly moved us to the post and shortly afterward we rented a house in a little town called Trenton Kentucky which had a population of 600 until we increased it to 603. We transferred our membership to the Baptist church that the people we rented from belonged to.

We were unhappy with the post quarters, and on our way to Fort Knox to visit Claude and Freda Hager, we took a back road and discovered that little town of Trenton. As we passed through we both agreed that this would be a nice place to live. On our way back from Fort Knox we decided to drive through there again. As we passed through, we saw a for rent sign on a big house. We stopped and asked the next door neighbor about it and she told us that the owners

Euell White

lived on a farm on the same road. We rented the house for $40 per month and the precious couple that we rented from, were apologetic for charging us so much.

Every time I went to pay the rent, they loaded me down with eggs, butter and usually a chicken. When they knew we were having company from back home the lady would bake a cake and send it to us. Other people in the community were also generous. We were the only military family in that little town. During the garden season we would come home from a trip and find our porch filled with fresh vegetables.

An incident that happened at Fort Campbell which-- was funny to me, but would not be funny to the animal rights fanatics-- involved the division mascot. The mascot for the "Screaming Eagles" is a real live eagle. In 1959 the mascot was murdered one night and the murder was a mystery for a time. I think the cause of death was strangulation, although I never saw the autopsy report. There was quite a stir about this. I don't know whether there was a reward offered for information leading to the identification of the perpetrator of this crime.

Some time later, a lieutenant came forward and confessed to the crime. General Westmoreland had administered non-judicial punishment to the lieutenant for some offense and he was angry about it. He couldn't strangle the general so he strangled his eagle. The revenge was empty, however, when no one knew that he had done it so he confessed. A new eagle was acquired and I don't know what happened to the lieutenant--- but I would bet that he never wore captain's bars.

The Life Of A Soldier

4.
Third Enlistment
May 1960-April 1962

In 1960 my enlistment was up and I re-enlisted for Hawaii because there was an opening there for me to get in a position to be promoted. At least that was what I was told. I was assigned to a tank battalion, but I didn't get the position that I expected. After realizing I had been bamboozled, I took a job teaching in the division Noncommissioned Officers Academy.

While on leave before going to Hawaii in 1960, I bought a new 1960 Chevrolet Corvair . It was the first model ever built and it had an air-cooled engine. We headed out for San Francisco before the engine was broken in good. We left early enough to take our time and do some sight-seeing on the way, but my impatient urge to get there prevented it.

The car didn't have air conditioning and the weather was hot, so we decided to drive at night and sleep in daytime. This didn't work as well as we expected because Sherry would sleep while we were driving at night then she wanted to play all day while we were trying to sleep.

We arrived at Fort Mason in San Francisco several days before our flight to Hawaii. We held on to the car until the last day before turning it in to be shipped and did some sightseeing in and around San Francisco. We drove across the Golden Gate Bridge to Oakland and other towns and cities. We enjoyed the time in San Francisco. The only problem was the weather. We didn't have anything but short sleeve clothing, and it was cold in San Francisco, especially in the evenings. We went to the Post Exchange at the Presidio of San Francisco and bought sweaters for Euna and Sherry, but I just toughed it out.

We flew from Travis Air Force Base near San Francisco to Hickam Air Force Base in Honolulu on an Air Force plane. We arrived late at night and there seemed to be someone there to meet every passenger except us. I felt disappointed and was beginning to have some misgivings about my assignment. I found a phone and called the unit I was assigned to, a tank Battalion in the 25th Infantry Division. The duty officer assured me someone would be there shortly to meet us. Soon, Battalion Sergeant Major Furlow and his wife arrived and took us to an Apartment Hotel near Waikiki Beach, across the street from the Ala Wai Canal in Honolulu, where we lived for the next two months.

This foul up of not having anyone waiting for us when we arrived, really turned out to be a blessing because it opened the way for a personal relationship with the Sergeant Major. He and his wife were from Jacksonville, Alabama and they were almost old enough to be our parents. They had no children and they very attentive to us.

Later when I became unhappy because I didn't get the position I was promised when I re-enlisted, Sergeant Major Furlow helped to me get a job as instructor at the Division Noncommissioned Officers Academy. I had reenlisted at Fort Campbell for Hawaii because there was supposed to be a Platoon Sergeant position for me that would give me an opportunity to be promoted.

The Life Of A Soldier

When I arrived I found an old Master Sergeant named Hart, who had never been assigned to a combat unit, filling the position. His experience was in personnel and he was supposedly being trained for a military occupational specialty (MOS) in armor. I think the reason was to qualify him for the rank of First Sergeant. This man had congestive heart failure and was unable to get on and off the tank by himself. I was assigned to this platoon apparently to be his caretaker for awhile. While I had compassion for his disabilities, he was not qualified technically nor physically for the job. I resented him taking the position that I had been promised and uprooted my family and traveled to Hawaii for. I had a basis for a complaint, but decided not to pursue it. The Biblical promise that all things work for good proved to apply to this situation.

When I went to the academy to work, I was still assigned to the tank battalion and on special duty to the academy. With this job I was home for supper every night except for occasional field trips, and was off every weekend.

When I first arrived at the academy I was assigned as an instructor. While I was still going through the process of rehearsing for a class before other instructors, a new Assistant Commandant was assigned. He was Captain Schirra, a West point Graduate who had been awarded the Silver Star for action in the Korean War. He immediately reorganized the school and put me in charge of half of it. The school was like many others, with an academic department and a tactical department. Each class was divided into two sections and each section was under a senior tactical NCO. The tactical NCOs took care of the students in the barracks. The academic department was divided into two sections also.

Captain Schirra combined the tactical with the academic and put me in charge of half of the students, half of the tactical NCOs and half of the instructors. Overnight I became the boss of the one who was my boss. Everything went smooth, however, and when I decided to apply for a direct commission, Captain Schirra gave me a super recommendation.

The nearest I ever came to being a casualty because of the cold was in Hawaii. On a field training exercise, we climbed Mt. Kaala, the highest point on Oahu. When we arrived at the top just before dark, we found that it was flat and like a swamp. If you stood still you would sink in the mud up to your knees. We had no equipment or clothing with us for the cold weather and it became very cold that night. I tried to make a bed from my poncho but just sank in the mud. I have slept in the snow in Germany in 30 degrees below zero weather, but there I had the clothing and equipment to protect me.

In the summer of 1961 I learned through a neighbor who was the Division Personnel NCO, of a procurement program whereby qualified applicants could apply for a direct appointment as Second Lieutenant. I applied and was commissioned as a reserve second lieutenant in January 1962 with an active duty date of 6 April. I was assigned to a tank battalion when I applied for a commission in the infantry. I had to be interviewed by the battalion commander and he was very much interested in why I didn't apply for the armor branch.

The Life Of A Soldier

I submitted my application in the Summer of 1961. I had a very flattering recommendation from the Captain who was my boss at the noncommissioned officer's academy at Schofield Barracks. I had to appear before a board at Fort Derussey in Honolulu, then my application was forwarded to Department of the Army in Washington. The age limit for appointment was 27. My 28th birthday came on 26 December.

With no word about my application, when my birthday passed, I was certain it would be returned disapproved or requiring a waiver for my age which would delay the whole process. I became somewhat discouraged, but one day in January 1962, I was summoned to the battalion commander's office. (I had returned to the battalion). When I reported to the battalion commander, he said, "raise your right hand" then administered the oath of office to me.

Euell White

Taking the oath of office

My active duty date as a second lieutenant was set for 6 April 1962, and I had to report to Fort Benning on 10 April. This didn't leave us time to ship our car home and travel from San Francisco by car. I traded my Corvair in for a new Chevrolet Impala at Aloha Motors in Honolulu and had it delivered in Florence. It was waiting for me when I arrived. Aloha Motors allowed me to use the Corvair until I left. I was instructed to park it in front of the government building in Honolulu and lock the key in it.

The Life Of A Soldier

Those last two days in Hawaii were hectic, to say the least. The day that I put on my gold bar, every noncommissioned officer in the battalion went out of his way to salute me. A personnel warrant officer who worked at battalion headquarters had tried to put out obstacles to my being commissioned. It started when I got hold of the procurement circular before it came to him through channels. Like most bureaucrats he didn't like losing his power or having it diminished. The Sergeant major took charge of my application and made sure it was endorsed by the battalion commander and forwarded without undue delay. The day I put the bar on, I thought about what fun it would be to go and stand that warrant officer at attention and chew him out real good. After thinking about it for awhile, I did just the opposite. I went by to see him and thanked him for his help. He was speechless because he expected something different.

In Hawaii, we had just a little taste of what it is like to be discriminated against because of your race. All of the ads about rentals in the Honolulu newspapers, had at the end of the ads, "No Haoles." I couldn't figure out whether that was their word for pets or for black people. Then I learned it was their word for us--all of us, no matter what color—that were not local.

We found a nice house in Waipahu, about 15 miles from Schofield Barracks, but the ad said "No Haoles." I managed to get the Japanese-American couple who owned the house to meet me and there I convinced them that in spite of being a Haole, I was a nice guy and would take good care of the house and pay the rent on time.

Euell White

Sherry attended kindergarten at Waipahu Elementary where she was one of three white children in the class. All of our neighbors were Filipinos and we arranged through some of them for Sherry to ride a van that transported children to school. We later learned that because we were Haoles we were charged more.

Sherry's Kindergarten Class. At August Ahrens School in Waipahu, Oahu. She is second from left, front row.

The Life Of A Soldier

After a few months we moved to Schofield Barracks where we had a two bedroom house. It was old, but very comfortable costing less than the new apartments. Behind our house was the regimental parade field for one of the infantry regiments. On Friday afternoons the regiment paraded just before retreat. One day I came home while the regiment was passing in review and saw Sherry who was 5 or 6 with a little neighbor boy marching in between two of the battalions. The soldiers were carrying their weapons at right shoulder arms. Sherry and her friend were carrying Euna's broom and mop at right shoulder arms.

Of all my assignments, Hawaii was undoubtedly the most enjoyable one for our family, but not for the reasons most people would naturally assume. We went to the beach only a few times while we were there. Sherry hadn't learned to swim yet and I never cared much for swimming in salt water. One reason we enjoyed Hawaii so much is that we were able to be together as a family more than on any other assignment. Another is that we found a church where we formed many friendships The church was a Southern Baptist mission church when we joined it, but it became a church while we were there. It exists today as the First Baptist Church of Waipahu. The church was a double melting pot. Every ethnic group on the island of Oahu was represented as well as all of the uniformed services—Army, Navy, Air Force, Marine Corps, Coast Guard, the Public Health Service and the Coast and Geodetic Survey. We made many friends there, among the local people as well as the other military families.

Euell White

Our daughter Sherry, whom we adopted in Germany, was naturalized In Honolulu while we were there. In her typical take charge, independent manner, when the judge administered the loyalty oath, he said I could repeat it for Sherry, but she objected and said she wanted to do it herself. It was both amusing and touching for us to hear our little five-year-old daughter take an oath to bear arms if called upon to do so, and to defend the nation against all its enemies. She was sincere and to this day she loves her country.

The first and best friends we made in Hawaii were Doug and Bernice King. They lived in the same neighborhood of Waipahu as we did and they were very active in the First Baptist (mission) Church. Doug was an entrepreneur. Years earlier while stationed in Hawaii with the Navy, Doug had begun a coin operated laundry then branched out to other enterprises. His businesses became so successful that He left the Navy.

When we arrived, Doug had a laundromat, a furniture store, an apartment hotel, and sold cemetery plots. He owned the WORD Records franchise for the state of Hawaii to sell a phonograph record package containing hymns, and other spiritual music as well as Bible stories and inspirational materials for children, youth and adults. In his spare time Doug was DJ for a country music radio program and a reserve policeman for the Honolulu Police Department. .A description often used for someone with superior selling skills is "He could sell ice cream to the Eskimos." This description fit Doug King. He loved the challenge of selling

The Kings had two sons and two daughters. Doug passed away a few years ago. Bernice and the children now

The Life Of A Soldier

live in the Bakersfield California area. The Kings were originally from Russellville, Alabama, and Bernice sometimes visits us when she comes to visit her relatives there.

    Kazuo and Rena Arakawa were also special friends. Kazuo and his family owned Arakawa Department Store in Waipahu and he and Rena were members of First Baptist Church. I had a layover on Oahu on my way to Australia in 1973 and spent an entire day with Kazuo. I learned a lot from him that day about the history of Oahu and especially Waipahu.

Euell White

Dining at Ishii Garden Japanese restaurant in Honolulu as guests of the Arakawa's. The other couple are Frank and Mary Cross. Sergeant Frank cross was killed in Vietnam.

The Life Of A Soldier

5.
First Infantry Division–The Big Red One
April 1962–April 1964

When we left Hawaii in April 1962, I attended the basic Infantry officer's Course at Fort Benning, Georgia before going to my assignment in the First Infantry Division (the Big Red One) at Fort Riley, Kansas. This is the only stateside assignment I ever had outside the Third Army area, which was basically the Southeastern states. During the two years with the First Infantry Division, I served as platoon leader executive officer and commanding officer of a rifle company, and as Executive officer of a service company. I was assigned to Company E, 1st Battle Group, 13th Infantry which later became the 1st battalion 18th Infantry in an organization change.

    I didn't play the role of the dumb second lieutenant very well. When we arrived at Fort Riley for my first assignment as an officer, I reported in to the 1st Battle Group, 13th Infantry late in the afternoon. I was greeted by the adjutant and the deputy battle group commander, then assigned to Company E. First Sergeant Wicker came and escorted me to the company and I leaned that the company was out on a field exercise and would be out there for another few days. The following morning I drew field equipment from the supply room and told First Sergeant Wicker that I needed transportation to the company's location in the field. He tried to discourage me from going out there, and I correctly guessed that he had been told by the company commander to keep the new lieutenant there until the company returned. I insisted, however, and the first Sergeant took me out in a jeep.

When we found the company commander, First Lieutenant Forrest Woods, he shook my hand then stopped an armored personnel carrier and introduced me to a Master Sergeant who was the 3rd Platoon Sergeant. I mounted the Carrier and we drove a short distance to a night defensive position. After the squads were in place I told the platoon sergeant to assemble the squad leaders. I introduced myself and a little later it was time for supper.

It is a tradition in the combat arms that in the field, the leaders do not eat until after the last man has been fed. I went to the mess area and told the platoon sergeant to notify me when the platoon was fed. In tactical situations the troops would be rotated. Half would eat while the other half manned the defensive positions. After he told me the platoon had been fed I ate and then returned to the platoon area to find that one fire team had not been fed. As soon as we made sure they were fed, I had a private straightforward talk with the platoon sergeant. In a way this foul up was a blessing. I had sensed a resentment from him for being displaced as the platoon leader and this gave me an opportunity to let him know that from that moment I was in charge of the platoon.

After supper, we received word that the company commander wanted all platoon leaders at his command post (CP) to receive the order for the following day. The platoon sergeant was getting ready to go but I told him to give me his map and I would go. When I arrived at the CP the company commander showed surprise by his expression and asked where the platoon sergeant was. I replied that he

The Life Of A Soldier

was with the platoon where he belonged. The remainder of the field exercise went well. The only thing that kept it from being perfect was the sullen attitude of the platoon sergeant.

The day following our return from the field I reported to the company commander, formally, in his office. Later on after we had become friends, Forrest told me that he had indeed told the first sergeant to keep me in the barracks and was surprised that I came out there. He made captain soon after that.

Upon our return from six months in Germany, Captain Woods appointed me as company executive officer over a first lieutenant. Then when he found out that he was being reassigned he tried to have me assigned as company commander. In the several months I served under Forrest, he never once found it necessary to reprimand me.

Soon after my arrival we went to South Carolina for maneuvers. We traveled by truck convoy from Fort Riley to South Carolina. We had an overnight at Fort Campbell on the way down and I visited with Sergeant Don Walker who had been my platoon sergeant in the SPAT platoon before I went to Hawaii.

The South Carolina maneuvers provided a good breaking in for me as a platoon leader. There was a parasitic plant indigenous to the county we were in and the agriculture department was watching to make sure we didn't spread it. It was called "Witchweed." The witchweed patches were marked on our maps and we were not supposed to set foot in them. In the excitement of a mock battle, however, troops sometimes forgot or misread the map. When this happened, the unit that was involved would be stopped until decontamination teams could come and spray their boots. I am not certain that some of the incidents weren't deliberate because it was an opportunity to rest for a few hours.

Soon after our return from South Carolina we received word that the Battle Group was to deploy to Germany for six months temporary change of station, during the winter of 1962-63. At that time we had not found suitable quarters and our furniture was still in storage. I took leave and drove Euna and Sherry back home where they stayed with Euna's sister Virginia while I was gone. Euna had never learned to drive so I taught her to drive while on that leave. She passed her drivers test just in time to drive me to the train station in Sheffield to return to Fort Riley.

We had three months at Wildflecken and three months in Berlin. Wildflecken is a very hilly place. The little post where we stayed was beautiful. We stayed busy training, and that is where I really got to know my platoon.

I remember that one of the young sergeants in my platoon named Chavis, who was a fire team leader, left his men behind one morning when we went out to a training area about 8 miles from the post. He simply forgot to see that they were on the truck. The men were guilty too, because they knew we were going.

I sent him back by jeep to get them, and required him to march them out on foot. After that I invested a lot of time in that young man. He had a fear of teaching and was finding a way to dodge that when he was assigned a class to teach. I helped him through that by personally having him to rehearse his classes to me. I taught him about leadership

The Life Of A Soldier

one-on one. I required him to write and rewrite essays on the eleven principles of military leadership and fourteen traits of a leader, applying each one to himself. I am sure there were times that he wished he had never become a sergeant, but it paid off.

One day in 1972, at Fort Benning just a couple of months before I retired, the Sergeant Major came to the door of my office and told me there was a Master Sergeant Chavis wanting to see me. When he came in I recognized him. He had seen my name in the post daily bulletin. He told me that he wanted to thank me for the attention I gave him back there ten years earlier. He had been promoted to Master Sergeant E-8 as an ammunition specialist, on a waiver when he was shy of the required time in service and was then on the list for Sergeant Major with a waiver for time in grade and service. He gave me credit for his success. That visit from Master Sergeant Chavis was more meaningful than any of the medals I was awarded.

We left Wildflecken just before Christmas of 1962 for Berlin. I took a day off and rode the train to Fulda to do some Christmas shopping. I wore my uniform for that trip and was truly amazed at the reaction of the German people in that town. In every shop I was invited to spend Christmas with a German family. I had to refuse because I knew I wouldn't be there for Christmas. The owner of the last shop that I visited, accompanied me to the Bahnhoff (train station) and sipped coffee with me and chatted while I was waiting for the train.

During our time in Berlin I had duty as Officer In Charge of the checkpoint between the U.S. and Soviet zone. For details of this special assignment, see Appendix C: Unusual and Interesting Duties (Checkpoint Charlie, Page 305).

    I went from Wildflecken to Berlin with the advance party. Although the main body came by vehicle convoy, the advance party went by train from Frankfurt to Berlin. For those who are not up to date on the geography and history, the city of Berlin was like an island inside Communist East Germany, and Berlin was divided into four sectors, The Soviet Sector, The American Sector, The British Sector and the French sector. The Soviet sector was referred to as East Berlin and the remaining three sectors comprised West Berlin.

    To travel by land from West Germany to West Berlin you had to pass through Communist East Germany. It was an interesting trip. Ever time we stopped in East Germany, Communist soldiers surrounded the train with their rifles and machine guns pointed at the train. It was a little intimidating, but mostly amusing. They were poised for action as though they expected these Americans to try to escape from our own army and join them.

    Our battle group commander when we went to Germany was Colonel Robert Dickerson. I came to know him more than the average second lieutenant would have. He was a World War II veteran who commanded a rifle company in the Normandy invasion in one of the airborne divisions, and landed by glider. Colonel Dickerson was fluent in German, a fact that I doubt was even known by his staff. He was from Kentucky and his favorite pastime was playing the guitar and singing country music. I had heard some of the officers making fun of this behind his back. One evening at the snack bar we called our officers club in

The Life Of A Soldier

Berlin, he gave a blanket invitation for anyone that wanted to come to his room and he would play and sing. Nobody responded so I told him I would very much like to hear him play and sing. I was doing it because I felt sorry for him. He was obviously a lonely man. However, I really enjoyed it. He was very talented and played and sang the old songs that I had heard my dad play and sing.

Although he was a Catholic and drank wine with his meals, the Colonel strongly disapproved of excessive drinking by his officers, and he had some on his staff who had this problem.

One day soon after my visit to his room, the assistant adjutant, a second lieutenant who was really more like the Colonel's aide, called me and told me that Lieutenant Wardell Caesar Smith was running a race at the Olympic Stadium on Saturday afternoon and the Colonel would like for me to accompany him to watch the race and for Lieutenant Smith and me to go out with him for dinner afterward. I accepted, of course, and the lieutenant told me the colonel's staff car would pick me up at a certain time. Caesar did real well in the race and the Germans loved him. Colonel Dickerson took us to a quaint little place and ordered for us. I remember sauerbraten and potato dumplings. There was more and the food was delicious. There was a violinist playing and the Colonel made requests all during the meal.

Caesar Smith and me at Andrews Barracks, Berlin

The battle group adjutant, a Captain who was nearing retirement eligibility, was a drunk, and drinking buddy with some of the other staff officers., including the major who was battle group Operations Officer. One night while I was on duty as the Battle Group Staff Duty Officer, the Berlin Command Provost Marshall came by and told me that he had arrested the captain and placed him in arrest of quarters. He had been arrested for public drunkenness and causing a disturbance in some German establishment. I recorded the incident in the Staff Duty Officers Log which was exactly what I was required to do.

    The next morning the Battle Group Operations Officer sent for me and chewed me out. He told me we should keep these things from "the old man." My response was that I didn't have the authority to decide what the

The Life Of A Soldier

commanding officer should know about what is going on in his command, and neither did he. He was very angry and subtly threatened me, but I didn't let it bother me. I told my company commander, Captain Woods, about the incident and he assured me I did the right thing. A day or two later Colonel Dickerson sent for me and told me he appreciated my loyalty and diligence. I don't know how he learned of the confrontation with the major but he obviously had.

The captain got himself into such a fix with drinking and gambling that he embezzled money from a welfare fund of which he was custodian. I heard that he was tried by a general court and lost all pay and rank and received a dishonorable discharge. I am not sure whether he went to prison. This is an example of what happens when people are enabled rather than confronted with such problems.

After we returned from Germany to Fort Riley, my company commander, Captain Forrest Woods, appointed me as his executive officer and made the first lieutenant that held the position a platoon leader. I was glad that he had such confidence in me and realized the first lieutenant was incompetent, but he was a friend and I felt bad for him. We remained friends, however. He understood that it was not ambition on my part that caused the change. Maybe incompetent was not the correct description, He was a very smart and educated man, but was physically clumsy and impulsive. It seemed that everything he tried to do somehow got fouled up. I won't use his real name. I will call him Lieutenant Priest. He was a good man. He had a heart of gold and really wanted to please, and it seemed that was part of his problem.

One of the missions we had in Berlin was to have a riot control platoon on standby, ready to go on a moment's notice. This duty rotated among the rifle companies and I think we had it for two weeks. The riot platoon had to have an officer for platoon leader and the only officer platoon leaders in the company were Lieutenant Caesar Smith and me. Captain Woods assigned Priest, who was the executive officer, to be a platoon leader for the third rifle platoon so that Smith and I didn't have to double up on the duty.

The first night that Lt. Priest had the duty, he got in trouble. A second lieutenant from one of the other companies who was always playing practical jokes, decided to have some fun with Lieutenant Priest. He called him and with an affected German accent told him there was a riot in progress and he was needed. He gave Priest a grid coordinate location in East Berlin and identified himself as an Oberloitnant (First Lieutenant) with the West Berlin police. The prankster heard Priest say, "Get em out Sergeant" then Priest laid the phone down and never came back on. Hearing all of the noise to indicate the platoon was being loaded onto vehicles, the lieutenant called the Battle Group headquarters and told the duty officer to stop it. He had intended to tell Priest that he was joking but he responded so fast he didn't get the chance. The platoon sergeant covered for Priest and told the troops that it was a practice alert.

Captain Woods was furious with Priest and with the lieutenant prankster. Priest should have known that any orders to deploy the platoon would come from Battle Group headquarters, and not the West Berlin police.

The Life Of A Soldier

When I had been a second lieutenant exactly one year, Captain Woods called me to his office and told me that he was being moved to the Battle Group staff and had recommended to the Battle Group Commander, Colonel Dickerson, that I be given command of E company. He said he told the Colonel that He believed I was the best qualified lieutenant in the group for company command. The Colonel agreed with him but said it would create a morale problem to give a second lieutenant a company with so many first lieutenants wanting to command a company. The Colonel said if you can find a way that we can promote him now to first lieutenant, we will promote him, then give him the company. This couldn't be done, however, because there was a statute that said a second lieutenant must serve 18 months before being promoted except in time of war. It made me feel good just to know I was considered, and it turned out that when I did make first lieutenant 6 months later, I was given command of the company.

When Captain Woods left the company I assumed temporary command of Company E. One day the adjutant called and told me to come and pick up my company commander. The man that I met was a stranger to me. I will call him Captain Riverbuck. This began one of the most challenging duties I ever had. For details see Appendix B: Unforgettable Characters (Captain Riverbuck, Page 290).

One interesting character that I encountered in the Big Red One was Brigadier General Monk Meyers. I can't remember his first name but he was known as Monk from his football days at West point. He was Assistant Division Commander and apparently didn't have much to do, or didn't know what to do. Besides football at West point, which meant nothing to the troops of the division, Monk was famous for riding around the post, seeking soldiers who failed to salute him and seeing that they were punished, regardless of whether their slight of him was intentional or unintentional.

One day during our preparation for a live fire demonstration that "E" Company was doing for all of the R.O.T.C. cadets of the 5th Army, Lieutenant Caesar Smith and I were at the bleachers site checking the sound system. After we checked it we forgot to disconnect the microphone. We saw General Meyers drive up in his jeep to the control site that was about a hundred yards down the hill from us. Caesar and I started talking about him referring to him as "old Monk" and generally discussing how useless he was. After awhile a lieutenant whom I knew and who was the general's aide walked up and disconnected the microphone and said, the next time you want to talk about the general you should be sure that you are not talking into a live microphone with a speaker right next to the general's ear. He said the general heard everything we said and told him to find out who it was. He suggested that we get out of the area so that he could go back and tell the general he didn't find us. We jumped in our jeep and left. We never heard any more about it.

I was promoted to First Lieutenant in October 1963.Shortly after that promotion, Captain Riverbuck was transferred to the staff of a Brigade being formed, and I was Given command of Company E.

The Life Of A Soldier

Euna Penning my Silver Bar

Euell White

**Euna having coffee with Colonel Malone,
Battle Group Commander**

Later on while I was commanding Company "E", one of my soldiers, a Private First Class, came to see me and was really scared. He said he was in big trouble. He had been standing in a soldier pickup shelter that was provided for those who needed a ride to wait for transportation. General Meyer drove up in his jeep and surprised them. Nobody called attention nor saluted him. He instructed his aide to get all of their names and units. My soldier told me he meant no disrespect but was caught by surprise and couldn't think what the right thing to do was in a shelter like that.

I realized that I would soon be hearing from Battle Group headquarters so I called the First Sergeant in with the company punishment book. I administered non-judicial punishment and gave the man a verbal reprimand. Within

The Life Of A Soldier

the hour the Battle Group adjutant called and said the general wanted the man busted to private. I told him it was too late because I had already given him a verbal reprimand under article 15 of the Uniform Code of Military Justice. He said the general wouldn't like it and I said that's too bad because it was not the general's prerogative but mine as company commander. I never heard anymore about that. I have always believed that Monk Meyers' only real expertise was in playing football and he lived on his fame as a football player.

Euell White

The Life Of A Soldier

6.
Okinawa
First Special Forces Group (Airborne)

Lieutenant Wardell Caesar Smith from Iowa, became a close friend. Like me, he had prior enlisted service, and unlike me he attended officer candidate school. Caesar was a runner. He had tried out for the Army Olympic team, and although he didn't make the team he was good. While we were in Berlin, Caesar ran with the Germans at the same stadium where the Olympics were held in 1939 and Hitler refused to honor Jesse Owens because he was black. Caesar is black and the Germans loved to see him run.

Caesar and I were both parachutists and wanted to have an airborne assignment. We were always kidding one another about who would be first to get an airborne assignment. I filled out an assignment preference sheet and requested an airborne assignment. The response from the personnel infantry branch was, in effect, don't bother us, we will tell you where you want to go.

While I was commanding Company E I received a call from division personnel one day telling me that I would be receiving orders for the First Special Forces Group (Airborne) in Okinawa. The call came late in the afternoon and I didn't see Caesar to tell him about it, so I called him that evening at home to boast about it. The next morning he was having coffee with several officers in the Battle Group and told them about my coming assignment. A First Lieutenant named Jim White said that sounded like his assignment. Jim was a Military Academy graduate and He had a friend in personnel at the Pentagon who was getting him the assignment. I later learned that the division personnel office had called the Battle Group and asked for information on Lieutenant White. They didn't say which Lieutenant White so my file was pulled and the information was provided. When they realized their mistake, rather than admit it, they asked me to volunteer for the assignment which I gladly did. That is how I got into Special Forces, by saving face for the bureaucracy.

In the Spring of 1964 I Attended the U.S. Army Special Warfare School at Fort Bragg North Carolina in preparation for my assignment to the First Special Forces Group (Airborne) on Okinawa. I completed two courses, the Special Forces Officer Course and the Special Warfare Staff Officers Course.

The Special Forces training was very interesting. The concept for the training was that special forces teams would be inserted behind enemy lines to organize, train and equip guerilla forces. You could say that we were trained more to be part of an insurgency than to conduct counter-insurgency operations. The special forces "A" team consisted of two officers, a captain, commander and a lieutenant, executive officer, plus 10 noncommissioned officers with two each of five specialties. These were, operations and intelligence; weapons; demolitions; communications; and medical.

These NCOs were truly experts in their field. Between the two weapons NCOs they knew all about every small arms weapon and mortar in the world. The communications NCOs knew all about the CW (Constant Wave) radios of the world. The medics could do anything

The Life Of A Soldier

from delivering babies to emergency surgery. The demolitions guys could efficiently blow up anything you wanted blown up. All of the NCOs were cross-trained so that they could fill in for another in a pinch.

At that time there was no special forces branch for officers. We came from different branches; therefore we didn't have near the technical expertise of the NCOs. I would not have attempted to operate the radio unless there was no one else to do it. I never developed any speed and could not read the incoming messages sent at the normal speed. We didn't spend much time on this. I learned a lot about demolitions in the school. I had also been schooled in the weapons and demolitions when I was an NCO so I could have done a fair job in these areas.

For our field exercise, we jumped at night into the Uwharrie National Forest in North Carolina. One night the group that I was with set up in the forest for the night. I strung my hammock between two trees and went to sleep. We had been on the move with little sleep for several days and I was very tired. The next morning at about 0800 hours the sun woke me and there was no one there but me. I saw the shell casings from the blank rifle ammunition and litter from the grenade simulators all around the area where I was sleeping. Obviously there had been a great battle there but I slept right through it.

I was not in a leadership position at that time and didn't even have a map. I had no idea where the unit had gone. For the first couple of days after our jump we had camped by a lake. I thought I knew the way back to that point. I walked through the forest all day. That forest was infested with rattlesnakes and I thought all day that if one of them bit me, nobody would find me in time to save me. Shortly before dark I arrived at the lake and found two Special Forces Sergeants there. I was never more glad to see someone. They were cooking supper and invited me to eat with them. I never enjoyed a meal more, although it was mostly heated C rations. A day or two later my unit returned to that location. They hadn't worried about me because they assumed I had been captured by the aggressors in the attack.

During this exercise I was struck by lightning. I was in charge of a small patrol with three Sergeants and we were in a pasture when a storm came up. We saw a barn nearby and decided to get in the barn for shelter. We had to cross a barbed wire fence to get to the barn. One of the sergeants crossed the fence then used his M-1 Rifle to hold down the wire for me to cross. I was astride the fence with my hands on the wire when lightning struck the fence beyond where the sergeant was standing. A ball of fire came rolling down the fence. When it reached the sergeant it knocked the rifle out of his hand but did him no harm. I received a considerable shock but no damage was done. Apparently the sergeant wasn't touching the metal parts of his rifle. I shuddered to think what would have happened if he hadn't been there with his rifle across the wire.

After graduation and a leave, I went to Okinawa. It was August when I arrived in Okinawa and I was assigned to Company "C" First Special Forces Group (Airborne) First Special Forces. Soon I was assigned to an "A" team that was training and preparing to go to Vietnam with the mission of building a camp. The team was already formed

The Life Of A Soldier

except for a lieutenant executive officer and I became the outsider new guy.

The captain commanding the team--I will call him Captain Alan Chase--was obviously planning to line his pockets with government funds. Having been in the Army thirteen years by that time, I was fairly perceptive. It became obvious that the master sergeant who was the team sergeant had been given the assignment to find out whether I would go along with Captain Chase's plans.

Standing operating procedures for teams that went to Vietnam was for the executive officer to be accountable for funds. It could be anticipated that with the construction of the camp there would be thousands of dollars in my hands to pay contractors, purchase materials, etc. The team sergeant would make comments to me such as' "If we work it right there will be plenty of money for the team take R & R." My reply was consistent each time he made such a remark. Like a broken record, I replied: "If I am charged with the responsibility of the funds, they will be administered in accordance with the regulations."

As time progressed Captain Chase became more and more cool toward me and so did the rest of the team. We went to a training site where we stayed for several days. The captain never spoke to me and if I tried to converse with him he ignored me. If I sat down at a table with him or any other member of the team, they would either move or ignore me. I began to dread the thought of spending six months with this team. The captain never once counseled me to give me any indication of what he didn't like, but I knew it wasn't about my military skills or performance as an officer, but about my unwillingness to compromise. In fact, during that period, we never really had a conversation. This is unnatural for a commander and his second-in-command.

After we returned from the training area, just a few days before we were to depart for Vietnam, we were on the hand grenade range and I was told to report to Lieutenant

The Life Of A Soldier

Colonel Monger, the Commanding Officer of Company C. When I Reported to him he told me he was taking me off Captain Chase's team. Then he asked if I had any questions. I said "Yes sir, I want to know why you are taking me off the team." He replied that Captain Chase told him I was not qualified. I reminded the Colonel that I had more than 10 years as an NCO and was considered outstanding enough to be given a direct commission, and that as a platoon leader, company executive officer and company commander I had received near perfect scores on my efficiency reports. I also pointed out that some of the 2d Lieutenants that were going with teams were right out of school.

    Then I asked if Captain Chase gave him any specifics about my not being qualified. Then he said the captain said I couldn't throw a hand grenade very far. I reminded the Colonel that one of the events for the annual physical fitness test was the hand grenade throw, and told him that I always earned a perfect score on that event. By this time the Colonel was getting very uncomfortable, and said that he didn't want to send a team to Vietnam with an executive officer that the team commander didn't want. I realized that Colonel Monger didn't really know why the Captain didn't want me and it was not my place to tell him because it was not something I could prove. I also privately agreed with his decision. I was glad to be off the team, but it was a humiliating experience.

    I was replaced by a captain and I won't give his name either. I will call him Luke Johnson. Captain Johnson had just arrived and was hot to go to Vietnam. He volunteered to take my place and I thought it strange for a captain to volunteer to take a position that called for a lieutenant. All of the professional officers were eager to get the combat experience on their records. I didn't get to know Luke Johnson before he left for Vietnam but we later became friends.

When I returned from Vietnam to Okinawa in 1965 and was released from the hospital I was assigned to the C detachment staff as S-4 (supply officer). Luke Johnson was the S-1 (personnel officer) and Chase who was now a major was S-3 (operations officer). Johnson and I became friends and one day I asked him if he knew why Chase didn't want me on his team in Vietnam. He said he did know and would tell me after Chase left the island, but not before.

One of my duties as S-4 was coordination with the transportation officer at Naha Seaport for the shipping of household goods and hold baggage. One day the Transportation Officer called and asked me if I had a Major Chase in my unit. When I acknowledged that I did he told me that the major had acquired some furniture from Hong Kong and had arranged for an enlisted man to ship some of it in his name because the weight of it exceeded his allowance. In the process he had not only defrauded the government but had also encouraged an enlisted soldier to do the same.

The Transportation officer had impounded the furniture. He told me he would leave it up to me. If I didn't want to intervene, he would initiate charges against Major Chase and that would at best end his career and at worst send him to prison. But if I wanted to save him, he would allow him to pick up his furniture. The Transportation officer gave me 24 hours to let him know my decision.

The Life Of A Soldier

I must admit that I thought of how satisfying it could be to finally see this man who had humiliated me suffer for his misdeeds. I decided, however, to let him of the hook. I had seen what vengeance does to the one who seeks vengeance. I called and told the transportation officer that Chase would be down to pick up his furniture. I went to Chase's office and told him he must pick up the furniture immediately or he would be in big trouble. I didn't stay and chat. I just walked out. I never told Chase that I had such power over his fate and showed him mercy rather than take revenge.

After Chase left the island, I asked Luke Johnson for the answer to the question I had asked earlier and he said: "You were too honest." Then he told me he was ashamed that he conformed. He said Chase would come to him and get large sums of Vietnamese currency and he, Johnson, would make phony vouchers to cover it.

In 1967 while at the special warfare school at Fort Bragg, taking a course in preparation for an advisor assignment in Vietnam, someone told me that Colonel Monger was commanding one of the Special Forces groups there and wanted to see me. He had been promoted to full Colonel. I went to see him and he seemed genuinely glad to see me. He told me that I was much too good as a Special Forces officer to be assigned as advisor to a regular unit and offered to make contact with someone in Vietnam who could have the assignment changed once I arrived. I told him I appreciated it but preferred to just let it go. Colonel Monger did everything but just come right out and apologize to me for the incident with Chase.

Euell White

The primary reason I turned down Colonel Monger's offer was that there was a perception that too much time in Special Forces could get in the way when it came time for consideration for promotion to major. The emphasis was on company command time in combat for infantry captains and I understood that being a battalion advisor to the ARVN would count for this. As it turned out I was promoted to major toward the end of that tour. There was no special forces branch for officers at that time. We came from other branches and some of the officers of the various branches were resentful of the "elite" special forces.

In the fall o 1964 I participated in a guerilla warfare exercise in Korea with the ROK Speical Forces. For details of this exercise, see Appendix D: Guerilla Warfare Exercises (Korea 1964, Page 318).

While in Korea in November 1964, I received a letter from Euna telling me that she and Sherry had received their travel orders to join me in Okinawa.. They arrived by ship a few days after our return to Okinawa. I had rented a house, bought rattan furniture, had drapes custom-made and hired a full-time maid named Ukiko.

Sherry had been exposed to the measles aboard ship and came down with it a few days after their arrival. Ukiko caught the measles from Sherry but she came to work everyday. She said if she didn't come to work her father would make her work in the rice paddies. Sherry had to give up her dog when they left home and that is what she wanted for Christmas. Sherry had her 9th birthday a week before Christmas. I found a Japanese Spitz that an American diplomat in Naha wanted to find a home for. His name was Fuji and he was a peculiar dog. He didn't like the

The Life Of A Soldier

local people and would growl when they passed by the house even if he was inside and couldn't see them. He tolerated Ukiko. When she came in a room where he was, Fuji would move to another room. Ukiko thought it was her duty to feed him but he would not touch the food she set out for him.

> Euna learned in dealing with Ukiko that Asians don't always understand as well as they seem to. We were in need of a table cloth for our dining table. The one we had would barely cover the top of the dining table furnished by the quartermaster. Euna mail-ordered one from Montgomery Ward that was too large. Ukiko's sister did sewing so Euna sent it to her to alter. She explained to Ukiko — or at least thought she did — what size she wanted it to be. When Ukiko returned it, the new table cloth was the same size as the one that was too small in the first place. Fortunately Ukiko had gone home when Euna discovered the defect. Euna cried a little but then started laughing about it and we endured a short table cloth for the remainder of our tour in Okinawa. It was a humorous story to tell our guests when we used the dining room table.

Our best friends on Okinawa were Dan and Wilma Biggs. I met Dan while we were classmates at the Special Warfare School. We were in the same company on

Euell White

Okinawa and for more than a year we were neighbors. Dan was from Rogers Arkansas and Wilma from Roseboro, North Carolina. We maintained contact with them over the years. After being released from active-duty with 13 years service, Dan worked for the Army Corps of Engineers in procurement at Huntsville, Alabama and is now retired from that Job. He stayed in the reserves and retired from the Army at age 60 as a Lieutenant Colonel. Wilma was a school teacher. She died of cancer a few years ago and Dan has since remarried.

On 28 July 1965, I made my first jump with the T-10 steerable parachute and it was also my first jump into the South China Sea. We jumped a few miles off Bolo Point on Okinawa, and it was a memorable experience. We jumped, or more accurately, Scooted, out of a Hughey helicopter. For the jump we wore athletic shorts, T-shirts, Tennis shoes and a shark repellent kit attached to our leg.

With the steerable parachute you have to continually face into the wind to slow your descent. For the water jump we were instructed that when about a hundred feet from the water you were to place one forearm through the risers and with the opposite hand, release the riser quick release and hold the riser with the forearm until just before your feet hit the water. Then when our your feet touched the water, extend the arm so that the parachute would collapse, thereby preventing the opened parachute from dragging you through the water.

This was my 61st parachute jump and I had learned to judge my altitude above the ground, but the water was different and I released my quick release too early. My parachute turned so that I was not facing the wind and I was still pretty high up. Before I thought about it I reached

The Life Of A Soldier

up to steer the chute back into the wind. When I did this of course, my left riser slid away. I reacted real fast and managed to catch the riser buckle in my hand and held it until my feet touched the water. Our Group operations officer did the same thing but he didn't catch his riser buckle. His chute collapsed and he fell free for quite a distance. He wasn't injured, but the Group Commander, Colonel Kelly, saw him and he had to pay a fine. We were picked up by rubber lifeboats with outboard motors and taken to the Green Beret boat. It was more than a two hour ride back to the dock.

The water jump was instituted by Colonel Francis J. Kelly as a requirement for the first jump with the steerable parachute. I personally thought it was a great idea and except for the long boat ride back to the island, would have preferred it to jumping on land. The drop zone on Okinawa was near Kadena Air Base and was covered with coral rock, resulting in a lot of injuries. The word among the troops in the Group was that Colonel Kelly's motive for the water jump was for his personal comfort. I never thought this was true, but it was their perception. I understood that the Colonel earned his jump wings to qualify for the assignment as commander of the First Special Forces Group, and he was injured in jump school. He was no spring chicken at that time. The troops nicknamed him "Splash Kelly." He was very dramatic and the troops seemed to find this more amusing than inspiring.

When a team was leaving for Vietnam Colonel Kelly would give them a pep talk before they left. At the conclusion of his talk he would give a thumbs up with both thumbs and yell, "Kill the VC." The expected response was for the teams to yell "Kill the VC." When he gave the talk to our team and two others that were going at the same time, nobody responded the first time. We hadn't been told that we were expected to respond. He repeated his chant and finally got a weak response. There were no kids on these teams.

One day when the Colonel called a meeting of all officers and senior noncommissioned officers at the Sukiran theater, someone told him that his officers and NCOs called him "Splash" behind his back. The sensible response would have been to either ignore it or make some humorous remark about it, but he chose to chew out the entire assembly about it. After that he would come to his office some mornings and find reminders on his desk. One day there was a pair of thumbs carved out of wood with the words, "kill the VC" on it.

This incident reminded me of an experience I had as a second lieutenant in Germany with the 1st Infantry Division. I was platoon leader of one of the rifle platoons and the weapons platoon was being led by the platoon sergeant. Some exercise that the weapons platoon was participating in required a commissioned officer platoon leader. I was assigned this task and the platoon sergeant didn't agree with my way of doing things. I listened to his ideas but was not convinced that his way was better than mine.

He became very angry and approached me one day while we were in the forest and no one else was around. He asked could he speak to me man-to-man. My reply was that since we were both men that would be fine. I expected to hear some criticism of my leadership, but instead he

The Life Of A Soldier

came on like a child in a tantrum and asked me if I knew that the men called me "Mister Clean." I thought it over for a moment and realized that this could be because of my bald head and they were referring to the animated character in a TV commercial for a cleaning product. I also thought they might be referring to my lifestyle. My response to the platoon sergeant was that I would take this as a compliment. This seemed to really frustrate him, but we never had another man-to man talk and he seemed to give up his resistance to me.

In the early summer of 1965, I participated in a Guerilla warfare exercise in Taiwan with the Republic Of China Army Special Forces. For details, see Appendix D: Guerilla Warfare Exercises (Taiwan 1965, Page 324).

In the late summer of 1965, I deployed to Vietnam as executive officer of an A team. For details of this tour see Appendix E: Vietnam 1965 (Page 358)

While on Okinawa, I was assigned to be defense counsel for a special courts martial. For details of this assignment see Appendix C: Unusual and Interesting Assignments (The Courts Martial, Page 310).

In the summer and fall of 1966, I participated in the annual guerilla warfare exercise with the Republic of Korea (ROK) Special Forces. This was the last significant thing I did before returning stateside. For description of this adventure, see Appendix D: Guerilla Warfare Exercises (Korea 1966, Page 340).

Euell White

The Life Of A Soldier

7.
Stateside 1967

We left Okinawa sometime in January 1967. My new assignment was The Infantry School at Fort Benning Georgia. We had bought a house and 10 acres of land from my brother Almon, next door to my Dad's house near Rogersville, Alabama just before I left for Okinawa. Euna and Sherry had lived there until they joined me in Okinawa, and had left the furniture in place. When we came back we just moved back in and they lived there until we bought a house in Columbus, Georgia.

I was assigned to the Platoon Tactics Committee as a team chief. The committee chairman was Lieutenant Colonel Francis Bray. He was a good man and an avid fisherman. He taught me how to fly fish for bass. He had a terrible temper and when something went wrong he would pound on his desk with a swagger stick that he always carried and break the glass. After we started fishing together I could walk into his office and start talking about fishing and calm him when he was having one of his temper tantrums. Immediately he would decide to go fishing, and often invite me to go along. It was not unusual for someone to come to my office and ask me to go talk to the colonel when he was giving everyone a hard time.

I had two field problems and one classroom problem that I was responsible for. In the field I had Rifle Platoon in the Attack and Reinforced Rifle Platoon in the Attack. In the classroom I had Rifle Platoon in the Defense. When Colonel Bray visited my field problems, I would meet him at his jeep and start talking to him about fishing. He would never get around to inspecting the training.

Euna came and stayed with me in the bachelor quarters for a few days while looking for a house. We bought a new house and they allowed us to move in while the GI loan was being processed. Before the deal was ever closed, I received orders alert to go back to Vietnam after attending the Special Warfare School's Military Advisor and Assistance Course at Fort Bragg.

The Infantry School was supposed to be a stabilized assignment for a certain number of years, I can't remember how many. When I received the alert, I called the Infantry Branch personnel and asked what the deal was. Their reply was that I hadn't yet been to Vietnam. I asked them how did I get the combat infantry badge, the purple heart and bronze star for valor medals. They then replied that I was on temporary duty in Vietnam for a six month tour. My "wise guy" response to that was that the North Vietnamese machine gunner who shot me didn't seem to care that I was there on temporary duty. It turned out that we lived in the house free for the few months we were there, and closed the deal just in time to sell it. I moved Euna and Sherry back to our house in Rogersville.

When I reported to the Infantry School, I was required to attend the instructor course. The class was divided into small groups with a group instructor. My group instructor was a Captain Burr who was junior to me and a graduate of West Point. He had a problem with officers like me who had enlisted service and made more money than him. His pay grade was O-3 and mine was O-3E. The E meant at least six years enlisted service and there was a significant difference in the pay.

The Life Of A Soldier

One of the assignments he gave us was to give speeches on controversial issues and allow the class to debate the issue. He assigned someone the subject of why West Point graduates' four years at the academy should count for service longevity. Truthfully I had never even thought about this so I didn't have an opinion, but I got into the debate and gave good arguments against it. I didn't know that this was a personal issue with him. I doubt that I would have said any less had I known that. He really became offended at me over that and gave me a hard time for the remainder of the course. I couldn't do anything right.

Then, for our final presentation we were required to speak on closed circuit television. He assigned me the subject of "Why we should resume nuclear testing immediately." This man had the opinion that anyone with a Southern accent was less intelligent than Him. One captain from South Carolina had the black southern accent and Burr gave him a very hard time. He actually tried to change the man's accent. With the subject of treaties, he thought, he had me. I called my brother John and asked him for some information on this subject and he gave me what I needed.

As I got into the preparation, I became passionate about the subject. On the day of the TV presentations, the colonel who was head of the instructor school department came to hear and view the presentations. After the presentations were finished, the Colonel said that my presentation was the best he had heard. The Captain had to give me an "A" for that one. And I know he hated that.

Euell White

In preparation for my assignment as advisor to the Vietnamese, I attended the Special Warfare School at Fort Bragg. The Advisor course was very good and I thoroughly enjoyed it. A large part of the course was the Vietnamese language. I had studied spoken German while in Germany and learned enough to ask directions and order my food in restaurant. Then I had 60 hours of Chinese Mandarin, but I quickly forgot all that I knew. The Vietnamese language seemed easier for me than any of the languages I have studied.

We had language classes every day and they issued each of us a reel-to-reel tape recorder on which to practice and study during the evenings. Our teacher's voice was on the tapes and the lessons were really helpful. I learned every word of the vocabulary we were exposed to and made a perfect score on the final exam. For the exam we had to define 50 words and translate several sentences from Vietnamese to English and several from English to Vietnamese. Then the teacher engaged each of us individually in a conversation without any prompting as to the subject. I didn't miss anything.

In Vietnam I was able to read most of the military documents I was exposed to and follow the conversations of the Vietnamese around me. Making myself understood was a different thing. The language is tonal to the point of being almost musical, and like our language there are words that look the same but have entirely different meanings. For example the word for water or liquid is nuoc. To describe a particular form you add to this word. A popular condiment in Vietnam is fish sauce. The word for fish is mam. The fish sauce is called nuoc-mam.

The Life Of A Soldier

I once told my houseboy to put ice water in my canteen and when I started to drink it later it was scalding hot. The words for ice and hot were the same except for accent marks and the difference in the way the words were pronounced was a matter of tone. The houseboy didn't think it unreasonable for me to ask for hot water on a hot day. When I worked with the Nationalist Chinese Army, we drank hot water all day long.

Regardless of the difficulty in speaking, being able to hear and read was invaluable. I always had an interpreter, but interpreters are generally diplomatic and won't tell you anything they think will offend you. It was a great advantage when the interpreter knew that I knew the language well enough to know whether he was being straight with me.

Euell White

The Life Of A Soldier

8.
Vietnam 1967-68

I arrived at Bien Hoa Air Base on 11 December 1967 and was briefed by a Second Lieutenant who was very impressed with his own importance. He reminded me of the character, Lt. Fuzz in the Beetle Bailey comic strip. The Lt. told us scary stories about the dangers of being ambushed enroute to Long Binh by bus convoy with a Military Police escort. The bus trip was, however, uneventful.

The briefing at Long Bien processing center in the wee hours of the morning by this same lieutenant while we were suffering from jet lag and sleep deprivation, included such essentials as the proper wearing of the uniform, military courtesy and the warning, "don't use the Colonel's private latrine," with this last item obviously being the most important since it was emphasized so much. After the briefing we were issued bedding and assigned a bunk, but I was unable to sleep because I was so depressed that I couldn't use the Colonel's private latrine. (Actually it was about 0400 hours which made it sometime in the afternoon back home).

At breakfast I met Jim Walker, who was the team leader of the Special Forces Team I went to Vietnam with from Okinawa in 1965. He had finished his tour and was on his way home. At 0845 those of us who were being assigned as advisors departed Long Binh for Koelper Compound in Saigon by bus. As it turned out we didn't stay at Long Binh long enough to violate any of the rules they gave us. I didn't see one single officer with more rank than me that I could fail to salute, nor did I have need of the Colonel's latrine. At Koelper Compound I was billeted on the 6th floor of an old hotel. The elevator actually worked but it made some frightening noises.

On 15 December I departed Saigon for III Corps headquarters at Bien Hoa where I was briefed by a Colonel Woelfer who was Assistant Deputy Senior Advisor to the III Corps Commanding General. He gave me a good pep talk, then secured a helicopter to take me to the 5th ARVN Division at Phu Cuong in Binh Duong Province, about 15 miles North of Saigon.

The first person I met there was Major Henry (White Eyes) Hardy. We were NCOs together in the old 11th Airborne Division. Hardy was commissioned directly from the ranks while we were in Germany. We called him "White Eyes" because his eyes are white. Henry was the Headquarters Commandant for the Division Advisory Team and tried to recruit me as his assistant, but I said "no way." It would be a nice safe job, but it would probably kill my chances of making major. Besides that, If I was going to be in the war, I wanted to be in a combat unit..

On 16 December I met Colonel Sonstielle, the Division Senior Advisor and he assigned me as Senior Advisor to the 3d Battalion, 7th Regiment, located at An Son. On 18 December I struck out on my own to my regiment where I met Major Steffaniw, the Regimental Senior Advisor, and Colonel Chong, the Regimental Commander. I spent the night there then went to An Son the following day. The battalion commander Captain Hoang Kim Ninh showed me around then we had lunch together.

The Life Of A Soldier

Dai-uy(Captain) Ninh is the one to my right with the map in front of him.

The battalion advisor team was supposed to consist of a captain a lieutenant and two Noncommissioned officers (NCOs). There was a lieutenant there but he was just holding the fort until my arrival. I had three NCOs. The senior one was Platoon Sergeant Morales. The other two were staff sergeants, Czap and Ludwig. Czap was experienced and trained in explosive ordnance disposal.

Euell White

In the afternoon I met the operations officer who spoke fairly good English and received a briefing from him. The An Son area was basically a fruit plantation area, about 5 miles by 2 miles.. The Eastern boundary was Highway 13. The Northern boundary was the Ba Lua River. The Western boundary was the Saigon River and the Southern boundary a stream with no name on the map that was what we would call a creek.

This was a re-development area. An Son was called a Village and contained hamlets. South Vietnam consisted of Provinces. I believe there were 22 of them. Provinces had districts, districts had towns and villages, and villages had hamlets. The province and district chiefs were military officers, but the village and hamlet chiefs were civilians. The primary mission of our battalion was to make it safe for the people in the village to live in peace. One hamlet raised fish, another pigs and others were involved with farming and marketing the fruit. The battalion had three rifle companies. 9th, 10th and 11th. At night they outposted the area to prevent the Viet Cong (VC) from coming in to harass the people.

On 23 December the District Chief and his advisor, Major Stallings, whom I had met the day before, were out with a popular force company, and were attacked while taking a break. Major Stallings was critically wounded and his lieutenant and two NCOs (Americans) were killed, along with 15 of the Vietnamese Popular Force troops. The district chief and 37 of the Popular Force troops were wounded.

On 24 December in the afternoon the battalion had a Christmas party for the troops and the families of the ones who were able to be there. My NCOs obtained some extras

The Life Of A Soldier

for them and they were truly grateful. There was food as well as toys for the children. They had a public address system set up and the Dai-uy introduced me. One soldier came to the microphone and made a speech in broken English. He said he spoke for all his friends and they were very grateful that the Americans are in Vietnam to help them. He sounded so sincere that I believed him.

When the toys were passed out to the little children my eyes got full of tears. I don't know whether I was feeling sorry for them for being so poor or for myself because I am wasn't home for Christmas. Maybe it was a little of both. This was the second Christmas I was away from Euna and Sherry. The other one was 1962 when I was in Berlin, Germany.

All of the officers except one per company came in to the CP at midnight for a party. A little humorous thing: the Battalion executive Officer, who was the only Buddhist on the battalion staff, was put in charge of organizing the Christmas party. He told me about it and thought it was a lot of fun.

During the party with the officers, Lieutenant Anh, the battalion intelligence Officer, made a speech in which he expressed their appreciation for the United States helping them to be free from the oppression of communism and expressed confidence that we would never let them down. Nearly all of the officers in the battalion were originally from the North and they had come south to escape communist domination. After Lieutenant Anh's speech I was expected to reciprocate. I was on the spot and the easy way would have been to give them assurances, but my heart wasn't in it. I told them that I surely hoped that we would never let them down, but that because of the nature of our government, the natural impatience of our people, and the fact that the government is responsive to public opinion, there was a possibility that if the war lasted too long we wouldn't stick it out. I wrote in my journal that I sincerely hoped history would prove me wrong. But it didn't.

Lieutenant Anh and his wife. They were married in December

The Life Of A Soldier

On Christmas Day, Colonel Sonstielle, the Senior Division Advisor, flew in about 1000 hours with our Christmas dinner, and wished us a merry Christmas. The III Corps chaplain, a protestant colonel, and his deputy, a catholic lieutenant colonel flew in about 1700 hours for a short visit. My 34th birthday was on December 26 and the officers gave a gift.

On the night of 29 December our 9th company was attacked. For the details of this action, see Appendix F: Significant Battles, Vietnam 1967-68 (The attack on 9th Company, Page 391).

I aquired a puppy named Lady and she seemed to realize that she belonged to all of us. She would sleep under one bed for awhile, then move to another one. I was afraid she would bring the Vietnamese bad luck like the monkey the sergeants had before.

> The sergeants had a pet monkey and the Vietnamese soldiers decided there was a lot of bad luck and the solution would be to kill the monkey. The sergeants wouldn't hear of that, then it was decided that if they cut off the monkey's tail that might break the curse. The sergeants wouldn't go for that either. The final solution was to sneak the monkey out under the cover of darkness and move him to another advisor team to keep for the sergeants. The Vietnamese thought he had been killed. Amazingly, the accidents that were being blamed on the monkey sharply decreased right away. This illustrates the power of superstition.

Euell White

Some of the battalion officers.

The Life Of A Soldier

Battalion officers & senior NCOs. The old man in the black pajamas is the Village Chief.

On 8 January I learned that we were being haunted again. Previously, before my arrival, someone started throwing rocks at the outpost of one of the companies at night The soldiers are convinced that it is the ghost of a soldier who was killed while disarming one of their own booby trapped grenades. They would not believe it was the VC or one of their own soldiers doing this. An officer who was there, Lieutenant Parish, was fluent in the language, and went with the outpost one night to prove that it was one of their own throwing the rocks.

Euell White

Parish had everyone accounted for and took them out before dark. Right after dark, with all of his soldiers accounted for, a rock came through the firing aperture of the bunker and hit the American officer right between the eyes. In effect, he proved that their superstition was correct–that the ghost of the dead soldier was haunting them. The haunting and the bad luck associated with it had subsided when the monkey was dealt with, but it started again.

The Battalion commander and most of his officers knew better but the troops believed in the superstition. My interpreter, SGT Tu, who was of Chinese descent, explained it this way: Anything that they don't have an answer for must be the work of ghosts. It was amusing in a way, but it seriously affected the morale. They were afraid to set booby traps because of this. We can laugh at superstition, but to the people who live by it superstition is serious business.

On 8 January, the cavalry squadron and an infantry battalion conducted an operation north of us and found some sort of VC headquarters. We received a message that night that a large number of VC were believed to have crossed the Ba Lua River into the edge of our area. It was beyond the capability of this battalion to completely defend our borders. We had to patrol the area and rely on intelligence. We conducted a thorough search of the area all the way to the river but found nothing. No doubt we saw some VC working in the fields but we had no way of determining who they were. We searched sampans and houses and Checked the identity of all the occupants.

The Life Of A Soldier

Anson was really a rich farming area. They raised rice, pineapples, bananas, grapefruit, peppers and some other fruits that I don't know the name for, in this small area. They also raised sugar cane but they had to cut the cane because it provided too good a hiding place for the Viet Cong. Along Highway 13, at the edge of our area was the town of Bung. It was about 15 miles from Saigon and people come out from Saigon to buy food at the market.

The Life Of A Soldier

**Breakfast of North Vietnamese Soup at a little café' in Bung.
The North Vietnamese Soup is delicious but very hot with peppers,**

On 13 January at 0730 hours two of our soldiers ran into a VC booby trap. One was killed and the other seriously wounded. I requested a medevac at 0850 and was told VNAF would fly the mission. I called division and told them VNAF would surely be too slow and I didn't want a repeat of what happened 29 December when 9th Company's commander died because he didn't get to the hospital in time. At 0920 Colonel Sonstielle's helicopter came and evacuated the wounded man. At 0950 the VNAF helicopter came. That extra 30 minutes could have made the difference in life and death for the soldier who had wounds in both legs, both arms, belly and head. He may have died anyway but at least we gave him a chance. I felt as much responsibility for saving the life of one of my Vietnamese soldiers as I would have if commanding an American unit.

On 18 January I was visited by the district advisor and 3 American civilians, one from COORDS and the other two from some agency contracted to report on the progress of the New Life hamlets. I can't remember what all of the letters in COORDS stand for, but the C is for Civilian the R is for Revolutionary and D is for Development.

I took the visitors to one of the hamlets so they could talk to the people and find out what they wanted to know, then I took them to meet the village chief. It was the longest and most interesting talk I have had with the village chief. This whole An Son area is one village and includes four hamlets. They wanted to know why the village chief lives away from the village. Why he didn't live at his headquarters. He told them he was elected village chief by his people and felt it was his duty to his people and the nation to serve. He said he was 70 years old, had 7 sons, all of whom had sacrificed their lives for the nation. That he and his wife had the responsibility of raising their grandchildren, and for that reason, he was not ready to die. He said if he lived in the village at night, the VC would kill him. I admired the old man for accepting the job.

The chief told me that 70% of the people in that village were nationalist (or supported the government). 20% were neutral and 10% were Viet Cong or Viet Cong sympathizers. The chief said that if any strangers appeared he knew it because he knew everyone there. He as good as admitted he knew who the VC were there. When we started to leave he said "I am very grateful for you

The Life Of A Soldier

Americans who risk your lives trying to help our nation." I believe the old man was sincere.

On 21 January we participated in an operation that was a pretty big show. Our battalion was in a blocking position along the Ba Lua River. Another unit landed by helicopter across the stream and another by boat up the Saigon River. One of my companies fired across the river into a sugar cane field pretty close to one of the other friendly units, and they reported they were receiving fire from the VC. I immediately figured out what had happened and got it all straightened out without any casualties. The unit had given the wrong coordinates of their location–in fact they didn't know where they were on the map.

We captured one VC suspect and for the first time I witnessed the ARVN method of interrogation. I won't describe the details but it was not pleasant to watch. It was my duty to try and prevent them from using such methods. The commander told me that he understood that but not to waste my time. He said the U.S. method worked for U.S. units, but these methods wouldn't work for them. One of the other units on the operation killed one VC and found some weapons.

On 26 January a popular force outpost on highway 13 between our camp and Lai Thieu District was wiped out. They weren't really attacked, they were assassinated. I heard firing in that direction but didn't find out until the next day what it was. The VC caught the PFs asleep and killed six. Apparently the seventh man was one of the VC and left with them. All of their weapons and radios were captured.

Euell White

I was very fortunate as far as getting along with my counterpart. A common advisor complaint was the inability to keep informed. I didn't have that problem at all. Captain Ninh constantly worried about the safety of my sergeants and me and wouldn't allow any of us to walk around in the woods without a security detail. He kept telling me he wanted to send all of us home to our families alive and well. I trusted him completely. This would indeed have been a miserable job if I were with a commander I couldn't trust. Or couldn't get along with.

The gate to our compound at Anson. The camp was named for the company commander, Vu-Xuan-Phung who was killed on 29 December.

The Life Of A Soldier

The eve of the Vietnamese New Year, called TET, was on 29 January. This was the most important holiday they had. The only way to compare it with ours is to combine all our holidays into one. The Vietnamese were all excited about it. The grownups were as excited about this holiday as I was about Christmas as a child. They were busy putting up decorations and preparing food for the party which began that night and lasted until after midnight. The holiday lasted until 1 February.

The Officers Mess Tent prepared for the TET celebration.

  My Sergeants helped with the food for the holiday feast. They scrounged fresh eggs, tomatoes, potatoes and canned meats from the American Mess Sergeants. I didn't ask what they traded for the food.

  There was a truce in our area effective at 1800 hours on 29 January for TET. It was to last for 36 hours, but the enemy violated it somewhere in the area and it was terminated at 0945 hours the morning of the 30th. I had received an intel report that said the VC would violate the truce and that they would use ARVN (Army of the Republic of Vietnam) uniforms and possibly ARVN

The Life Of A Soldier

vehicles as well as the fireworks in celebration of TET as a cover for their attacks.

We had a nice time that night. I had supper at 1800 hours with the officers in their mess tent. Captain Ninh's wife and 10 children were with us. Lieutenant Anh's wife was also with us. We had a good meal of rice, vegetable soup, chicken cooked four different ways, candied fruits, oranges and bananas. Chicken is the Vietnamese's favorite meat.

After supper Captain Ninh and his family came over to our "house" and we watched television. There was an Armed Forces station in Saigon and we got it for a few hours each evening. We watched a 90 minute Vietnamese drama which reminded me of "As the World Turns" and some of the other soap operas American women like to watch. Following the oriental custom of masking real emotions with false ones, Ba Ninh and the older daughters laughed real loud at the tear jerking scenes. During station pauses we were entertained by the Dai-uy's youngest daughter who was four and as cute as a button. She sang little songs in English and acted them out, which she learned in school. One was about musical instruments. She would sing. "Pia, pia, pi-ano" while making like she was playing the piano. Then "vio, vio, vio-lin." All of his children spoke English.

At midnight the battalion commander fired the remainder of the firecrackers. Then we all retired for the night.

Euell White

*Ba Ninh and her children. One of the older girls is her niece.
They have 10 children.*

The Life Of A Soldier

The Ninh's youngest daughter holding my TET gift to her. It is customary to give the children money in a red envelope on this day.

The night of 31 January the VC didn't bother us, but they did mortar the 4th battalion and several other locations. I picked up the tail end of a newscast on Armed Forces Network and it appeared the VC attacked our embassy in Saigon. Captain Ninh was more shaken than I had ever seen him. He believed there was a Coup D' Tat (Overthrow of the government by force) in the working. He had some reason for believing this I was sure, but I thought it best not to pursue the subject too aggressively.

The VC had built up strength all around us. I received a report from Division TOC (Tactical Operations

Center) about 1000 hours that intelligence reported 300 VC about 800 meters north of the Ba Lua River. The Ba Lua River was our northern boundary. They sent out a reconnaissance aircraft and he confirmed it. He reported that he saw VC banners all over the place and people standing around. I couldn't do anything about it except wait for them to cross the river into our area, which I expected them to do that night.

Later that day an air strike was conducted across the Ba Lua River. At 1715 hours one of our companies on a reconnaissance patrol saw the people evacuating An My Hamlet. The people wouldn't tell them why, but we knew the VC has told them. All intelligence received indicated an attack from three directions that night. Every other unit had the same picture. There have been battalion and company size units sighted all over the place moving in all different directions, with some of them in ARVN uniforms. The VC mortared that the VC mortared Phu Loi (1st U.S. Infantry Division base) on the night of 30 January. And attempted a ground assault, but it only lasted a few minutes.

On 1 February, a lieutenant who went to the advisor school at Bragg with me and arrived about a week after I did, was killed at a bridge along highway 13 between our camp and Binh Duong. He was assistant advisor to the 1st battalion of this regiment.

As of 2 February we still hadn't been bothered by the VC. (I need to explain that I used the term VC for the enemy. Sometimes this was Viet Cong -- Communist Guerillas-- sometimes North Vietnamese Army, and sometimes an integrated unit with both.). We received an order to clear and secure a portion of highway 13. The stretch of highway we were securing extended from where

The Life Of A Soldier

the road leading into our area intersected the highway, south for about five kilometers toward Lai Thieu.

We moved out with two companies plus headquarters, leaving one company behind to secure our compound. We found our own road blocked with obstacles of rocks and trees and cleared it on the way to Lai Thieu. I left one of my NCOs with that company. As our lead element reached highway 13, District was getting ready to fire artillery on us thinking we were VC. The VC had been wearing ARVN uniforms. Regiment had failed to inform District of our mission. My friend Captain Rickman, who was my classmate in the advisor course at Bragg, in the 4th battalion across the Saigon River heard them calling for artillery and told them I was in the area. I later learned that they had the rounds in the tubes ready to fire when he stopped them.

We cleared the stretch of highway 13 as ordered. The VC had felled concrete utility posts, trees, etc. to build obstacles along the highway. They had also removed furniture from the schools at Bung and used it to build obstacles. After clearing the road and securing it all day, we moved into the town of Bung, right at the edge of our boundary on Highway 13 between Anson and Lai Thieu..

Bung was the headquarters for the regional and popular Forces who man the outposts at the bridges in this area. They had an American Lieutenant and four enlisted men as advisors with them. We moved in with them The only action we had on the night of 2 February was with the Regional Force/Popular Force (RF/PF) outposts. They attacked a bridge on the road to An Son and at another outpost. One Popular Force soldier was killed and two civilians seriously wounded.

On 3 February we participated in an attack with the 1st battalion of this regiment, but we had very little contact. Our only casualty was one lightly wounded soldier. Both battalions approached the VC from opposite directions and boxed them in, then we called an air strike. Twenty VC bodies were found. The reason I mention the number found rather than the number killed, is that they try to recover their dead as they withdraw so we never know for sure how many were killed. On the night of the 3rd, one of our ambush patrols on highway 13 made contact with the VC but the VC withdrew without much of a fight.

The Life Of A Soldier

Euell White

On 6 February we moved our command post to the Bung School. We were involved in a search and destroy operation with two other battalions. The other two battalions had contact with small VC units off and on all day, but we didn't get involved other than to put one of our companies in a blocking position. I received an intel report from the province advisors that morning which confirmed my suspicions that they are not in the same world with the

The Life Of A Soldier

rest of us. The report warned that we must be very careful because the VC is mingled with the local population and has identity papers. That is really big news since this has been the main problem of identifying the VC ever since this war began.

We picked up 22 suspects. We check the papers of all the young men. If they can't answer the questions they are arrested and made laborers (prisoners) until they are turned over to the national police for investigation. I noted in my journal that I hoped the offensive would soon be over so that we could move back to An Son because I was tired of eating C rations.

We moved our CP to Bung School right after dark on that night and I noted in my journal that this moving from the school to other points and back is supposed to keep the VC from knowing our location at night--at least that is the regimental commander's theory, but in reality we would be better off to keep it in one location and fortify. The enemy knew there were only so many places we could be along the stretch of highway we were securing. The attack at Bung School on 5 March proved my opinion to be correct and the Regimental Commander's over–controlling cost us several lives, including my Sergeant Ludwig.

Our area of responsibility was extended to Phu Van where the Regimental headquarters was located. The battalion commander was given complete authority over everyone, civilian and military in the area. He armed the laborers and I had never seen such a happy bunch of prisoners. They were serving from 2 to 5 years for desertion but they seemed to be pretty good soldiers. As prisoners they wore shirts with LCDB which is an abbreviation for (Lao Cong Dac Biet) and identified them as prisoners. In our army these would be classified as AWOLs rather than deserters. The Battalion commander had the authority to pardon them if they made a good showing in battle. They were really proud to get the weapons and become soldiers rather than prisoners. One of them came to me begging for extra magazines for his carbine. I had a few extras and gave him three 15 round magazines. You would think I had given him a million dollars.

    On 6 February I was called to division to make an evaluation of my Vietnamese counterpart, Captain Ninh. I gave him a good evaluation and recommended him for military schooling in the U.S. In 1970 I attended the Infantry Officers Advance Course as a major and Major Hoang Kim Ninh was in the class. I was his sponsor and he visited our home frequently. He and his family escaped from Vietnam after the fall of Saigon. I located him by mail once. They were in California. I misplaced the address and was never able to contact him again.

The Life Of A Soldier

On patrol at Anson with my Houseboy

Euell White

On 7 February the 2nd battalion across the Saigon River at Tan Than Dong came under heavy attack at about 1400 hours. There were 4 U.S. wounded, cut off outside the camp by the VC. Three of the wounded were from the U.S. 1st Infantry Division. They were a mobile training team working with the 2nd battalion. I heard the most pitiful

The Life Of A Soldier

thing on the radio One of the NCO advisors with the 2nd battalion along with two from the 1st U.S. Infantry Division out with an ARVN patrol about 800 meters from the camp were all wounded. They were not right together. The sergeant on the radio said he was paralyzed from the waist down. He was panicked and begging for help. The senior advisor, Captain Newcomb, kept reassuring him over the radio that he would get him out. The VC had him pinned down. Everyone who tried to go out and get him received so much fire they couldn't get to him.

Finally an observer plane and 2 helicopter gunships came and fired suppressive fires to allow the litter team to get him out, but the ARVNS were afraid the helicopter would shoot them—it has happened before. After about 3 hours with the SGT still alive and pleading for help and the captain reassuring him it was coming, a litter team finally picked him up and moved a short distance with him before a VC mortar round hit, killing the Sgt and killing or wounding the litter team. While all this was going on a medevac chopper was orbiting, waiting for them to get him someplace he could land to pick up the wounded man. The observer plane and the gunships took several hits but none of them quit until they found out the SGT was dead, then they expended all their ordnance, leveling the building where the VC were located. The observer plane waited until the Air Force observer relieved him. The Air Force observer brought in a flight of fighters and really tore up the place. Later they discovered the VC had built bunkers inside the houses.

Euell White

My jeep driver Looie and cook came back on 7 February. I had let them off for TET and the curfew had caught them so they couldn't return. Looie was in Saigon with his family and almost got caught by the VC. They searched his folks' house and he hid in the attic. He said people were sleeping in the streets whose homes are destroyed, and the dead were lying in the streets bloated like water buffalo from being there so long. I noted in my journal that Iwished our so-called peace advocates who insisted on calling the VC the National Liberation Front could see how they liberate.

The Life Of A Soldier

**At the Old French Villa in the town of Bung.
Looie, my jeep driver**

    At 0750 hours, 9 February our company which we left at An Son reported two companies of VC in the hamlet where one of our companies was beaten so badly on 29 December. They reported that the hamlet chief had been shot. We quickly developed a plan and started moving in that direction and I requested air and artillery support. After we were halfway there the regimental commander ordered the battalion commander to return to our original position then send in a squad from the company at An Son for recon. I called the regimental advisor and told him I didn't agree with this, that we needed to get closer before sending in a squad because if the report was accurate the squad would be wiped out before we could reinforce it. His reply was, "Maybe they will and maybe they won't, maybe there are no VC there." I told him he was starting to think like his Vietnamese counterpart and that if we wanted to play it that way we could just sit on our butts and disregard all intel reports. This seemed to be his weakness. He didn't believe in intelligence and had been sarcastic when I turned in intel reports to him. I suspected that this was a weakness in the entire system. The prejudice that makes people think that no Vietnamese can be trusted. I later learned that the hamlet chief died and the hamlet agriculture official was also killed.

On 13 February we participated in an operation that was certainly interesting. and eventful. For details see Appendix F: Significant Battles, Vietnam 1967-68 (Pete Egan's Cavalry Troop, Page 394).

On 19 February elements of the 1st U.S. division operated a little southeast of us. They killed 42 VC and captured 2 AK-47 machine guns. In fairness to the ARVN units (and their advisors) it should be explained that when U.S. infantry units conducted an operation they had unlimited support exactly when they needed it. They could have an air strike in preparation, artillery preparation and helicopter gunships orbiting nearby to give them immediate support. The battalion commander had a helicopter from which to observe his maneuver elements and control them.

The Life Of A Soldier

When we had an operation we had the rules of engagement to contend with. Unless it was a very large scale operation, we couldn't have the artillery preparation unless we could say definitely that there was a target there. We couldn't get a team of gunships until we were in contact.--exchanging fire with the enemy-- then by the time it arrived it was often too late. The ARVN had a mixture of weapons that were obsolete and a limited supply of ammunition. There were times when there was one 105mm howitzer to support three infantry battalions with a very short supply of ammunition.

Euell White

> **From my Journal on 19 February 1968**
> It is my opinion that instead of increasing the U.S. troop strength here, we should divert more of our air and artillery to support the ARVN units. Giving the VNAF more air capability will not solve the air support problem. They have basically the same problems in coordination and cooperation between the air force and army that we had only few years ago and still have to some degree. What is worse, all of their aircraft, including helicopters belong to the air force and no army commander has any authority or control over them. I remember when I was a young paratrooper the air force troop carrier crews thought they were doing us a big favor by flying us for our parachute jumps. Now the army and air force work more as a team, although it could still be improved, especially in the area of close air support. The ARVN artillery should be given an unlimited supply of ammunition or US artillery placed under advisor control. With this battalion if I were assured of the support I need when I need it, I could compete with a US battalion of the same strength. Of course it would take a while for the ARVN to gain his confidence that he will have the support when needed.

While I was attending the Infantry Officers Advance Course in 1970, I was part of a panel for the class on close air support presented by the Air Force Liason

The Life Of A Soldier

officer. I told of my experiences that indicated the Air Force didn't understand the importance of making their strikes at the planned time. The Air Force Liason officer wrote a letter of commendation for my input.

My jeep driver, Looie, was a funny character. He built a house beside the regimental headquarters from ammunition crates and other lumber that the advisor team had provided long before my arrival. He drove the jeep home at night and returned in the morning. We never got out in it after dark anyway. One day soon after my arrival, Looie brought his family to meet me. His little boys were all dressed in army fatigue uniforms and had their shoes shining like soldiers. When Looie presented them to me they snapped to attention and saluted like soldiers. He had trained them well. Sometimes he would try my patience and I would show my anger. Then he would go and tell the sergeants, "Dai-uy hot."

> **From my journal on 23 February, 1968**
> Today my driver Looie and I were coming from Phu Loi and were going to stop at Lam Son (division headquarters) on the way back to pick up supplies. Looie speaks his own language to us. It is a mixture of Vietnamese and English, and it is sometimes hard to know which words are of which language. He started telling me something. He formed his hands like he was describing a big hole, and said what I understood to be; "Dai-uy, one people chet." The word for killed in Vietnamese is "chet" so I thought he was trying to tell me that one person had been killed and it had made a big hole in him. He just kept on repeating it and I finally told him I understood to get him to shut up. I could tell he was frustrated and knew I didn't really understand. When we arrived at the supply room, Looie pointed to the toilet paper and the supply sergeant got us a case of toilet paper. He was saying, "Dai-uy one paper___, calling the toilet paper by the same name used by the American GIs. One of the sergeants had told him to be sure and get some.

Our battalion had a very eventful and successful day on 25 February. For details see Appendix F: Significant Battles, Vietnam 1967-68 (The VC in our Blocking Position, Page 397).

On 2 March we had the mission of blocking for the 1st battalion and the Province Recon platoon for an

The Life Of A Soldier

operation in the An Son area. We received a report that morning of VC force estimated as 2 platoons located in the same area where our 9th company suffered such a defeat on 29 December.

They fired a great deal of artillery in there then the 1st battalion moved in. The VC fired mortars into one of the companies killing the company commander, a US lieutenant and a US sergeant. Several ARVN soldiers were wounded. The lieutenant had arrived sometime last month and replaced the lieutenant who was killed on 1 February. I believe the mortars that fired on the 1st battalion were across the Ba Lua. There is a sugar factory there and I believe that is where the mortars were. The counterfire analysts said the crater analysis showed that the mortars were to the north. The range of the VC's 82mm mortars is about 4,000 meters. They probably had their data already set on the mortars and waited for the ARVN to arrive. I think they probably told the locals to report that they were there although they weren't, to get the ARVN to that location.

On 3 march we participated in a police operation with the national police and popular force troops from district. We surrounded some of the hamlets near here and they checked every male between the ages of 16 and 45. Forty four suspects were apprehended. Five of them were immediately identified as VC, one as a hard-core cadre I knew there was at least one important VC in that hamlet or nearby from documents we captured in a school building near there a few days ago. One with instructions to committee leaders. We have received intel that the next big offensive will start soon. a training center at Lai Thieu is under attack. I don't know how heavy.

I submitted recommendations for the award of the bronze star for valor for SGT Czap and the army commendation medal for the 9th and 10th company commanders and soldier who killed the 2 VC after being wounded himself for the battle on 25 February. The army commendation is the highest US award I could recommend for an ARVN soldier. I never knew whether they received these awards..

On 5 March, the VC attacked our battalion at Bung school. I was wounded and one of my NCOs was killed. For the details of this battle, see Appendix F: Significant Battles, Vietnam 1967-68 (Battle at Bung School, Page 403).

The situation changed in the six days I was away in the hospital. There were 2 battalions from the 1st US infantry division operating in my An Son area. My battalion had been moved a little south of Bung and was blocking for the US units during the day. I went over the afternoon of my return from the hospital on 14 March to the CP of one of the battalions to coordinate with them, but nobody with any authority was around. I was assigned a lieutenant while I was away and was glad to get him. I was planning to take leave in April go to Okinawa.

My Battalion captured a VC 82mm mortar and a few more weapons while I was away. We learned that the unit which attacked us on 5 March was 2 companies. We had the unit identification. We knew which companies of which battalion of which regiment and division. They were NVA and apparently had no local guerillas with them because we left the bodies lying along the road all day and

The Life Of A Soldier

not one body was recovered for burial. If any of them had been locals their families would have claimed them for burial As it was, we buried them in a common grave. I was told by Captain Tom Johnson, the Assistant Regimental Advisor that I was being recommended for the Silver Star medal for gallantry in action, but instead I received my second Bronze Star for valor. I have no complaints. I appreciated the effort but doubt that I deserved it anyway.

The day I returned from the hospital I went by the battalion CP of one of the Big Red One battalions that were operating in the An Son area to get acquainted and coordinate. My NCO at our An Son base had tried to effect coordination with them as to the location of our mines and booby traps but they were not interested. The Battalion commander wasn't around and nobody seemed to be interested in talking to me. In fact they were discourteous and snobbish, so I just left. They tripped some of our booby traps and needlessly suffered casualties from them. Additionally the VC squad in the area inflicted several casualties on them and they killed only 2 VC in about four days of operations. The next day they were leaving to return to wherever they came from and I went by again. This time I caught the battalion commander, a lieutenant colonel. When I finished talking with him I realized we were not fighting the same war. I was appalled at his attitude and sincerely hoped it was not typical. This officer told me that the people knew the VC are here but didn't report it. I could have told him that before he started. He said if it were up to him he would just kill every civilian who doesn't tell where the VC are. If we did that what would be the difference in us and the communists? I would expect such comments as those of the colonel from one of his uneducated soldiers, but not from an officer.

    I didn't bother trying to explain to him that the people who are not VC are in the middle and that when they inform they do so with the realization that it may cost them not only their own lives but the lives of their families as well. In spite of this many of them do give us information. As a matter of fact, the most useful intel we have had has come from the local population,

    On 17 march we moved our CP back to Bung, and the Battalion commander had us a bunker built to operate from. We received all sorts of intelligence reports about VC in the area planning to attack us, but nothing happened.

    On 18 march we conducted a recon in force operation in An Son. We made contact right after leaving highway 13 with about 6 VC. They fired and ran. We fired mortars and artillery in the direction of their withdrawal. It looked like an outpost trying to draw us into an ambush, but we called for artillery and a light fire team and decided to take the bait to establish contact. We advanced and established contact with that same small unit again and they ran further to the south toward the Saigon River. Then we came upon some fresh dug bunkers, enough for a company. There we found 2 big bags of rice, 250 rounds of ammo for the AK-47 machine gun, 25 fuzes for the 82mm mortar ammo and 100 bottles of penicillin for shots, made in U.S.A. and no doubt supplied by some of the VC sympathizers in the US. We moved to the river and never did find the VC again. We suffered no casualties and neither did they as far as we know.

The Life Of A Soldier

I received a message from division in the evening of 18 March that the following day was a VC holiday. It had been designated as "Hate the U.S. Imperialist Day" or something like that. It struck me as funny and I replied that we should make the following day, "Hate the VC Day." Then Major Steffaniw chimed in and told me that if I happened to see some VC walking around with posters reading, "Hate the US" or "Yankee go home", not to pay any attention to it, but consider it a peaceful demonstration .I don't think the duty officer at division appreciated our humor. He thought was giving us some serious hot information.

Platoon Sergeant Morales, who was on my team when I first arrived but was moved back to regiment then went on emergency leave just before the TET offensive began, was sent back to me on 5 march as a replacement for SGT Ludwig who was killed. On the night of 6 March the VC tried to attack us again with no success because we discovered it before they could get it off the ground. Morales went all to pieces just as he had done on the night of 29 December when one of our companies was attacked. He got on the radio and reported that we were surrounded and being overrun. I had to take the microphone from him and order him to sit down and shut up. He broke out in a cold sweat and shook like a leaf.

He had never really been in hard combat as far as I could determine. He always managed to avoid it. I moved him to An Son to replace SGT Czap with the company there just before I went to the hospital and ordered Czap not to change places with him while I was gone, I also told Major Steffaniw of the situation.

    All the time I was gone he called every day on the radio and begged Czap to trade places with him and called the major too. He called up the night of 18March and reported they were under heavy attack from 2 directions, when actually a small patrol fired 3 M-79 (40mm) grenades at the camp. The company commander there who is a real good one, said all of the automatic weapons fire was his own. Then the next morning at 0400 Morales reported they were under heavy attack again. The company commander said a dog tripped one of their booby traps, which is a common occurrence, and he showed Morales the dead dog, but he still maintained they were attacked. I sent SGT Czap out there by helicopter to take him some supplies.

    By that time Morales had started picking out the men in the company who he thought were VC and even had the company commander on his list of suspects. The battalion commander mentioned it to me after I had removed Morales. I sent SGT Czap out to relieve Morales and had the chopper take him back to division. I wrote a letter to the division senior advisor recommending that Morales be reduced for inefficiency or discharged for unsuitability. A man cannot lead a platoon in combat if he can't control his own fears. And it is not fair for someone who can't cut it to hold the rank that someone else should have.

    The big switch between the 7th and 8th regiment took place on 20 March and it gave the VC a chance to move around and do whatever he pleased in the area since nobody was out looking for them.

The Life Of A Soldier

On 22 March I walked through the building where we were attacked on 5 March. It hadn't been cleaned out or anything, it was just as we left it. After this walk through I couldn't figure out how any of us got out of there alive. I found holes in the porch wall all around where I was, apparently made by machine gun bullets. I took some pictures, but ran out of film before I finished. Sgt Ludwig's blood was still there and the fatigue trousers of my houseboy who was wounded.

At 2045 hours on 25 march the VC attacked or tried to attack our base at An. They approached from the south and west and fired mortars, M-79 grenades and automatic weapons. We called in artillery illumination ALOFT, and a team of helicopter gunships which is referred to as a Light Fire Team. The ALOFT pilot is a new one and wasn't much help. He was too afraid of getting hit and wouldn't fly over the area where the VC were to spot them for the Light Fire Team. As soon as the Light Fire Team arrived the VC completely stopped firing and the ARVN soldiers in our south outpost bunker heard them shouting commands to dig in. The Light Fire Team did the best it could without any real help from the ALOFT, but just as they got going good, the artillery quit. For some reason I still haven't determined, division ordered a checkfire. It took about 15 minutes to get that straightened out, then the fire team was getting low on fuel. We had one wounded soldier and the medevac chopper arrived just in time to be supported by the fire team before he had to leave. We released the ALOFT and stopped the illumination and waited for the VC to attack again. But he never did. SGT Czap did an outstanding job again. This time I wrote a strong letter to try to get him promoted. I had already recommended him but he was on a list behind some of the dead weight they had at division who had more time in grade. Our CP was about 1500 meters away so I could see it pretty well. A search the next morning disclosed nothing except that the VC did dig in.

On 28 march we ran another operation in the same area where we had the big battle on 25 February, along with the 3rd battalion of the 8th regiment. They got lost and attacked one of our objectives, firing automatic weapons and M-79 grenades. I found out later that they didn't see any VC but just thought there might be some there. They wounded a woman in the leg whom we evacuated. Then they tried to deny that it was them. It took us 2 hours to get them out of our zone so that we could continue with our mission, primarily because they would not recognize the fact that they were in our zone.

The advisor told me on the radio that it is hard to tell where the boundary between zones is unless it follows a road or stream. I told him it is not at all difficult if you know how to read a map and know where you are on the map at all times.

The deputy division commander came by and told us we were going back to Anson for Revolutionary Development security on 1 April. As bad as I hated to be under control of the province chief, I was glad to get away from the 8th regiment. The major who was the senior advisor was crazy. The very first night that my battalion was under the operational control of the 8th regiment the major and I had a conflict. Every night we called in to division TOC our night locations. There were two very

The Life Of A Soldier

good reasons for this. First, it was so that we wouldn't be fired upon by friendly forces and aircraft who mistook us for VC. We almost got fired upon at the beginning of the TET offensive because someone didn't know where we were. The second is so that when we had a contact, division TOC already knew where we are to give us artillery and air support.

That first evening with the 8th regiment when one of my sergeants called in our locations, the major called me on the radio and told me that henceforth we would not call in our night locations to the Division TOC. (Tactical Operations Center) I told him that it was necessary for me to do this and I would continue to do it. The next evening when we called in the night locations he called and threatened to relieve me. I was not certain that he really had the authority to do that, but I told him to go ahead, that he might save my life by relieving me. Then he threatened to bring charges against me for disobeying an order. I told him that no one has the authority to order an officer to not do what he deems needful for the security of his unit. He told me that the reason that he didn't want us to report our location is that he didn't trust the ARVNs on the division staff. That he was afraid they would reveal our location to the VC. I told him that the VC always knew where we were, so that didn't matter.

After we finished talking, I had the Sergeants to cut some bamboo poles so that we could extend our antenna to reach Major Steffaniw at Paris Tan Quy on the other side of the Saigon River. When I told him about the situation, he told me not to worry about it. This major(the 8th

Euell White

Regimental Advisor) belonged to the Navigators, a Christian discipleship ministry. He went to church every Sunday morning at the division chapel no matter what was going on. I heard him on the radio announcing that he was going to church when we were in contact and could have needed him to get support for us. Going to church is commendable but that cannot be a first priority when lives are at risk and you may be needed. It seemed to be important to him for everyone on the radio net to know that he was going to church. He couldn't simply say that he would be off the air for awhile. He had to let everyone know he was going to church because it was Sunday.

The advisor at the division training center told me on 28 March that he had been told by the division senior advisor, Colonel Sonstielle, that I would report for duty there on 1 May. I hated to leave the battalion in a way but I had already had more combat than any other advisor in the division. I was the only battalion advisor on his second tour. This and the fact that I had 2 purple hearts was a factor in the new assignment. I didn't ask for any change at all.

On 1 April we arrived back in Anson and it was just like returning home after the gypsy life we led for 2 months. The Saigon River had a tide that rose every night and everything was damp. The ARVN latrine was near our quarters and it smelled bad. There was nothing pretty about that place, but after being away so long it was a luxury to be there. We had cots to sleep on and a roof over our heads. We also had fortifications for defense. I have learned that comfort and safety are very relative concepts. When I compared that place with home it was an absolute dump. But when I compared it with sleeping on the ground, it was a home.

ARVN Kitchen

The Camp at Anson

The Bung school where we were attacked by the VC on 5 March, reopened on 1 April. The Battalion repaired everything they could prior to its reopening.

The Life Of A Soldier

> **From My Journal**
>
> I heard President Johnson's speech on TV announcing that he would not be a candidate for re-election. I really don't know how to describe my reaction to it. I am amazed to say the least, followed by puzzlement. My thought is that a president who leaves office voluntarily with the country at war will be recorded as a failure. Therefore he will try anything to get us out of this war before his term expires. The Vietnamese are really shook up. They sense and fear a pullout by the US.

    On 3 April I went to Phu Hoa Dong. I went over there by helicopter then went to regiment at Paris Tan Quy by jeep, then back to Phu Hoa Dong with Major Steffaniw where we had lunch with Captain Rickman. Captain Rickman and I agreed on swapping our property since we both had about the same thing. Then I learned that we wouldn't be going to Phu Hoa Dong, but would swap places with the 2nd Battalion, located with Regiment at Paris Tan Quy on 5 April, then later go to Phu Hoa Dong.
The reason for the change was that the province chief wouldn't accept the 4th battalion in his area I felt sorry for Rickman. The advisor before him had been relieved for incompetence along with the battalion commander I was

afraid I was going there when I arrived. Now he was on his third Battalion commander and the VC was still making monkeys out of them. I knew Rickman was a good officer and was doing his best.. That battalion needed to be put into an offensive operation where they had to fight to survive. They suffered so many defeats they had no spirit left.

I liked what I saw at Phu Hoa Dong. The terrain around the base was fairly flat and open. There was a US radar site from the 25th Infantry Division artillery there to watch for the VC at night.

My battalion moved across the Saigon River on 4 April and rejoined our regiment at Paris Tan Quy. We were one of the blocking forces on 7 April for an operation. We made contact twice, once when moving into position, then again when moving back into position after withdrawing for an air strike. We had five soldiers wounded, and we killed one VC (or recovered one body) and captured one AK-47 machine gun as well as 2 sandbags full of documents. The 4th Battalion (Rickman's battalion) landed by boat to sweep the area. As of dark that night they had seven killed and 33 wounded and hadn't found any dead VC. They were caught by the darkness and had to spend the night. We sent one of our companies to Phu Hoa Dong to secure their base camp for the night. The next morning they found some VC dead, I am not sure how many, 90 rounds of 82 mm mortar ammunition and various other items such as rice, grenades etc.

The VC mortared them and us the next day and mortared them the following night, but I don't think they had a sight or firing table because the fire was inaccurate and ineffective.

The Life Of A Soldier

I took leave to Okinawa from 10-18 April where I visited my Sister, Rose McAuliffe, and her family. Rose and Charles' home was a busy place. Rose Nell was like a magnet for people with problems. She gave a listening ear and words of encouragement. Sometimes she and Charles gave financial aid that they really couldn't afford. One woman who came by while I was there had a husband who was gambling away the money needed to support his family. Charles and Rose gave her money to buy food for the children. I told Charles if it were me I would report the man to his commanding officer or first sergeant, but that was just not their nature. Charles was a Sergeant and worked in the housing office.

> On 5 April I was on my way to Phu Hoa Dong to coordinate with the senior advisor of the 4th Battalion for our move to that location, when I was informed via radio that Martin Luther King, Jr. had been assassinated. When I arrived at Phu Hoa Dong, the only American at the camp was a black Sergeant. When I arrived, the Vietnamese soldiers from the 4th Battalion were acting weird and gathered around to watch us. We learned that from what they were hearing on the radio they assumed that the sergeant and I would have a shootout. They were surprised to see that there was no animosity between us.

Euell White

Upon my return from leave I found my battalion yet at Paris Tan Quy with the regimental headquarters. My battalion gave a good account of itself while I was away. On the 15th they killed 22 VC and captured several weapons with only one lightly wounded. Sergeant Czap told me that the man who was wounded was grazed in the arm and ran back to the medic, got a bandage on his arm, then rejoined his company.

The VC attacked the 4th Battalion at Phu Hoa Dong one night while I was away. They fired mortars and small arms fire into the compound but didn't actually try a ground assault. The only damage done by the small arms fire was to make a bunch of holes in their shower barrel. One mortar round landed right in the doorway of a bunker killing one and wounded three inside the bunker.

On 19 April we had an unusual and exciting day. We kicked off a big operation which would have really amounted to something had it not been called off just as it was a getting started good. For a description of this see Appendix F: Significant Battles, Vietnam 1967-68 (. The High ranking Hoi Chan 413).

On 24 April the battalion moved to Phu Hoa Dong. It was good to have a base to work from, but we inherited the fruit of the 4th Battalion's failures. The VC were strong in that area and defeated the 4th battalion every time they moved. It was my hope that our battalion would never go back to An Son for New Life Hamlet or Revolutionary Development or whatever other name they came up with for it. In my opinion it was a big fat failure. They supposedly reorganized it every time they gave it a new name, but it had failed every time. It was now headed by a civilian and had a bunch of highly-paid civilians in the

The Life Of A Soldier

system who were more concerned with their own personal comfort, safety and the almighty dollar than anything else. Their only qualifications were degrees from Harvard, Yale, or some other institution.

We had an operation with the 4th Battalion and a battalion of US 25th Division. We were blocking and the other two battalions landed by boat. When the US battalion landed, the boats fired into us with their 20mm guns. They didn't hit any of us but one woman working in the field just a few yards from where we were with the battalion command post was hit in the head and killed instantly. Our medical officer ran to her but she was already dead. There were 2 men and another woman working alongside her and they just ignored her, until the battalion commander started yelling at them. Then the 2 men put her on a stretcher we provided and took her away. This seeming passivity was strange. There is no doubt that these people were somehow related as they were working in the same field. In my mind I contrasted their response, or lack of response, to the old lady who wept over my wounds about 2 months earlier.

The operation turned out to be pretty much a waste of time. The 4th battalion didn't make contact with the VC. They did find some bunkers, but typically for them, they didn't take any demolitions along with which to destroy them. The US battalion had a small contact and found some 122mm rockets.

I had a unique experience on 1 May. For the first time to my knowledge, I had lunch with a Vietcong. A Hoi Chan turned himself into one of our companies that morning. The words Chieu Hoi means open arms and the person who turns himself in is called a Hoi Chan. We were obligated to treat them well. I found out during lunch that he belonged to the battalion that attacked us on 5 March at Bung School and that is the same unit which the battalion of the US 25th Division engaged on 30 April and suffered 5 killed and 19 wounded. The Hoi Chan was from North Vietnam and he had been in the South only a few days. He found a leaflet signed by the VC Colonel who defected a few days earlier. He said the trip from North Vietnam was long and hard and about 50 percent of the replacements sent from the north die en-route. They were told that except for Saigon all of the civilian population were behind the VC. He said the people in the north didn't have enough to eat and weren't aren't allowed to use motor-driven transportation, only bicycles.

The soldiers were told that the US commanded the South Vietnamese and our motive was to colonize the country. When I was introduced to him he smiled real big and said he had seen me driving through Phu Hoa Dong. The Hoi Chan told us that the VC had orders to take no prisoners, and to kill all Americans or ARVN soldiers, even if they surrender. Our officers, except for one, were originally from North Vietnam. They are always eager to talk to someone from home. One of the things I disliked about Phu Hoa Dong was that we had no way to go anywhere without passing through the town.

On 4 May a Hoi Chan turned himself in and a big battle ensued. For details see Appendix F: Significant Battles, Vitnam 1967-68 (The Battle in the Rubber Plantation, Page 417).

We didn't have any contact with the VC on 5 May. We had intelligence that the VC had moved a 300-man

The Life Of A Soldier

force into the area where we fought on 4 May. I had the radar scanning 360 degrees. They could complete the circle in three minutes. The radar was here when I came. They were from the US 25th Infantry Division Artillery. After I arrived, I found out that the only man of the 3-man crew who really knew how to operate the radar was the repairman. I had a talk with them and told them that they had better learn how to operate it or I would send them back to Cu Chi. I told them if they would do a good job with the radar, we would feed them well and require nothing else from them. They all learned how to operate it, and I began using the 25th DIVARTY (Division Artillery) for (H & I) harassing and interdiction fires. Anytime the radar reported that they saw a target, DIVARTY would fire. I sometimes helped them to see a target where I suspected the enemy might be.

One thing I liked about the area was we had no trouble getting medevacs. The 25th US Infantry Division was at Cu Chi, a short distance from us. We called their Dustoff control direct and didn't have to go through with the farce of requesting a VNAF medevac. On the other side of the Saigon River, the medevac unit always wanted to know if the casualty was US and often wouldn't come if there were only ARVN casualties. The Cu Chi medevacs never asked and when they got ARVN casualties they asked us what hospital we wanted them to go to. Captain Ninh always wanted them to go the Cong Hoa Military Hospital. If they went to a US hospital it was hard for him to find them and easier for them to desert. Those guys that flew the medevacs were great. They would come in if you asked them to even if they are receiving fire, but I wouldn't let them land under fire.

Early in the evening of 10 May my radar spotted a long column of VC moving toward a bridge on the road between Phu Hoa Dong and Paris Tan Quy. Artillery from the US 25th Division at Cu Chi fired about 200 rounds on it and the radar couldn't detect any more movement. I keep referring to the radar as mine. The 25th Division thought it was their radar, but it was mine.

The Phu Hoa District headquarters was very close to us. They caught three VC among their soldiers on 11 May. Each of them had tear gas grenades and said that their mission was to throw tear gas into the bunkers when the VC attacked. One of them supposedly had the entire plan of attack which was to take place at 0200 hours on 12 May against the district headquarters and our battalion. He said the VC had an infantry battalion, a company of artillery, and 82 mm mortars. They were to attack us from the southwest. The whole deal sounded phony to me. I couldn't believe a VC commander would disclose his plan of attack to some joker he planted inside the compound to toss tear gas grenades. However everyone got shook up. We were ready for the VC to attack every night, but we took advantage of the panic and requested extra harassing and interdiction artillery missions and they fired them. Major Green the district advisor was new and he was not a combat arms officer. I think he was from the quartermaster branch. He got excited over everything. I didn't doubt that the VC planned to attack district headquarters and possibly us, but they were not going to make it quite that easy for us to find out what time and from what direction. On 14 May the district adviser. Major Green. came by and told me that

The Life Of A Soldier

they had discovered 13 VC among their popular force troops. They found three a couple days before and started checking them all. That made me wonder how many we had in our battalion.

> I was awarded the Vietnamese Cross of Gallantry with Silver Star at a ceremony at division, for my actions on 5 March at Bung School. The following is a translation of the citation: Euell T. White-Captain –US ARMY – an excellent, much combat experiences officer Advisor. Especially noteworthy was in the VC attack against location of 3/7 Bn predawn of 5 March 1968. Subject officer was very brave and remained side by side the Vietnamese counterpart in command and maneuvering the troops to counter attack, same time, he requested timely and accurate Air and Artillery support repelling Enemy. After 30 minutes contacting, there were 38 KIA, 11 AK 50, 4 BAR, 5 B40, 2 B41, 1CKC and numerous documents confiscated.

On 15 may the 2nd Battalion of the 14th Infantry (US) moved into the western part of my area . Their S-3(Operations Officer) came to coordinate then sent a lieutenant for liaison who stayed with me while they were in my area of operations.

Euell White

On 12 May one of our ambushes killed a VC officer near us.. He was an intelligence officer for Cu Chi VC District. He had a sketch of our compound showing the location of the advisors' bunker, the battalion commander's bunker and the command bunker.. I went to district on 14 May and they told me that all of 13 of the VC had been Hoi Chans. Then I was wondering whether my troops didn't have the right idea. They didn't believe in the Chieu Hoi (open arms) program and they would kill them when they tried to surrender unless there was an officer with them, then say that the Hoi Chan had a grenade in his hand. They just did not understand why they should treat someone like a brother who had been trying to kill them and maybe had just killed one of their buddies.

The Battalion Commander of the $2/14^{th}$ Infantry (US). LTC Nunn, came by to visit. He came right at lunch time so I invited him to eat with us. He wanted to have a combined operation with us, and wanted his troops to work with the ARVN.

I found out on 17 May, how the VC among the district troops were discovered. While the regimental staff was examining the documents taken from the bodies of the NVA/VC killed in the rubber plantation, the regimental interpreter discovered a photo taken from the body of one of the NVA soldiers, The photo was of that soldier and one of his buddies, both of them in NVA uniform. The other soldier looked exactly like the jeep driver for Major Green, the district advisor. They called Major Green and asked him to come to regimental headquarters. When they told him his driver was an NVA soldier he adamantly resisted it.

I was told that when they showed Major Green the photo, he turned white. He wanted to have the man arrested

The Life Of A Soldier

immediately but they convinced him to ride with him back to district and report it to the district chief. When they interrogated the man he identified the others. All of them had access to the headquarters personnel including the Americans. One was the barber who cut the Americans hair and sometimes shaved them with a straight razor.

The 2nd battalion of the 14th Infantry (US) made a heliborne assault in an area to the east of us on 17 May. I really learned a great deal by listening to their radio traffic. Their battalion commander had less authority and freedom of movement than I did, although he was a Lt. Colonel commanding an infantry battalion. The brigade commander was on the radio meddling and giving instructions and asking stupid questions all the time. By the time it got to the company commander he was a puppet on a string.

In May when the time finally came to issue the 5th ARVN Division M-16 rifles and M-60 machine guns -- which is standard for US units--our battalion was at first issued enough to equip one platoon of each company. Captain Ninh, the battalion commander, decided that he would prefer to outfit one company rather than one platoon from each company. There was a big ceremony involved in the issuing the weapons.

The weapons were issued to 10th Company which was commanded by Lieutenant Tien, the battalion commander's son-in-law. This company was occupying an outpost at Phu Hoa Dong. Soon after the new weapons were issued, Sergeant Czap went to Cu Chi and acquired from the 25th US division a truckload of Bouncing Betty

Euell White

anti-personnel mines. The mine got its name from the fact that when someone steps on it the mine bounces into the air at the right level to disperse deadly metal fragment inflicting wounds on all in the immediate vicinity. Sergeant Czap helped them emplace the mines around the outpost perimeter.

That night, in what seemed almost bizarre in its irony, the VC attacked that outpost in strength. The soldiers were so confident with their new weapons, they not only fought the enemy but at one point got out of their emplacements and went out to close with them. Sergeant Czap, who was with the company, had to call a cease-fire for the spooky and shift the artillery fire because they were in such close combat. This was a North Vietnamese unit and they had been told that all they had to do was attack and the ARVN would turn on their American advisers and kill them, then surrender themselves. These prisoners really believed this and were shocked that it didn't turn out that way.

The Life Of A Soldier

During the Tet offensive when we had the mission of securing a stretch of Highway 13, and moving our night position, we stayed one night in the home of a Vietnamese family. They lived just off the highway and across the little stream that was our southern boundary. I never went to sleep that night. I talked with the Vietnamese man that was the head of the household all night. They were catholic and had their walls covered with pictures of popes. The old man told me over and over that he was grateful for the Americans sacrificing the lives of their young men to assure freedom for them. A few days later, one night while we had our CP at the old French villa at Bung, one of our ambushes killed a young boy. He was dressed in the black pajamas of the Viet Cong, armed with a Viet cong weapon, and obviously part of the Viet Cong unit that was trying to attack us when they ran into our ambush. The next morning the boy was identified as the 14-year-old son of the man who had been our host a few days earlier. The boy had eaten supper with us. I told Captain Ninh I wanted to go and see that man, but he didn't want to go. My interpreter, Sergeant Tu didn't want to go either but I insisted that he go with me. I wanted to make sure I didn't say the wrong thing. The man told me that he had lost his son to the VC when he was 7 years old. I did all I could do. I told him I was sorry for his loss.

Euell White

The home of the Vietnamese family
who lost their 14-year-old son

The Life Of A Soldier

Sometime in May I moved to the Division Training Center, after an R & R to Hawaii where Euna met me. The 5th ARVN Division Training Center was located at the junction of Highway 13 going North and South with another road going East to the 5th ARVN and 1st US division bases. The captain whom I was relieving was still there and stayed for a couple of days until time for him to return to the states.

The first night I was there the departing advisor and the training center commander, Major Huy, kept me awake most of the night shooting firecrackers. They had problems getting along and they were trying to get rid of the evil spirits before they said their final goodbyes to one another. When I saw this I began to dread this assignment. If there was bad blood between these two it would probably be difficult for me to establish a good relationship with the commander. I was relieved then when, a few days later Major Huy was replaced by a Lieutenant Colonel.

The colonel and I had a good relationship for the four months I was there. Events later confirmed my feeling that Major Huy would have been difficult to get along with. When he left the training center he was assigned to the division G-3. He seemed to really want to be friendly with me. He left in midweek and invited me to have supper with his family on Saturday evening. I accepted and he told me he would send his jeep driver to pick me up at a certain time. I got dressed for the occasion and waited for the jeep but it never arrived. When I saw him the next week he was very offended. I had made him lose face with his family. I explained that his jeep never showed and I had no idea where he lived. He apparently had called and left a message that the jeep wouldn't come and that the commander's driver at the training center knew the way. I didn't get the message and assumed he had forgotten. I did my best to be friendly with him but he never again invited me. I was grateful that he was gone from the training center.

The training center was about 15 or 20 acres fenced in with firing ranges outside the fence. The advisory staff included three NCOs and there were two or three from the US 1st Infantry Division on special duty. I quickly discovered that there was not much advising and assisting going on but a lot of drinking and other unhealthy activities. The advisory team quarters had a pretty extensive bar and it was known as a watering hole or stopover for Americans of the two divisions traveling to and returning from Saigon. My sergeants from the 3rd Battalion, 7th Regiment had told me about the bar and also that they had warned the sergeants at the training center I would probably close the bar.

The first night after the other captain had left, one of the Sergeants asked me if we were going to have a meeting to learn of my policies. I sensed this was something they had all talked about so I said OK if you think that is needed. I had really planned to observe them for a few more days before saying anything. During the meeting one of the NCOs from the 1st US Division asked what was my policy about women. I said I didn't know we needed a policy about women. I said I am married to a woman my mother was a woman and I have a daughter that is fast approaching womanhood, so I am in favor of women.

The Life Of A Soldier

Then I asked what does my policy about women have to do with being advisors at this training center? He then told me that my predecessor allowed them to bring women in once in awhile. I made it clear that we wouldn't be doing that and that I didn't want our place to be known as the place one could come to get drunk. I told them the whiskey bar would be closed. That they could drink beer so long as it didn't interfere with their duties.

I told the sergeants from the 1st US Infantry Division to pack their bags to return to their units the next day. Then I told the others I expected to see them out where the training was going on every day and I wanted daily reports on what was going on as well as recommendations for improvements. My impression was that all of them, including the captain, were just lying around enjoying themselves.

Very soon after the change of command, the Lt. Colonel training center commander invited me to his quarters one evening for tea, and this became a regular routine. Visiting with him was educational and fun. He was very particular to have his tea at exactly the right temperature. Usually the houseboy had to take it back at least once to get it right.

On my second visit the colonel showed me a secret entrance from his bedroom to a tunnel that led to the command bunker some 300 yards away, and told me that should we come under attack I should use the tunnel to get to the command bunker. As it turned out there was never an occasion to use it, but if there had been it could have been a life saver. When I told the sergeants about the tunnel they had never even heard of its existence.

When I inspected what was called the defensive bunker next to our quarters I think I learned why they didn't know about the safety tunnel. I found four M-60 machine guns as well as various other weapons and defensive devices in the bunker. The training center was conducting training at that time on the M-60 because it was being issued to the battalions, and they didn't have near as many as they needed for the training. When I asked why these weapons were in this bunker, which I assumed was for temporary protection from artillery and mortar attacks, I was told that their plan, devised by my predecessor, was to defend that bunker against everything that moved outside it in the event of an attack.

I ordered them to turn those machine guns and other defensive devices over to the training center supply to be used for training and defense of the perimeter. I told them that if the training center is attacked, our job is to help defend the perimeter and the only use for the so-called defensive bunker would be for temporary protection during an artillery or mortar attack.

I cannot remember the name of the Lt. Colonel who commanded the training center, but he was an interesting character. We had from 1,000 to 2,000 trainees there at any given time, plus the training center staff and their families. There was a good water well with a pump, but no pipelines. A truck with a tank on it spent the whole day filling barrels at the various buildings throughout the compound every day. The commander was not satisfied with this arrangement and one evening at tea, he told me that we needed a water works and if I could help him get

The Life Of A Soldier

the needed pipe he could do it. He knew how much he needed for the mainline which had to be a large pipe, but he said the branch lines could be various sizes because he could weld pipes together that were not the same size.

I told my sergeants about the need and the next day they showed up with a truckload of pipe, including enough of the big pipes for the main line. When I asked where they found the pipe they replied that we needed a water works more than the division advisory team needed a swimming pool. Later I heard the people at division talking about their missing pipe.

Early one morning, soon after the pipe arrived I was awakened by someone yelling over a loudspeaker. I went outside and found the colonel with a bullhorn, a welding truck and a bunch of trainees at work. He worked them in shifts day and night until the project was completed. The first branch line was to our quarters. We were nearest to the well.

A few days after the water works was completed we were visited by the division commander, Major General Thuan, and the senior American advisor, Colonel Leach. The training center commander and I had a standard briefing that we gave all VIPs that visited us, with charts etc. If the senior visitor was Vietnamese, the colonel did the briefing in Vietnamese and I translated it to English. If the senior visitor was American I presented the briefing and the colonel translated. It was a canned presentation—meaning that we knew exactly what we were going to say.

After we gave the briefing to General Thuan and Colonel Leach, the training center commander wanted to show them the water works. We got in jeeps and took a tour through the compound then stopped by the well.

As they were admiring the water works, the training center commander told the general in Vietnamese that I had furnished the pipe for it. Colonel leach didn't understand Vietnamese, but the general then turned to me, shook my hand and in English, said, "Thank you Captain White for furnishing the pipe for the water works." Colonel leach looked at me and I knew from his expression that at that moment he knew we had misappropriated the pipe for his swimming pool. I fully expected to be called to division that very day, but nothing was ever said about it.

Before I left for Malaysia a couple of months later, the swimming pool was completed. I suppose they had no problem getting more pipes. After we got running water I decided that I wanted to have a flush toilet. Getting a commode was no problem but the plumbing was another matter. My sergeants had befriended an American civilian named Barney from somewhere in Alabama, Selma, I think. He worked for Pacific Architects and Engineers, called P.A. & E. They were the contractors for maintenance. Barney came to spend a few days with us and brought some heavy equipment with him. He built a septic tank from 55-gallon drums in a big pit that he dug with his equipment, that worked perfectly, and I had a flush toilet.

The Life Of A Soldier

Barney

When I arrived at the training center, the advisors had a big chicken pen with about a thousand chickens, almost frying size. My predecessor had the idea that this would be a way for the ARVNs to raise their own meat and save on their food budget. He had arranged with an American agricultural advisor at Binh Duong Province to get some baby chicks from the Philippines with all of the food and medicines to raise them. He had planned to get it started then let the Vietnamese to take over the project, but they were not at all interested.

Euell White

After the new commander arrived, I approached the subject with him and he was not interested. He said the meat from chickens raised like that is no good. That chickens need to roam free so they can eat rocks etc. He had a valid argument but I still thought the plan had merit. One of my NCOs, Sergeant Newton, from Kentucky, was an excellent cook. We planned a party and invited all of the Vietnamese training center officers as well as the Vietnamese officers and their American advisors from the division G-3 staff.

Sergeant Newton, assisted by the other NCOs and our Vietnamese cook, fried chicken that would put Colonel Sanders to shame, and made biscuits, gravy and mashed potatoes. Everyone ate to their hearts (or stomachs) content. I especially watched the Vietnamese officers to see how they ate because they had never seen chicken cooked this way before. Chicken is their favorite meat. They ate as heartily as did the Americans. A day or two later, I approached the colonel again on the subject of raising chickens and he still said no. We started eating the chickens and gave some of them to the families of the training center staff who were not so particular as to how the chickens were raised.

The Life Of A Soldier

> The Following is a letter I received from Dai-uy Ninh, shortly after I moved to the Training Center:
>
> Dear Capt. White
> I can't tell you how excited I was when I received your letter. During the time you and I worked together we had faced many dangers. You and I faced misery, sometimes winning, sometimes losing and still we worked together as friends. Only in the army can there be such great friendship. Beside everything you have done, you have help the 3rd Bn in any way you could. I think good friend like you aren't too many, but I hope the Americans will as you have done.
> In behalf of my troops in this Bn and my family I wish you, your country more strength. So maybe your country become the rule of the world.
> I wish you and your family happiness and all of God's love. If I have chance and time I will come to Phu Van to see you at the Training center.

When I first arrived at the 3rd Battalion, 7th Regiment, I met Trung-uy (First Lieutenant) Huang who was the operations officer. I had just finished an intensive course in the Vietnamese language at the Special Warfare School and wanted to follow up. Lieutenant Huang knew a lot of English but also wanted to know more. We made an agreement to meet every night when the situation allowed, to teach each other. One night we would speak only English and the next time only Vietnamese. When the Tet offensive started, Huang was moved to one of the rifle companies as a platoon leader. One night while we had our base at the French villa in Bung, a patrol from Huang's platoon was ambushed and withdrew to their base minus one man. Lieutenant Huang went back to get the man and lost both his legs in the process. I have always regretted that I never visited him in the hospital. I received a very touching letter from him while at the training center.

> Conghoa Hospital
> August 12, 1968
> Dear Sir:
>   By the occasion my houseboy go to Phu Van I hurriedly have some words for you. First, I beg your pardon about the silence so long with you. I'm so well now but I can't go right now. I'm practicing to use two sticks to go-- and I wonder that I can't know when I can again have occasion to see you 1 more time before you leave Vietnam. But as I'm very happy to be a closed friend of yours and always I think of you. Announce me when you promote major. I want have something for you in that promotion. I send you all my respects of a high friendship by ending this note.
> Very sincerely yours,
> Lt. Huang

The Life Of A Soldier

Trung-uy (1ˢᵗ Lt) Huang

Euell White

The four months I was with the training center were largely uneventful insofar as combat is concerned. I was at the training center until late September or early October. I was called to division personnel one day and told that there was a requirement to send a captain to Penang, Malaysia as a liaison to a US Navy detachment there. I was offered the opportunity to volunteer because I had more combat time than any other captain. I was also the only one in the division who was on his second tour, and had two purple hearts.

The assignment amounted to a 60-day vacation. I respectfully declined, and forgot all about it. Then one day about a month later personnel called me and told me that I was to report to the American Embassy in Saigon the following day to get a passport, and board an Air Vietnam plane the day following that for a flight to Singapore then take a Malaysian Airlines flight from Singapore to Penang. I reminded the personnel officer that I had declined the opportunity to volunteer and he said I was already on orders, that there must have been a foul-up, but it was too late to change it. I had to go.

The Life Of A Soldier

Saigon 1968

Sometime in November from Penang, I called the Infantry Branch of Department of the Army Personnel to find out what my assignment would be when I returned to the states in December. I had been called in from the field in Vietnam a few months earlier because of what was described on the radio as an emergency. I was frightened when I received the call, thinking something had happened to my wife or daughter. When I reported to Division Personnel they wanted me to fill out a form called the assignment preference sheet and often referred to as a dream sheet. I was angry about the deception and skipped all of the blocks where I was supposed to list first, second and third preferences and in the remarks section wrote that I wanted an assignment where I could commute from my home at Route 1, Rogersville, Alabama.

I was shocked when I learned that my new duty station would be at Huntsville, Alabama, about 40 miles from my home. Then the officer that I was talking to said, "By the way, you will be promoted to major on 18 November ." My promotion date came while I was still in Penang.

I returned to Vietnam in December, just in time to process out for my return to the states. I spent the night with Dan Biggs in Saigon on the way.

The Life Of A Soldier

9.
Stateside 1969-70

I returned home from Vietnam sometime in December 1968 on leave en-route to my new duty station at Huntsville, Alabama. My orders assigned me to the Army National Guard Advisor Group in Montgomery, Alabama with duty Station in Huntsville. There was nothing in the orders concerning the unit or the location address within Huntsville. I knew there was a National Guard armory on South Memorial Parkway so I reported there on 18 December. No one there was expecting me but one of the officers called Montgomery and learned that I was to be the senior adviser to the "C" Detachment of 20th Special Forces Group (Airborne) of the Alabama National Guard. The group headquarters was in Birmingham and this "C" detachment which was designated, company "A" was at another location in Huntsville at an old armory shared with a unit of the 115th signal battalion.

It seemed that blessings were overtaking me. I had no Idea I was getting an assignment that would allow me to be on parachute jump status. To be on jump status was in itself a morale booster and the extra $110 per month was yet another blessing. At that time $110 was a good percentage increase of my pay.

I must say that I was really surprised by the level of proficiency of the officers and senior noncommissioned officers of the 20th Special Forces Group. In the Huntsville unit all of the staff officers had been in the unit long enough to rotate through most of the staff positions which amounted to being very well cross-trained. Although they didn't have actual combat experience I would have had no qualms about going to combat with that unit.

I had one regular army Special forces NCO to assist me. He was Master Sergeant Ledbetter. Sergeant Ledbetter was an excellent NCO. He was a good soldier and devoted husband and father.

My boss was Major Lee Mize who was the adviser to the group headquarters in Birmingham, until he returned to Vietnam. Major Mize and I attended the Special Warfare Special Forces Officer School together in 1964, when he was a captain and I a 1st lieutenant, but I didn't get to know him then.

He and MSGT Ledbetter had worked together in Vietnam and were close friends. When Major Mize left for Vietnam he arranged with the Army Adjutant General not to be replaced so that he could return to that position after Vietnam as his terminal assignment before retirement. Mize was a medal of honor recipient from the Korean War. Lee Mize's position at Birmingham became my additional duty when he left.

The "C" detachment in Huntsville had a subordinate "B' detachment in Montgomery and another in Pell City. Both Colonel Cobb , the group commander and his deputy commander, Lieutenant Colonel Bishop later became the Adjutant General of Alabama. Colonel Cobb owned an automobile dealership in Montgomery and was an agent for New York Life Insurance Company. LTC Bishop owned a plant nursery in Alexander City. The commander of Company "A" in Huntsville, a Lieutenant Colonel whose name I can't remember , was a medical technician who

The Life Of A Soldier

worked for a Huntsville doctor. The executive officer of Company "A" was Major Tom Sharp who owned Tom Sharp Tire Company in Huntsville.

A few months ago I joined the Alabama chapter of the Special Forces Association. Lieutenant Colonel (retired) Joe Miller is the president. He was Captain Miller on the C detachment staff while I was the advisor. The local chapter of the Special Forces association is named for Colonel Lee Mize.

The truth is that there was not much for Sergeant Ledbetter or myself to do except during the MUTA weekends. MUTA stand for Multiple Unit Training Assembly. At least that is the way I remember it. The units were on duty for the entire weekend once a month. Company "A" had two NCOs who were civil service employees and called A.S.T.s. These men, Sergeants Creasy and Irvine were administrators and very efficient. After Major Mize left I spent part of each week with the group headquarters in Birmingham, where they had a larger A.S.T. staff and at least three regular army special forces NCO advisors.

Once each month we had a meeting with the advisors from Huntsville, Birmingham, Montgomery and Pell City. The guys from Birmingham would bring parachutes with them to Fort Mclellan and after a jump, we would go to a restaurant for lunch. Colonel McKean who was commander of the 5th Special Forces Group when I was in Vietnam in 1965, was Post commander at Fort McClellan and we could get one of his helicopters anytime we wanted to make a jump. Master Sergeant Bill Edge whom I knew from the 1st in Okinawa was one of my NCOs at Birmingham for awhile. He was a freefall parachutist with hundreds of jumps. I believe he was later a member of the Golden Knights Army Parachute Team. Sergeant Major Edge died with cancer a few months ago.

In the summer of 1969, the 20th Special Forces Group had its summer camp on the Coosa river. Later on that summer I was detailed to help out with two summer camps at Camp Shelby Mississippi. For one camp I was adviser to a tank battalion from Clarksville Tennessee. For the other I was adviser for a military police battalion from Clanton and Eufaula Alabama. I enjoyed both of these assignments.

When I was in Germany with the 76th Tank Battalion, I was for a time the assistant operations Sergeant. During that time Seventh Army sent us a part of the draft for a tank gunnery manual to edit before publication. I had become the editor for everything in the S-3 section so I inherited the job. The part that I edited was for the Tank Crew Proficiency Course (T.C.P.C.) This was an annual test for each tank crew and it was considered a main measurement of the combat readiness of a tank battalion.

In editing this manual and having been a tank platoon leader, I knew a lot about the tank crew proficiency test. When I joined the Clarksville battalion they were beginning the T.C.P.C. The officers were shocked when this infantry major wearing the green beret of special forces and the crossed rifles of an infantry officer started asking questions and making comments about their performance in the T.C.P.C. The T.C.P.C. was a live fire exercise that required firing all of the tank's guns, the 90mm cannon, and 50 caliber and 30 caliber machine guns. They could

The Life Of A Soldier

not figure out how I knew so much about what they were doing. It was a good battalion and they did well. My respect for the National Guard that I had gained from the 20th Special Forces Group was not at all diminished by my experience with the Clarksville tank battalion.

The military police battalion from Clayton, Alabama was commanded by Major Henry Gray. Henry was a graduate of an Ivy League university and a big dairy farmer in Eufala. He was intelligent and personable. It became evident that he was politically strong in the state. When we would enter a room for a social gathering he was given more attention than the major general who was in charge of the summer camp. Henry later became the adjutant general of Alabama, He also headed the Alabama Alcoholic Beverage Control Board, and the Mental Health Board.

During this camp, Hurricane Camille hit. I had been home for the weekend and was headed back to Camp Shelby on Sunday afternoon. On the interstate there was a constant stream of traffic moving north to get away from the coast. I arrived at Shelby that Sunday afternoon just before dark and moved into a building that no one else was occupying. I parked my car under a big oak tree outside the building. The windows were rattling in the building from the wind. I was tired from the trip and went to bed and to sleep immediately. I awakened the next morning and found the building adjacent to me gone. I thought sure my car would be ruined but except for being covered with leaves and acorns it was fine. It was Hurricane Camille.

Euell White

Henry's M.P. battalion was given a mission to secure some of the small towns that had been destroyed by the tornado in the hurricane. They were to prevent looting. I asked Henry had the battalion been federalized and had the governor of Mississippi formally requested their help. When he answered no, I told him that if one of his men shot a looter, as battalion commander he could be held personally responsible and liable. He didn't seem to be sure that I knew what I was talking about so I told him to contact the Judge Advocate General (JAG) lawyer. He did, then immediately withdrew his troops from the towns.

I did a lot of fishing in 1969. I was at that time a determined, although not successful, fisherman. I was living next door to my Dad and he decided that together we should have a garden. I had never enjoyed anything connected with farming and gardening and I didn't really want to do it. But I wanted to please my dad and I wanted to have some time with him so I agreed. Many times when I would come home with the idea of going fishing my dad would be waiting for me and say we had work to do in the garden. We had a good garden but I can't really say that I enjoyed that aside from the aspect of being with my dad and pleasing him.

I had the honor and privilege of administering the oath of office as a WO1 (Warrant Officer 1), to my nephew, Gary A. White on 20 October 1969 at Fort Rucker, Alabama. Gary retired in November 1988 as a WO4. In 1970, He served in Vietnam with the 2nd Battalion, 20th Aerial Rocket Artillery, 1st Cavalry Division, flying the COBRA. Gary was awarded the Distinguished Flying Cross with oak leaf cluster-- which in

The Life Of A Soldier

plain English means he was twice awarded the medal-- and various other medals.

Another of my Nephews, Michael Butler, served in the 1991 Gulf War as a gunship pilot. Michael enlisted in the army in 1970 and served over 24 years, retiring in 1994 as a CWO4. Michael flew the APACHE with the 1st Battalion, 227th Aviation Regiment of the 3rd Cavalry Division. He was shot down by a SAM (Surface to Air Missile). Both he and his co-pilot were rescued by one of their buddies in another Apache. They had only minor injuries from the crash. Michael was awarded the Purple Heart, Bronze Star, Air Medal and various other medals.

On Veterans Day 1969, I addressed the Lauderdale County High School (LCHS) at Rogersville. Although I had dropped out of school there in the 9th grade, my home room and English teacher, Mrs. Essie Goad, was still teaching there and was the faculty advisor for the student council. She arranged to have me invited to speak on that day. In my speech I told about a sergeant who was on my team when I went to Vietnam in 1965 that sacrificed his life to save his buddies in Project Delta. He was wounded and couldn't walk. He urged his buddies to leave him and go to the point where the helicopter was to pick them up. When they wouldn't leave him he shot himself in the head so they wouldn't be killed trying to get him out. I heard the story from an eyewitness, another sergeant who was with him. Years later, LTC (retired) Bo Gritz who was trying get the POWs out that were allegedly abandoned, told the same story in a fund-raising speech and was attacked by Ted Koppel on Nightline and called a liar among other things.

  I became bored with the advisor assignment and missed being active in the Army. Early in 1970 I called Infantry Branch at Department of the Army personnel and asked if they had any plans for me to attend the infantry officer advanced course at Fort Benning. The assignment officer seemed surprised that I wanted to leave this plush assignment but he said they would send me if I wanted to go.

  I reported to Fort Benning in late March or early April 1970 for Infantry Officer Advanced Course Class 5-70. The very first day I discovered Major Hoang Kim Ninh, my Vietnamese counterpart from 1967-68 in Vietnam. I had recommended him for the school but never dreamed we would be classmates. All of the Allied officers

The Life Of A Soldier

were assigned sponsors so I volunteered to be Major Ninh's sponsor.

In the classroom Major Ninh and I were seated near Lieutenant Colonel Mamdouh from Jordan and his sponsor, Major Nick Sellers. The four of us worked together as a group for the tactical exercises on the terrain board and we had a lot of fun.

Nick was single and he brought Colonel Mamdouh and Major Ninh to our house frequently for visits. We bought a house in Columbus and moved while we were still in school. On Halloween of 1970 Nick and the two allied officers came to the house with masks on and said trick or treat. They brought gifts for Sherry and she just loved all of them.

During the war in which Israel defeated Jordan although Jordan had them outnumbered, Colonel Mamdouh was a tank battalion commander and lost all of his tanks. We replayed that battle on the terrain board in class. Nick would say, "Lets put the tanks out front" and Colonel Mamdouh just couldn't stand this although it was only and exercise. He would say, "No!...No!...No! We must put the infantry out front to protect the tanks. Nick Sellers would say. "Oh what the heck, they only cost about a million dollars." I thought Colonel Mamdough would have a stroke.

On the first day of class there was a disturbance over seating. A captain from one of the Arab nations, was assigned a seat adjacent to an Israeli captain and went into a tantrum over it. Colonel Mamdough took the initiative to calm the Arab officer. There were about 200 officers in the class so I didn't get to know everyone. Recently when I looked at the roster of the graduating class, there was no one from Israel on the list. I suppose they moved that Captain to another class. Apparently, even then we were appeasing the Muslims.

When we were about half way through the course a personnel team came down from Washington to speak to all of the infantry officers and bring us up to date on what was happening and what we could expect in the future.

After hearing the briefing I was fairly sure that my next assignment would be another tour in Vietnam. I tried to prepare Euna for this but she wouldn't hear of it. She said, surely they wouldn't send me again after I was wounded on both of my earlier tours. She said this would not be fair. I explained to her that fair had nothing to do with it, the needs of the service prevails. She knew this already in her head but her heart wouldn't agree.

A couple of months before graduation a personnel team came to tell us what our assignments would be. The day before the team arrived, I tried to prepare Euna for what I was certain would be my assignment, but she still wouldn't believe it. When the day came I was proven right. When I went home and told her she became very upset. She was certain that I would be killed this time.

I hated so much to see her so upset that I made an attempt to get out of this assignment. There was a Major Black who was to go to Vietnam at the same time and his orders were canceled because they didn't need him. Major Black wanted to go because he had never been to Vietnam. We got together and called infantry branch and asked that they let him go instead of me. The answer was "no" because the requisition for my assignment required a "3" prefix to the military occupational specialty which means to be airborne special forces qualified. I knew that special forces were being phased out already in Vietnam and therefore it was unlikely that I would get a special forces assignment, but the bureaucracy wouldn't budge. I was right. I didn't get a special forces assignment and Major Black could have filled the position as well as I.

From left: LTC Stone, my faculty Advisor in the Advance Course, Mrs. Stone, Major Ninh and me at a reception for the allied officers.

Euell White

The Life Of A Soldier

10
Vietnam 1971
101st Airborne (Airmobile)

This departure from home was one of the hardest and probably the hardest one ever for me. Not because I was afraid of what would happen to me, but because of my family. Sherry had just turned 15 and I needed to be there for her. My last act as her father before leaving was to ground her from any social life except at school because of something she did.

I graduated from the Advanced Course on 23 November, 1970 and didn't leave for Vietnam until sometime in January 1971. There wasn't much to do, as far as duty was concerned, in the meantime. I attended one day of Lieutenant Calley's trial, but it was such a hassle to get into the courtroom I gave it up after the first day.

I arrived at Long Binh early in January. I know that I departed there for the 101st Airmobile Division on 8 or 9 January. As I predicted I didn't get the special forces assignment they claimed they needed me for. When I found this out at Long Binh I tried to get transportation to Saigon but they were suspicious and wouldn't let me have a jeep. I had the name of a colonel in Saigon at a hotel who could get my assignment changed to adviser for a unit in the ARVN Airborne Division.

When I arrived at division headquarters it was very rainy and muddy. The First Brigade was nearby and the 3rd Brigade at Camp Evans, between Hue and Quang Tri. The division personnel officer, who was an old friend, sent me to the First Brigade to be interviewed. When I arrived I was met by the deputy brigade commander. The brigade commander was on leave.

This lieutenant colonel took the attitude that I was applying for a job and told me he had 2 openings for a major. One battalion needed an executive officer and the other an operations officer. He then asked me which would I prefer. I told him I would prefer to be an executive officer. He acted like this was a test and I gave the wrong answer. He started grilling me about why I didn't want to be an operations officer. This made me angry. I was already in a bad mood because I was required to go to Vietnam to fill a position that didn't exist, as a special forces officer, and was instead in an airmobile division. I told the colonel that I did not say that I didn't want to be an operations officer. I was simply answering his question. I told him if he assigned me as operations officer I would be the best one they had but if given the choice I would prefer to be an executive officer because it is a senior position and I thought I would be good at it. The colonel told me he would contact me later.

I went back to division personnel and told the personnel officer I did not want to be a assigned to that brigade. The following day he told me I was going to the 3rd Brigade at Camp Evans. At some point I learned that I would go to the 3rd Battalion, 187th Infantry (Airmobile) as executive officer and that the Battalion Commander was Lieutenant Colonel Bryan Sutton. Bryan and I were together in the First Special Forces Group on Okinawa when he was a captain and I a lieutenant.

The Life Of A Soldier

Captain Bryan Sutton, 1964

When I arrived at Camp Evans in mid-afternoon I reported to the brigade commander Colonel David E. Grange. I liked him immediately and never changed my mind about that. He told me that he had just received word that his son, Lieutenant David E. Grange, Jr. had been wounded. He was assigned to one of the battalions in the 3rd Brigade. He said his son would be okay but he was probably in trouble with his mother for arranging to have him assigned there. When Colonel Grange left Vietnam he took command of the Ranger school at Fort Benning Georgia. I visited him once after I returned to Fort Benning. He was a brigadier general at that time. When I last heard from him he was a Lt. General commanding 6th Army. His son, now a retired brigadier general is one of the media terrorist experts.

I learned that Colonel Grange especially trusted officers who had served as noncommissioned officers prior to being commissioned. I assume this was because of his own background. He served with 517th parachute Infantry in Europe during WWII as a NCO and was commissioned from Officer Candidate School in 1950, then served in the Korean War. General Grange is highly decorated and member of both the Ranger School and Officer Candidate School halls of fame.

Captain Lykens from the 3/187 picked me up at brigade headquarters. When I arrived at the battalion headquarters Colonel Sutton was not there. He was out in the field with one of the rifle companies and wasn't expected to return to base for 2 or 3 days. Major Ron Scharnberg, the operations officer, was there and he called on the radio to tell the Colonel I had arrived. The secure radio set was not working, and Scharnberg tried to tell Bryan who I was without using my name because of radio security. Finally I took the handset and made reference to the green hat from an island and a boat trip after a jump. Immediately, Bryan knew who I was. We had made a parachute jump in the South China Sea off Okinawa from a helicopter and was picked up by a boat for about a 3 hour ride back to the island. That was the day that we really met,

The Life Of A Soldier

although we had seen each other before. We talked for the whole boat trip and were friends thereafter. After learning who I was, Bryan told me he had a job for me-- to increase his foxhole strength because he was in trouble with division about it. Foxhole strength was a slang term for the number or percentage of the total strength in the field, or fighting strength.

    I instructed the adjutant, that we would have a meeting after supper and I wanted the senior person from each company that was at the base, with a list of all personnel and their current location and status. I also instructed Major Scharnberg, the operations officer, to alert Brigade that we would need helicopters the next morning to deliver troops to the companies. It was an interesting meeting and we sent a bunch of them back to the companies the following day. I don't remember how many.

    I really made an impression and it was described as a "purge" by some. One lieutenant company executive officer reported himself to me later on that day. One of his men tried to refuse to board the chopper. The lieutenant put a pistol to his head and told him he was going to pull the trigger if he didn't get on the chopper. The lieutenant was really scared that he was in trouble. I told him to write it down as a statement and we would just wait to see if the man complained. We never heard any more about the incident. I believe this was Lieutenant Sloane, but I am not sure. The last time I heard from Lieutenant Sloane, he was a colonel in the army reserve. The foxhole strength was increased considerably that day and the battalion commander was very happy about it, but in a few days it would be back like it was before the "purge." I was to learn that the company commanders didn't really want most of those men I sent them, in the field. The drug problem was serious and the drug of choice was heroin which was dirt cheap. This was my first experience dealing with drugs. When I was a platoon leader, XO, and company commander in the 1st Infantry Division as a lieutenant, the drug problem had not yet begun. In special forces we didn't keep anyone with any kind of discipline problems. As an advisor in 1967-68 in Vietnam I had only a small team of Americans and there were no drugs. Before this tour was over however, I would have my life threatened and the lives of my wife and daughter threatened, for trying to interdict the drug trafficking.

  On 20 January, the battalion came back to the base for rest and refitting. On 21 January I went to division headquarters at Camp Eagle with Colonel Sutton and Lt. Enochian, our S-4 (supply officer), to a meeting with Brigadier General Smith, the assistant division commander for support. It was interesting to say the least. The division G-4 was there, along with the commander of the division support command. The drill was for us to tell them about our support needs and problems and they would solve them.

  When we started telling the general about shortages of equipment that we had requisitioned and re-requisitioned and hadn't received, the staff assured the General that they would take care of this immediately. When we took a coffee break, I told Lt. Enochian to call his warrant officer and have him send trucks with new requisitions for the things we needed. Before the day was over, the trucks arrived and returned practically empty. They still didn't

The Life Of A Soldier

have the things they told the general they would issue to us immediately. The critical item was wet weather suits. We were in the monsoon and needed rain suits. General Smith was an old timer, a veteran of WWII and Korea. He kept talking about getting ice cream out to the troops, but it was more important to get the rain suits to keep them dry and warm.

    The officers had a "Dining In" the evening of 21 January. We wore fatigues instead of the Mess uniforms that are traditionally worn for this event. Colonel Grange, the brigade commander, was the guest of honor. Michael Hasselberg's S-1 section enlisted men volunteered to serve, which probably means Michael volunteered them. He somehow managed to get some white waiters jackets for them to wear. The "dining-In" is a 187th Airborne regimental tradition that was also a tradition for the 1st Special forces group.

    Sometime in late January the Battalion was alerted that we would participate in an operation called Lam Son 719 which was an invasion into Laos by the ARVN. A young author, Keith William Nolan, published a book in 1986 titled "Into Laos" about this operation and all of the units involved. Nolan interviewed me by telephone for several hours. My memory of events were much clearer in 1986 than now, so I'll rely a great deal on what he quoted from me in the book.

    The operation was to begin on 8 February 1971, with several ARVN divisions and smaller formations, going into Laos. The 3/187 was under the operational control of the 5th Mechanized Brigade, commanded by

Euell White

Brigadier General John Hill. On a previous tour in Vietnam Bryan Sutton , on a special forces assignment, had worked with then Colonel Hill. The general who had a general dislike for special forces, was so impressed with Bryan thatbhe specifically requested the 3/187 for this operation. No American ground units were to go into Laos, The primary mission of the task force we were part of was to secure Route 9 that went from Quang-Tri to Khe Sanh. This road parallels the border with North Vietnam, and Khe Sanh is in the corner of South Vietnam, bordering both Laos and North Vietnam.

The night of 15 February we had two soldiers killed and one wounded. One of our lieutenants was critically wounded on the 16th. Our battalion had two more men wounded on 18 February. The battalion moved into a new area of operations further to the north of where they were and it really was hot. We replaced a battalion of the Americal Division that got pretty well whipped out there. We had one man killed and two wounded on the 19th.

I visited our wounded at the hospital at Quang-Tri on 20 February. One of our Vietnamese scouts who was wounded the day before was sitting next to a tent at the logistics base with a bandage on his head. No one was paying any attention to him and he wasn't complaining. I found out he hadn't been treated since the medics put the bandage on is head. I brought him back to Camp Evans with me and took him to the aid station where they took the bullet out of his head. I turned him over to our battalion surgeon.

Our operations officer, Major Ron Scharnberg was wounded on 21 February leaving me the only major in the battalion. He was wounded by mortar fire. It was really hot

The Life Of A Soldier

out there where the companies were. We had a total of 19 wounded and one killed that day. I called the hospital and learned that Ron Scharnberg wasn't critical and would probably be out of the hospital in a few days.

We had an IG (Inspector General) inspection on the 21st. I had thought that maybe those were suspended in combat zones, but we had it. I was really proud of the staff, especially Mutt and Jeff, the S-1 and S-4. The S1 was Lieutenant Michael Hasselberg. He is short. The S4 was Lt. Stephen Enochian, and he is over 6 feet tall. They were the best of buddies and always together when they were off-duty. They insulted each other all the time, but not seriously. They were filling Captain positions but I wouldn't have traded either of them for all the captains in the world. Michael was the epitome of efficiency. If you had a question about personnel he had the answer—if not in his head, then in his pocket.

Major Scharnberg was released from hospital on 23 February and returned to camp Evans. He still had open wounds. He wanted the doctor to sew him up so he could go back to the field. I had the adjutant to arrange for a 14-day leave for him starting on the 24th. He protested that he wanted to go back to the field, but I think he was glad to be going home. The troops really loved him, but they were also amused by his show of bravado.

I wouldn't let him go back to the field until his wounds were healed. I knew if I kept him at Camp Evans while he was healing he would drive me crazy. I finally told him to just shut up about it. He wanted to appeal to the CO but I told him Colonel Sutton didn't want to even talk to him until he got back from leave and his wounds were healed.

> **From my letter to Euna on 25 February**
> I am at the forward log base tonight, and the CO is here with me. My little puppy cried to come with me this morning. Night before last was the first time I had left her overnight. Lt. Hasselberg is taking care of her. He loves dogs. She wouldn't be pacified to stay in his room. Major Scharnberg had just returned from the hospital and Lady had never seen him before, but when he let her in his room she was pacified. Mike Hasselberg said she is strictly a field grade officers dog. We came out good on the IG inspection. This battalion had failed it for the past three years. The IG said we had the best supply and administration in the division. I already knew that.

We established a forward base at a place called the Rock Pile. Where the 5th Mechanized Brigade also had a base. It was a real challenge to get the log base up and functioning as it should have been. The Supply and Transportation Platoon leader was in charge and it was one mess. Everything was jumbled up and disorganized. He just didn't seem to be able to get it done. He had the mess tent set up right by the chopper pad so that every time a chopper landed the dirt was blown into it. We had our companies

The Life Of A Soldier

coming into the base one at a time for a couple of days of rest and resupply.

I went out there for two days and straightened it out. I had a bulldozer clear off an area then I supervised moving the tents and setting up everything. I was supervising details like a sergeant. I got up at 0430 on the second day and woke up the cooks. We had breakfast before first light and began work at first light. They had been sleeping til about 0800. When Colonel Sutton came back there and saw the difference he couldn't believe it. He asked me how did I get it done and I told him it apparently takes a field grade officer to supervise a work detail in this modern army. Lt. Enochian would have done it but he was preoccupied with the IG inspection at Camp Evans.

Euell White

One day while we were co-located with the 5th Mech Log base, and we were bringing our companies to the base, one at a time for a 24-hour stand-down, I went to their logistics officer and asked about getting some ice for the troops while they were in so they could have cold drinks. This major's office was in the equivalent of a large air conditioned camper trailer. He invited me in and offered me a cold drink, a choice of ice-cold beer or soda. Then while we were drinking our cold drinks—a beer for him and a soda for me—I asked about the ice and he proceeded to give me a lecture about how the troops need to be tough and learn to do without the niceties. He reminded me that we were in a war. I responded that maybe we should set them an example for doing without the niceties. He turned red in the face and I left, but the next day we had ice for the troops.

On 3 March I received notice that the battalion was moving and our forward base would be displaced to Khe San. I really dreaded it. It was difficult enough to support from the Rock Pile, but when the distance doubles the problems also double.

On 5 March I received a call from Bryan Sutton to come to the the base at the Rock Pile as soon as possible. The battalion base was moving to Khe Sanh. I really enjoyed going out to the field. I got tired of dealing with the troublemakers at Camp Evans and it was a pleasant diversion to go out there where the good soldiers were. The problem was that the troubles waited for my return to Camp Evans.

Bryan was scheduled to take his 14-day leave starting on 7 April. He had delayed it because of the operation. I told him that if he would prefer to have Major

The Life Of A Soldier

Scharnberg, the operations officer in command, while he was gone, even though I was senior, I wouldn't be offended. He said emphatically that he would prefer to have me in command. The reason I thought maybe he would prefer Ron was that they had been working together for 5 months I knew he esteemed Ron very highly as operations officer.

Euell White

> **From my letter to Euna on 10 March**
>
> It does seem that God is protecting me. I have driven over roads and nothing happens, then someone else gets ambushed or hit by a sniper's bullet. I do, however, exercise as much caution as possible. I have lost a little weight recently since I started spending so much time at the forward area and the mess hall started serving light bread rather than biscuits. My stomach is almost flat now. I am busy today answering congressional inquiries. We average one each week. Most of them from Ted Kennedy

On 11 march I had to repeat the "purge" that I did the day I joined the battalion in January. The battalion commander kept getting flak from division about having too many in the base camp, but at the same time they put requirements on us that made it necessary to have people at the base. I made all of the companies justify by name each man they had at the base.

The Life Of A Soldier

> **From my letter to Euna on 12 March**
> I am writing by candlelight in my bunker at Khe Sanh. I left Camp Evans by helicopter at 0700 this morning. I really sleep better up here because I feel safer. Back at Evans we live in buildings while up here we sleep underground. Everyone is aware of the enemy here and at Evans I am afraid they forget sometimes that the enemy is capable of attacking. Three 122mm rockets landed at Evans last night just before my bedtime. They hit near the brigade headquarters. I guess I'll stay here until Sunday and go back to Evans for a couple of days. The job of the battalion executive officer, besides being the second in command, is to coordinate the efforts of the staff. It is equivalent to the chief of staff at higher levels. This means I have responsibilities at both the forward base and the rear. When I stay at Khe Sanh too long, some trouble crops up there that I have to answer to the Brigade Commander for. If I stay here too long there is something wrong out there with the staff that needs my attention.

On 15 March Major Scharnberg returned from his leave. He told me that the news media back there were making it sound like the ARVN was incompetent or cowards, and that they were really taking a beating. The media reported the defeats but not the victories. Any army in war suffers defeats as well as winning victories. Such one-sided reporting can make any army look bad.

> **From my letter to Euna on 18 March**
> I didn't write last night. I just didn't have time and couldn't settle down to it. I am not supposed to write about it just yet but Colonel Bryan Sutton and Major Ron Scharnberg were killed yesterday afternoon when their helicopter crashed into the side of a mountain.

Nobody knew exactly what happened since the Warrant officer pilot was killed also, but they did determine that there was no indication of enemy fire. I received a call on the radio at about 1615 in the afternoon, right after it happened, from the assistant operations officer requesting me to come to Khe Sanh and informing me that they had crashed and were presumed dead. I grabbed a chopper went out there right away, but the new battalion commander was already there.

A replacement for Major Scharnberg arrived later that night, but I was not too pleased with him. Lieutenant Colonel Steverson, the new battalion CO was in the same battle group with me at Fort Campbell in 1958-60. He was a lieutenant then and I a Sergeant First Class. He was the

The Life Of A Soldier

Operations officer for the The 5th Mech and knew all about the operation, and the ideal choice for the assignment.

The major who was sent to replace Ron Scharnberg, nicknamed "Chief" had been kicked out of another division and had been hanging around brigade headquarters for some time. He came into the command bunker while we were all sitting there silently, not more than 3 hours after our battalion commander and operations officer were killed, loud and boisterous, saying how glad he was to get this assignment. It was tantamount to saying he was glad Ron Scharnberg was killed. Then he turned to me and said, "Well, White, so you are the XO. Let me tell you what I expect of the XO." I couldn't believe this guy. I very quickly told him it was Major White and that he had been assigned as operations officer, not battalion commander, and that it was not what he expected of me but what I expected of him.

I have had people close to me die before in this war, but his was more upsetting to me than any of them. I had a premonition of this. The night before they were killed I had a sleepless night. I had this uneasiness concerning Bryan Sutton and couldn't sleep. I wrote him a note that morning and put it with some papers I was sending out by courier for him to sign. In the note I told him about the uneasiness and I mentioned the problems we were having with division about our field strength. The courier pouch was delivered to him, he signed the papers and on the note that I had written him he wrote a note back to me and it was a note of encouragement assuring me that he was well pleased with the job I was doing as his XO. He apparently interpreted what I wrote as an indication I was feeling discouraged.

When I received the call from the helicopter pad where my AM radio was set up that Captain Grace, the assistant operations officer, wanted to talk to me on the radio, I knew then that something was wrong. But it was not because of the call. This was a daily occurrence to get calls from him. I looked out the window and saw that my jeep was gone, so I ran all the way to the chopper pad. When I got there Captain Grace told me on the radio that the chopper had crashed and that all 3 men were presumed dead. On my way to the chopper pad I knew that was what I was going to hear.

Our chaplain, Captain Tony Longval, escorted Colonel Sutton home and our intelligence officer, Captain Peale who was due to go home in a few days anyway, escorted Major Scharnberg.

In 2008, Bryan Sutton's youngest daughter contacted me. She was only two when Bryan died. She wanted to know about her Dad from those who worked with him. I communicated with her via email and told her all I knew about him, then put her in contact with some of the other officers of the battalion. Through her I established contact with Bryan's wife and have exchanged letters with her.

I was really pleased with Colonel Steverson as battalion commander. As I wrote earlier, we were in the same battle group at Fort Campbell when he was a First lieutenant and I was a Sergeant First Class. We went before the board for the Senior Parachutist Badge at the same time. He didn't pass the parachute inspection part of it and I did. I never reminded him of that. I know he made it later

The Life Of A Soldier

because both of us were wearing the Master Badge. He was really good on tactics and aggressive like Colonel Sutton. He was also the same size as Colonel Sutton, small. I gave him Bryan's field uniforms.

On 23 March he NVA attacked Khe Sanh . I anticipated an attack because they registered artillery from three different locations as well as their mortars the morning before, which is usually a pretty good indication of a planned attack. It was only a sapper company, however, that attacked. Eighteen of them were killed and one captured. Then on the 24th the COBRA gunships found more of them in a woods and worked them over.

I had problems with our Battalion Surgeon. He was a draftee and had no interest in helping the war effort. In his heart he was a war protestor. He was constantly issuing light duty prescriptions saying that a soldier couldn't go back to his company in the field because of some problem, real or made up. I instructed him over and over that he did not have the authority to determine where a soldier would perform his duty. I told him that he could prescribe duty limitations, but it is the company commander's prerogative as to where the soldier performs his duties. He continually ignored this and caused a lot of confusion. His real purpose I believed was to keep as many soldiers as he could out of combat.

I contacted the Division Surgeon and talked with him about it. He sent his deputy to the battalion to talk to the battalion surgeon about it. He spent a day with him. Before he left the assistant division surgeon told me that the doctor understood that his duty was to help keep the foxhole strength up rather than find ways to decrease it. His behavior changed for a few days, then we were back where we started.

One evening, I told the doctor to get packed to go to Khe Sanh the next morning. He tried to talk me out of it but I insisted he was needed there. The next morning we drove to Khe Sanh. He rode in the ambulance and I rode in my jeep. Along route 9 we saw burning vehicles that had been ambushed just a little earlier that morning, but no one shot at us. This really frightened the doctor. I kept him up there for a few days. He was there the night of the sapper attack. The sappers blew up a COBRA and the rockets from it and others flew wild. It was an impressive fireworks display and it really frightened the doctor.

The next day he told me he needed to go back to Camp Evans, but I said, no. Later on that day he came and told me he thought he had Dengue Fever. I felt of his forehead and he was really hot. I told him I didn't believe him and suspected he had somehow induced the fever, but I let him go. Then when I went back to camp Evans the following day he was completely free of the fever, confirming my suspicions. I told him that if he caused any more trouble, I would take him to Khe Sanh and make him stay there for the duration of the operation.

The Life Of A Soldier

> **From my Letter to Euna on 25 March**
> I will stay at Khe Sanh through tomorrow night. The battalion commander is going to camp Evans to spend the night and he is afraid to leave the Chief (operations officer) in control of the battalion even for one night. He is very headstrong and when left alone, makes decisions that he doesn't have the authority to make. I don't think he is going to last long here. He wants to run the battalion and Colonel Steverson won't stand for it. It has been a real strain for me trying to keep things running smooth, which is my job. This major came in with an attitude that he was here to straighten out the battalion. I have had to remind him several times that I am his boss. He has not only tried to question my authority, but the battalion commander's as well. You can't believe what the news media says. They report only one side of the news. They want it to appear to have been a mistake to go into Laos and they will make it come out that way.

The NVA woke us up on 30 March with their artillery. There was no damage nor casualties although all the rounds landed in my battalion area. Our companies out near the border saw the flashes and called in the azimuths to the guns. I worked out an intersection and the guns plotted just inside Laos.

On 3 April, Chaplain Longval returned from escorting Colonel Sutton home. He said the funeral was at Arlington National Cemetery with full military honors. I never received any report on Ron Scharnberg's funeral.

On 8 April we had a memorial ceremony for the 19 men we lost during Lam Son 719, including Colonel Sutton and Major Scharnberg. I was the commander of troops for the ceremony. It was a beautiful ceremony. Major Genral Tarpley, the Division Commander, and Major General Berry, the Assistant Division Commander for Operations, attended. General Berry complimented me on the ceremony.

We had our dining-in that evening and General Berry was our guest of honor. According to tradition it was my duty (and honor) to sit with the guest of honor. General Berry and I got along very well. Euna and I met him at the allied officers reception at Fort Benning, but I got to know him through his former aide, Captain Grace, who was one of our staff officers.

Lieutenant Michael Hasselberg left about the end of May and I really missed him. He was so efficient and I could really tell the difference after he left. I was not at all surprised to learn that Michael became the head of a big law firm in Peoria, Illinois.

On 7 June I was awakened by rocket firing. It was the first time since April they hit Camp Evans with anything. As usual, they were aiming for the brigade headquarters and the helicopters. There were 8 men

The Life Of A Soldier

wounded near the brigade headquarters. We sent one of our units out to the suspected location of the rocket site. It was out of our normal area of operations. The 122mm rockets have a pretty long range. The search was, however, unfruitful.

On 8 June the battalion was alerted to be ready to move to Fire Support Base Fuller up near the demilitarized zone. It was under attack and was being manned by a Vietnamese marine battalion. We had to be ready to move one company in one hour and the remainder in four hours. If it had happened, I was to remain at Evans and take command of three Vietnamese Regional Force companies and one Popular Force company that were then under our operational control, but the fire base was overrun the next morning. The last I heard, the NVA had taken over their artillery and was using it against them. The 1st ARVN Division launched a counterattack to retake the firebase.

On 26 June we moved the battalion (minus) to a firebase. It was a very busy and trying day for me, trying to get the firebase organized and at the same time keeping up with everything at Camp Evans.

On 9 July we moved to another firebase and that day I assumed command of the battalion while Colonel Steverson was on leave. By this time we had our new brigade commander. I cannot remember his name, but he was a good man and never made it home. After I left Vietnam he was promoted to Brigadier General and received a new assignment. He was killed by a direct hit by a mortar shell.

Colonel Steverson had finally gotten rid of the

Chief and our operations officer was Major Pierce. He was senior to me but Colonel Steverson wanted me to remain as XO. Major Pierce was the opposite of the Chief. He worked hard and cooperated with everyone else. I was certainly glad that I didn't have the chief to contend with while acting as battalion commander.

The only thing that was memorable during my brief tenure as battalion commander was a visit from the brigade commander. We had planned an operation that was very near the Ap Bia Mountain, that became known as "Hamburger Hill" where the 3rd Brigade of the 101st and some ARVN units battled the NVA in May 1969 resulting in 56 Americans killed and 420 wounded. A movie was made about the battle.

We had to submit all of our plans that involved the use of helicopters to Brigade for approval. After we submitted the plan to Brigade, the brigade operations officer called and said, the plan was disapproved and the Colonel would be out to explain why. The Colonel came to my CP, went straight to the operations map, took a grease pencil and drew a circle that included that area and marked "Off Limits" in the circle. He angrily told me that we should never even think about going to that vicinity ever, because the media identified it as "Hamburger Hill."

Although I could understand the Colonel's point, in reality the fear of that location was irrational. The heavy losses two years earlier happened because the NVA occupied the hill in force and we tried to take it. I wasn't planning to assault that hill but to act on intelligence concerning enemy troops located at a waterfall nearby.

I was reminded of the superstitions of the ARVNs on my previous tour as an advisor, that a certain area was bad luck. Looking back, I realize that the war was over and we just hadn't admitted it. The fear of taking casualties was dictating our actions and the enemy didn't have to be too smart to figure that out.

While the Battalion Commander was on leave, We received orders to move the battalion minus to Cam Ranh Bay to secure the rocket belt. The mission, obviously, was to keep the enemy from getting his rocket launchers to a point where Cam Ranh Bay would be within rocket range. The move didn't take place until after the Battalion Commander returned from leave, but I had to go, along with the Brigade Commander, to make a reconnaissance and coordinate with the local command. We flew down there in one of those 2-engine propeller driven planes that they used to transport VIPs.

I had my R & R to Australia planned for when the Colonel returned from leave. Euna and Sherry were already on their way to meet me there, so I had to send them a message through my brother John, who lives in Australia, that I would be late. I had to move the battalion before I went to Australia. It turned out well though. They enjoyed the visit with John and his family while waiting for me.

Euell White

> **From my letter to Euna on 19 August**
> I haven't had a letter from you since I returned from Australia, but it has only been seven days. It seems like a month or more. It will be so good to come home never to leave again. Things are getting tense around here. It seems the Vietnamese people are getting tired of us or at least the VC propaganda is working. They are having demonstrations in Hue, throwing firebombs at our vehicles, etc. We can't use the road at all now except for mission essential trips. Nobody from this battalion can get out the Camp Evans gate unless I sign their dispatch saying it is mission essential. I won't sign any. I knew this would come eventually. I wish I didn't have to be here to see it.

The battalion was at Cam Ranh until early October. I divided my time between Camp Evans and Cam Ranh. It was more complicated than going back and forth to Khe Sanh. Because of the distance, I had to hitch-hike on Air Force Planes and it usually took 2 days each way with an overnight somewhere between the two locations. When I was at Evans we communicated by AM radio, but there was usually only a few minutes of opportunity each day.

The Life Of A Soldier

When I would arrive at Cam Ranh, the CO would unload on me about the failings of the staff there and I would rattle some cages. Then when I returned to Camp Evans there would be a message from either the Brigade Commander or his deputy about something that had happened while I was gone. The only nice thing was the overnights between the two places. I usually was able to get a good night's sleep and nobody knew where I was to call me.

Cam Ranh was not good for the battalion. It was a resort area and there was too much opportunity for drugs. Adjacent to the battalion area was a drug rehab center whose mission it was to get the soldiers that were going home off drugs before they left. I don't know how successful they were. According to the statistics, our battalion was better off than any other battalion in the division before the battalion went to Cam Ranh Bay. Afterward we had as many dopers, if not more, than anyone else. The dope was so easy to get down there.

Colonel Steverson was out of his element at Cam Ranh. There was no enemy there to fight with. As far as I know most of the enemy fire the battalion received there was rocks thrown at them by Rangutangs during the night. The most serious casualties resulted from one of our own gunships firing on one of our squads. The young squad leader thought he saw a light and the battalion commander called for a fire team (two gunships). The squad illuminated their own position and one of the gunship pilots mistook it for the light which was their target. These pilots, I learned, had never really been in combat.

Euell White

I went to the aviation unit which was on an island, the following morning to begin a preliminary investigation, but the unit commander would not let me see the pilots. He used the excuse that they were sleeping. I left for camp Evans that day and never learned the result of the Friendly Fire investigation.

The drug problem was ever facing me. When I joined the battalion I knew about as much concerning the army's drug problem as any civilian at home who watched TV news and read the newspapers. I had not had any experience dealing with it, but I very soon became educated. The drug of choice then was heroin. Smoking was the primary way that the drug was used. They would put it in their cigarettes and they could smoke it in your presence and you wouldn't know it. It was frustrating, to put it mildly, to see a young man arrive who was clean and clean-cut and a few weeks later see that same young man , sloppy in appearance and looking like he was in a trance. I would ask them how it happened and most of them would tell me the truth. Usually, they were convinced by someone else to just try it one time. In my year with the battalion I never found one man who tried the heroin one time without becoming addicted. Often they would tell me that they were threatened by the other men around them that wanted them to use it so he couldn't rat on them.

Soon after I took over as XO of the battalion, which included for all practical purposes, being in command of the elements at the base camp, I established a policy that no new replacements would be sent out to the companies before I personally interviewed them. It was doubly frustrating when I talked to a young man and he assured me that he would never do the drugs because he wouldn't want

The Life Of A Soldier

to bring shame to his parents, or because he had a wife or wife and children, then a few weeks later see this same young man with all of the signs of addiction.

I love the army and I am proud of being a part of it, but one of the weaknesses in the army was the reluctance to acknowledge when they had a problem. The drug problem had the army stumped for awhile. Although I didn't know the answer, I knew that denial was not the answer.

In May or June of 1971, we received word that a government agency, I believe it was the GAO, was going to conduct a study concerning the drug problem in Vietnam. The instructions we received required us to have certain data available when the evaluation teams arrived. They would select at random, so many units to evaluate. To me this posed no problem and I had my staff begin to assimilate the needed information just in case they chose our unit. Then I received a call from the deputy brigade commander, whom I will write about in detail later on. He wanted me to provide a place for him to hold a meeting of all of the battalion XOs in the brigade concerning the drug abuse evaluation by the federal agency.

The Colonel started the meeting by saying that we didn't have as much of a drug problem as Washington seemed to think and that the main thing was not to tell the evaluators anything. Had I not already known this man was an idiot, I would have been shocked by his statement. I immediately challenged this. I told him that the other battalions may not have had a drug problem but my battalion did. I told him I could take him for a walk through the battalion area and point them out to him. I further told him that we had no right to withhold information from a federal agency that had been designated by the Congress to obtain information from us.

The other battalion XOs just sat there like dummies and didn't say anything. The Lieutenant Colonel turned red and talked for awhile about some trivial administrative matters, then the meeting broke up. At this time Colonel Grange had already gone back to the States. The next thing I knew, the battalion commander told me he would take care of our preparation for the drug abuse evaluation. He took all of it out of my hands. I didn't ask why. As it turned out our battalion wasn't chosen for the evaluation.

The First Sergeant of Company A, First Sergeant Peale, was my most dependable ally in the fight against drugs. It was a war we couldn't win, but we did win a few battles. Neither of us could devote our full time to the task. Instead, we periodically closed off the area and searched everyone coming and going. We never failed to catch some pushers when we did that. As I mentioned earlier, we could only prosecute them for possession. Because of our efforts, we were the targets for planned assassination. We would learn through what was called the "grapevine" that a hand grenade was stashed at a certain location that was intended to be used to kill either First Sergeant Peale or myself and we would find the grenade. I slept many nights with my pistol in my hand.

I learned that our military telephone system was used by the drug pushers. Periodically we would receive an update on the code words they used. If you weren't up on this your own clerk could transact business concerning drug pushing on the phone in your presence in your office without you knowing it was being done. The system was a bit too sophisticated to be set up by some uneducated dope head. I have no idea how high up the corruption was, but I did learn for certain that the Division Criminal Investigators were involved in the drug trafficking.

In April there was a shooting incident in the battalion area. I saw a man with a bandage on his head and when I asked him what happened, he gave me a story that didn't make sense. When I started checking into it I discovered that he had actually been shot with a pistol. After I had interrogated several witnesses with the assistant adjutant recording what they said, I stopped and called the CID (Criminal Investigators) at Brigade Headquarters.

Two agents arrived and I brought them up to date on what I had so far. The CID agents took the statements we had and started interviewing the witnesses. I was impressed that they very quickly learned that the weapon used was a 38 caliber revolver and found the weapon . I had assumed it was an issue 45 caliber because the sergeant that did the shooting would have been armed with that weapon. He was the Sergeant of the Guard for our part of the bunker line. I was observing the CID and hearing everything that was said. They were sailing along until one of the witnesses mentioned that the shooting was related to the drug trafficking. Then they immediately, dismissed all the witnesses and left. I asked for the statements that we had taken and they told me they would type them up and provide me a copy.

A few days later I went by their office and asked about the statements. They laughed and said. "What statements."

Then I asked about the pistol and they responded the same way and said there was no shooting. A few days later we caught three men distributing drugs on the bunker line. Acting on information from an informant, we actually saw a ¾-ton truck drive down the bunker line and toss the drugs out. We caught the three men who picked them up. We brought them to battalion headquarters and I had them under guard on the porch of the building where the offices of the battalion commander, Sergeant Major and myself were.

We called the CID and when they arrived, they started yelling real loud that the search we did was probably illegal, and saying other things to communicate to the suspects that they should not say anything. Then they came into my office and started arguing with me that I had no case against the men without knowing any of the details. What they didn't know was that Colonel Steverson had heard the commotion and was standing right behind them. He became so angry I was afraid he was going to have stroke. He ordered the two CID agents in no uncertain terms, using strong language , to get out of his battalion area and never return. Colonel Steverson then called the Brigade Commander, Colonel Grange and told him about it.

The following morning Colonel Steverson and I were summoned to Colonel Grange's office. When we arrived, The Division Provost Marshall, a Military Police Lieutenant Colonel, and the Chief Warrant officer who was in charge of the division CID were there. Colonel Grange asked me to tell what the problem was. I told him about the incident the night before and also about the previous

The Life Of A Soldier

incident where the two CID agents had killed the shooting investigation, then concluded by saying that these men were part of the drug distribution system.

The Provost Marshall strongly objected and started to verbally attack me. I was very near taking a swing at him when Colonel Grange said, "Cool it Euell." Then he told the Provost Marshall, "I want those two birds off my post and I don't want them to ever enter the gates again. Do you understand me?" The provost Marshall said, "Yes Sir." Then Colonel Grange asked who he had that could take up the investigations and try to salvage them. The Provost Marshall said the Warrant Officer could do it. To this day I am not certain whether the Provost Marshall was just being loyal to his men or was himself involved. I do know that both of the investigations died.

One of the solutions to the drug problem that was attempted was an amnesty program that allowed a person to come forward and ask for help with the assurance that he wouldn't be punished. Each battalion had to appoint a person to be a counselor, whom the drug user could come to and would arrange to get him off drugs. This man was not required to give any information to the commanders concerning the identities of the persons that came to him.

I located in our battalion a Specialist 4 that had a degree in sociology. He was ideal for the job, and had a compassion for the drug addicts. He was Black and that was a plus, because more than half of the drug users were Black and they were more likely to trust a Black man. The Specialist would report to me periodically on the progress of the program and provide statistical data without revealing any names. After he had been at this for a couple of months he came to me very frustrated and discouraged. He told me that when a man came for rehabilitation he would take him to the dispensary where he could be treated during withdrawal. But, he said, that if he didn't stay with the man constantly, some of the medics would give him heroin while in the dispensary.

Like any other profession, the military has its share of incompetents who somehow seem to slip through the cracks and hinder, rather then help. The battalion operations officer that was assigned to us when Major Ron Scharnberg was killed fit this category. I won't mention his name, but he nicknamed himself "Chief" and wanted to be called that. For more about this character see Appendix B; Unforgettable Characters (The Chief, Page 296).

I went home on leave in May and had a real good time. When I returned to the battalion, Colonel Steverson told me that he had been fighting division to keep me nearly the whole time I was gone. There was a requirement for an infantry major with a "3" prefix to his military occupational specialty for a classified mission in another country and the people at division thought I was the only major in the division with that qualification. The "3" prefix means that you are a parachutist and special forces qualified.

Colonel Steverson told me that if it hadn't been for another major who was qualified hearing about the requirement and identifying himself, I would have been drafted for it and he wouldn't have been able to stop it. I was not disappointed. I think it was probably Laos, but they never gave that information.

The Life Of A Soldier

I wrote earlier about the Brigade Deputy Commander and the effort to cover-up the drug problem. I will call him Colonel Dufus. That isn't his real name, but a good description of him. He was a pain in the neck and more of a hindrance than a help. For more about this man see Appendix B: Unforgettable Characters (Lieutenant Colonel Dufus, Page 299).

One of the extra duties that I had was the conduct of Article 32 hearings. See Appendix C: Unusual and Interesting Duties . (Article 32 Hearings, Page 315)

Our primary civil affairs projects in the Quang-Tri and Hue areas were two orphanages, one in each of these cities. There was one Vietnamese Missionary Alliance Pastor who oversaw both of these orphanages. There was also an American missionary family who lived in Hue that worked with him. The couple had a little girl about 4 years old. I visited their home in Hue and had them as lunch guests at the mess hall.

The missionary told me that he went about the countryside preaching the gospel but he was careful to not mention the Viet Cong because he knew they had spies in his services. We gave the orphans food, clothing and other items. My Civil Affairs Officer was Captain Thomas for awhile, then Lieutenant Mitchell Zais. Mitchell was a military Academy graduate and his Dad had been Commanding General of the 101st. I last saw Mitchell in Columbus, Georgia after I had retired and was attending Columbus College. He was stationed at Benning and we had him over for dinner. Mitchell retired as a Brigadier

General and is now president of a small college in South Carolina.

The orphans at Quang-Tri. The American soldier without a hat was my Jeep Driver

The Life Of A Soldier

The Pastor and Me

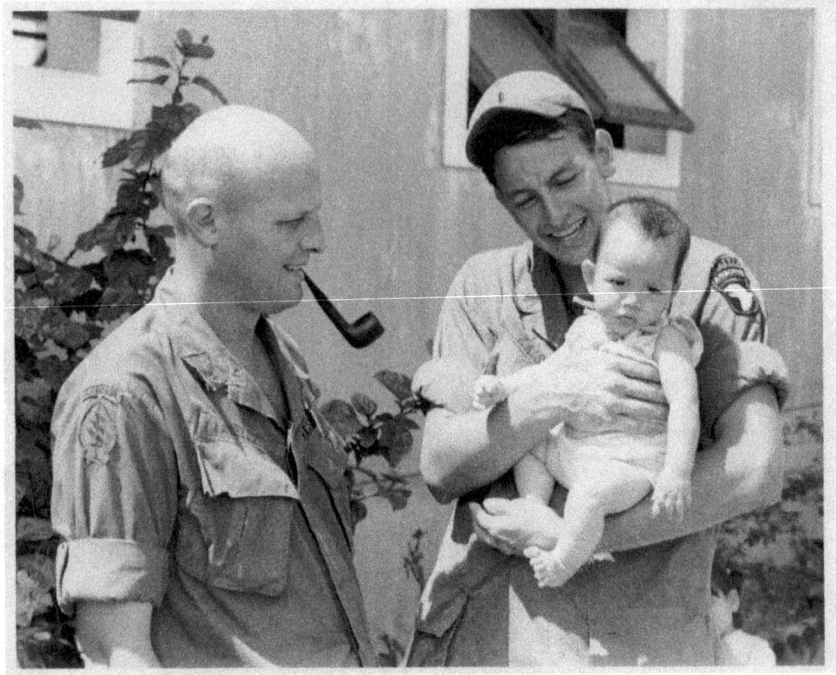
Lieutenant Mitchell Zais holding the baby

Sometime in late summer we were given an alert that the division would be standing down and when that time came the 3/187 would be the first battalion to stand down. We were given the requirement to prepare contingency plans for three scenarios. One was for the battalion to stand down and move to its stateside home which was Fort Campbell, Kentucky with all its troops and equipment. Scenario two was for the battalion to turn in its equipment an go to Fort Campbell as a unit. The third was for only the colors to be taken to Fort Campbell. Those who had more than 90 days left on their one-year tour would be reassigned to another unit in the division, and those with

The Life Of A Soldier

less than 90 days would be sent back to the states for reassignment, individually.

My money was on option three and the battalion commander's was on option one. As it happened, I was right. While I had the staff working on all three options, the battalion commander focused entirely on option one. It became almost an obsession with him. He would talk about us marching the battalion off the planes in their khaki uniforms with all of their medals on, with the band playing. After he rehearsed this fantasy to me several times, I finally told him that I not only didn't believe the battalion would return to Fort Campbell as a unit, but even if it did I wouldn't be with them. My wife and daughter were living in Columbus, Georgia in the house that we owned, and my retirement date was 31 May, 1972, which meant I would have only a few months left. I had requested Fort Benning as my final assignment and before General Berry left the Division to be chief of the Infantry branch at Department of the Army personnel, he assured me I would get the assignment.

For some reason that I cannot explain, I sensed when the stand down was near without any reason or evidence—not even a rumor. I knew that if I was there when the stand down came I could get caught up in it and have to stay past my rotation date which was January. I wanted very much to be home for Christmas, so I talked to my buddy at division personnel about how I could get out early. He said I could apply for an early release if I had a replacement. Then he told me about a Major Francis who was with the 5th Mechanized Brigade which had stood down already. Major Francis was still supposedly involved in the turn-in of their equipment, but the personnel officer told me that he really only had one jeep to turn in and he was using it for his own transportation. He was goofing off, to put it simply.

I found Major Francis and talked him into turning in the jeep and volunteering to be my replacement. The battalion commander didn't know I was doing this. I arranged for a helicopter to pick up Major Francis and bring him right to the door of my quarters. The day that Francis arrived I gave him my bed and I slept on a folding cot that night. I told the battalion adjutant to request orders assigning me to brigade headquarters company and introduced Francis to the battalion commander.

The next day I moved to Brigade, but before I unloaded my gear from the jeep the brigade adjutant started talking about needing someone to do an article 32 investigation. He told me that he knew I was trying to get out early but he was going to make sure I didn't. He was a non-combat major and we hadn't been close friends.

I got back in the jeep and went to the division Replacement Training Center and found me a place to stay there. I was really hiding out. The very next day the order came for the battalion to stand down. I contacted my buddy at division personnel and he said all I needed to do to get out was to have the permission of the brigade commander. I asked did it have to be in writing and he said no. I arranged for a helicopter to take me to division and while it was on the pad, cranked up and ready to go, I went into the brigade commander's office and told him I came to say goodbye. We exchanged the "It was good to have served with you" and I left.

The Life Of A Soldier

I was at division for less than an hour, getting my orders and my records, then flew to Danang. I stayed overnight in Danang and flew to Seattle Washington. I arrived there on Thanksgiving Day and sent the brigade adjutant a Thanksgiving card. I then went home on leave before proceeding to Fort Benning where I was assigned to the 197th Brigade until my retirement.

I learned later that I had predicted the correct scenario and that Colonel Steverson and the Battalion Sergeant Major escorted the Colors to Fort Campbell.

Primary Staff, 3/187th Rakkasans

Euell White

The Life Of A Soldier

11
Final Assignment, Retirement and Afterward

It was a beautiful Sunny afternoon in May 1972 when the official retirement ceremony was held at Fort Benning, Georgia, the home of the United States Army Infantry School. I wish I could report that this was a joyful time for me, but it was, in reality, a depressing time. I felt more like the rat abandoning a sinking ship than a soldier being honored for 21 years of loyal service to his country.

The Army was in terrible shape at that time. I won't go into detail except to say that the spirit of that period in history—the drugs, the anti-war, anti-military sentiment–had taken its toll on the Army.

I was pleased when I started to see, a few years later, signs that the army had recovered. I appreciate those officers, many of them that I served with, who brought the army back from the pits. Several of the officers that I knew became generals by the time the Gulf War came along. General Gary Luck commanded the 18th Airborne Corps during the Gulf War and later had assignments as Commanding General of The Special Operations, and as Commander of 8th Army in Korea. We were in the same tank company in Hawaii, he a lieutenant and I a sergeant first class about to be appointed as a lieutenant. Later we were in the Special Forces together.

General Henry (Hugh) Shelton was my classmate in the Infantry Officers Advance Course at Fort Benning in 1970 while he was a captain and I was a major. Shelton also served in Project Delta in Vietnam as a lieutenant, an assignment I had as a Captain in 1965. Before his retirement a few years ago Shelton was Chairman of the Joint Chiefs of Staff. There are several more that I knew but can't recall at the moment.

When I reported in to the 197th Infantry Brigade in January 1972, the Brigade Executive Officer, Lieutenant Colonel Robert Orkand, recognized me. I had written an article for publication in Infantry Magazine while in Infantry Officer Advance Course in 1970. Colonel Orkand was Editor of the magazine at the time. He nabbed me to be Executive Officer of one of the brigade's battalions although I had only four months to retirement..

Even after dealing with drug addicts in Vietnam this assignment was a shock to me. The Battalion Commander had a doctorate in statistics, but knew nothing about human behavior and leadership. It seemed the words "leadership" and "leader" had been replaced with the words "management" and "manager."

I soon learned that the Battalion Intelligence Officer had an additional duty as crime control officer which had in reality, become his primary duty. Almost every night there were thefts and burglaries in the barracks as well as in the parking lots.

The mission of the battalion was to support the Infantry School, but the Brigade was also at the forefront of modeling the New Volunteer Army, called VOLAR. Units of the brigade were going hither and yon, performing musicals and dramas as a recruiting tool, to demonstrate to the public that the Army was not about fighting wars, but about having fun and living comfortably.

The troops were allowed, for the first time in my experience, to have alcoholic beverages in the barracks.

The Life Of A Soldier

They were also allowed to display pornographic pictures and the Brigade even had a Playboy club for them. When I was an 18-year-old corporal and squad leader in the 82nd Airborne Division in the 1950s, I was in trouble if an inspecting officer found a photo of a nude woman inside the footlocker of one of my soldiers. It was called pornography and it was illegal.

Back to the retirement ceremony, which was not for me exclusively but for all who were retiring at Fort Benning that month, my guests were my wife, Euna, daughter Sherry, my dad, and nephews, Chief Warrant Officer Gary White and Randy White, with their wives.

My Dad was 79 years old and because of health problems was becoming feeble. His trip from Florence, Alabama to Columbus, Georgia to visit with us for a few days and attend my retirement ceremony was the last real outing he had before having to go into a nursing home.

The retirement ceremony was a big event in his life. He was so proud of his youngest son that when he would accompany me to the Piggly Wiggly he would introduce me to strangers, saying, "This is my son, he is a major." Of course in the military community where we lived , majors were a nickel a dozen, but Dad didn't understand that. I was embarrassed but I don't think he ever sensed it. My regret is that I didn't have more patience with him.

Dad really admired those who served in the military. He missed World War I because he was married with children. He told me many times about a cavalry unit passing through, stopping at the blacksmith shop where he worked when he was young and single. He shod their horses and the Sergeant in charge was so impressed with his work that he tried to recruit him. Dad said he was excited about it at first because the sergeant said he would be promoted fast, then he learned that what the sergeant wanted him for was to shoe horses. Dad said he was tired of shoeing horses and mules and didn't see any point in leaving home to do the same thing he was already doing.

After retiring from the Army I enrolled at Columbus College in Columbus, Georgia, (now Columbus State University) where, after two years I earned the B.S. degree in Business Administration. My daughter, Sherry Lynn, graduated from Baker High School there the same weekend that I graduated from Columbus College.

During my last quarter at Columbus College I had what can best be described as a visitation from the Lord that would ultimately change the direction and priorities of my life. I had approached the Christian life as a soldier. I had determined to be the best soldier that I could be and accomplished this through the strength of my own will. I approached Christianity the same way because I had never been taught that to be strong I needed to realize my own weakness and rely on the strength of the Lord.

For several years I managed to resist temptations in the strength of my own will, but eventually found myself yielding to temptations. I came to consider myself a failure as a Christian and for a few years I withdrew from active participation in church. A few months after retirement from the army while I was attending Columbus College, David Wilkerson came to town for a weekend crusade. I attended more to please my wife than for any other purpose. On Sunday Dallas Holm, a singer with Wilkerson's crusade, preached at Evangel Temple Assembly of God in

The Life Of A Soldier

Columbus. He was a good singer and we were curious about what kind of preacher he was. We attended and my life has never been the same. God touched me in a way that I had never before experienced, and I knew that day, more than 35 years ago, that I would never again turn away from God. I finally understood that to be successful in the Christian life I had to rely on His strength and not my own I don't mean to imply that Dallas Holm was the key to the transformation. It was simply my time. I couldn't have told you that day what he preached about.

After about three years at various jobs and turning down some very attractive offers because I couldn't put my heart into the goals of the business enterprises, I admitted to myself that the calling of God for me was full time Christian ministry. My entire adult life had been in "service."

In the fall of 1977 I enrolled in Bible College and graduated in 1979 with the Master of Theology degree. I later earned a doctorate in Christian Counseling Psychology. I was in full time Christian ministry until I retired again in 2001.

When we left Vietnam and the communists took over, the South Vietnamese military and those civilians who worked for the U.S. forces, were severely persecuted. Many were killed and the others were sent to re-education camps for years. Fortunately the commander of the infantry battalion I advised, Major Hoang Kim Ninh, escaped with his family, which included his wife, 10 children, and one of his company commanders who was his son-in-law, to the

Euell White

U.S. on a boat. Many of those whom I knew did not escape however.

A few years ago someone wrote in a guest editorial of the local paper that all who have served in the U.S. armed forces, with the exception of chaplains, were losers. This person described himself and others who avoided the draft as the real heroes.

It doesn't matter to me whether I am considered a hero, but to imply that the effort to save the Vietnamese people from slavery---no matter how ineffective it turned out to be—was a waste, and that those who gave their lives in the process are losers-- is unacceptable.

The Vietnamese people are as precious to Almighty God as are Americans, and those who served in Vietnam are as honorable as the World War II veterans.

There is always to me the question of how many lives were lost, both American and Vietnamese, because of the protests here which encouraged the communists to continue with the war.

After I retired from the army and was attending college, a young student asked me one day whether I had apologized for serving in Vietnam. This really shocked me. This was a young man who was having some difficulties in his studies and had asked me to help him. In fact he was at my home when he asked the question. My answer to him was that I had nothing to apologize for. I likened it to giving emergency aid to the victim of an automobile accident. If you do all that you can and the victim dies anyway, there is nothing to apologize for.

The Life Of A Soldier

Appendices

A. Tragic Accidents...................................276

B. Unforgettable Characters..........................284

C. Unusual and interesting Assignments.............302

D. Guerilla Warfare Exercises........................317

E. Vietnam 1965......................................358

F. Significant Battles, Vietnam 1967-68............390

Euell White

Appendix "A"

Tragic Accidents

1. Air Tragedy at Fort Bragg....................277

2. Vehicle Accident at Fort Campbell..........281

The Life Of A Soldier

Air Tragedy at Fort Bragg.

On 17 November 1953, there was an accident during a parachute drop involving the battalion I was assigned to, the 2nd Battalion, 504th A.I.R. It was the big national news story for a few days.

The battalion was scheduled to make a mass tactical jump as a demonstration for the Secretary of the Army who was to visit on 19 November. On 17 November we had a dress rehearsal for the demonstration. We were flying in C-119 "Flying Boxcars" in a "V" of "V"s formation. This means that three groups of three planes, each forming a "V", formed a "V" much like a formation of geese when they are migrating. One plane lost an engine and ran through the troopers in the air from another plane. No one in my plane was hit, but the ones who were hit were from another plane in our "V".

As I was descending to earth I noticed there was a lot of noise—people yelling, etc. which was forbidden on a tactical jump. I also saw pieces of paper and slivers of nylon floating in the air. This was puzzling to me but there wasn't time to think it through. When I landed and was getting my parachute off I saw a white parachute that was fully opened without anyone in it, land a few feet from me. My thought was that someone fell out of his parachute, then I realized that that this was a reserve parachute. Our main parachutes were green camouflage and the reserves were white.

This was puzzling to me, but before I could think it through, a friend of mine, Sergeant McDowell from another

Euell White

platoon of "F" Company, came by and very excitedly said, "Hey White, I just found half of a man." I asked, "What happened" and McDowell replied that the propeller must have cut him in two. Thinking he was referring to the propeller of the plane the man jumped from, I said that it was impossible because the jump doors were behind the propellers. Then about that time I looked in the direction the planes were flying when we jumped and saw the smoke from the burning plane at the far end of the drop zone. I then immediately knew what had happened. I picked up some of the papers and found they were from survival pamphlets that were in the cockpit of the crashed plane. I later learned that the first man the plane hit went through the windshield of the plane, and these pamphlets were blown out.

Our platoon had the pre-assigned duty of gathering up the parachutes, and we took on another duty of helping the graves registration unit piece together the bodies. There were heads, limbs and torsos scattered over the drop zone and it seemed that everyone who saw one of the body parts felt the urge to cover it. When we would pick up a parachute by the apex and twist it to get it ready to roll, a head or other body part might fall out.

We were very late getting back to the post and it was nighttime before I got home. I was certain that Euna would be frantic with worry because she knew that I was on that jump and it was bound to be on the news. When I arrived home, however, I found her sound asleep. She had become ill at work and came home early. She had been in bed all day and hadn't had the radio on. She didn't know anything about the accident until I told her. While I was glad that she hadn't had to worry about me, I was also a

The Life Of A Soldier

little disappointed that I didn't get the attention that I would have had she known.

I think the number killed was 19 including the crew of the plane that crashed. Included in those killed was our regimental chaplain who was the only paratrooper killed in the plane crash. I understood that the chaplain got some of his equipment stuck and couldn't get out.

Two days later we made the jump we were rehearsing for. To help overcome the fear, we were issued the new parachutes that had been tested for a few months. We had been using the model T-7 parachutes. These parachutes were deployed by the prop blast. The static line would pull the folded parachute out of the pack and the blast from the propeller would catch it and carry it out until the trooper swung under it. This resulted in a considerable jolt which we called the opening shock. If you weren't in good shape and/or didn't have your chin down tight against your chest, you would get a crick in your neck or worse. This parachute was 28 feet in diameter.

Another tragedy occurred on the November 18, I believe. A C-119 on its way to Fort Lee Virginia to bring the T-10 parachutes for our jump, crashed at Smoke Bomb Hill on Fort Bragg. I don't remember the number of casualties involved in that accident. These two accidents with the C-119 which was called the flying boxcar and was rumored to defy the law of aerodynamics to fly, certainly didn't help my confidence. I thought it was weird to get new parachutes when the problem was with the aircraft. This reminds me of the government giving more money to incompetent teachers and school officials expecting it to solve the education problems.

The new parachute that they issued us for the jump on 19 November, was the T-10. For months prior to this incident, one man out of every 20-man stick would jump with the T-10. To determine who would get to jump the T-10, we each drew a marble from a container that had 19 black marbles and one white one. The man who got the odd marble won the privilege. Everyone wanted to get the odd marble for two reasons. One was simply because it was something new. The other was that whoever jumped the T-10 was picked up by jeep with the parachute and taken to the assembly point. The T-10 parachute was 30 feet in diameter and deployed from a bag, with negligible opening shock. The accident, however, was because the plane lost an engine and had nothing to do with the parachutes.

On the day of the demonstration for the Secretary, one of my men told me before we left the barracks that he was not going to jump that day. I placed him so that he would sit next to me and be in front of me for the jump. We flew for about three hours and every few minutes he would remind me that he wasn't going to jump. Each time I would reply that he was going to jump. When the time came, he jumped without hesitation.

The Life Of A Soldier

Vehicle Accident at Fort Campbell

While I was assigned to the Assault Gun Platoon, one of my men was killed in an accident with the SPAT (Self Propelled Antitank Gun). Except for the NCOs, all of the men in our platoon were under 21. When the platoon was formed, the Platoon Sergeant, Sergeant First Class Don Walker, was allowed to hand-pick the men. I was also a Sergeant First Class and next in seniority to Don.

One of my men, 19-year-old Herbert Tate, who was called "Bo", from Virginia, came to me a few weeks before Christmas with a dilemma. He was engaged to a girl back home and she was planning to come and visit with him a few days before Christmas and travel back home with him for his Christmas leave. Her parents required that she be chaperoned and Bo asked if she could stay at our house. We had a big house in Trenton, Kentucky so we agreed. She arrived just before the weekend and we were going out on a field exercise on Monday. I arranged to allow Bo to stay behind for a day or two to spend some time with his fiancee.

The day that Bo was to join us in the field, Sergeant Walker went back to the base to pick up one of the SPATs that was in the maintenance shop. He took one driver with him, but it turned out that there were two SPATs ready to pick up. Bo Tate was the only man in the platoon who didn't drive. His Dad had been killed in an auto accident when he was a little boy and he had a fear of driving. In fact, he was half-owner of a car with one of the other guys in the platoon, but never drove the car.

Euell White

Technically his refusal to drive disqualified him as a crewman for the SPAT because every man was supposed to be cross trained to do any job. I had encouraged him to learn to drive but he wouldn't. Bo was such a good soldier, so dependable and loyal to the unit that an exception was made.

I never did learn how Don Walker persuaded him to drive the SPAT that day, but he did. On the way out to the training site the SPAT Bo was driving veered off the road and up an embankment, but stopped before it reached the top. Then it turned over on top of Bo and crushed him to death. If it had been an automobile it would not have turned over. The embankment was not steep enough to appear to be a hazard.

I was then faced with the responsibility of going to my home to tell his fiancee that he was dead. We put her on a plane for home and I escorted Bo's body home by train. Members of the platoon drove to Virginia at their own expense to be the firing squad for his military funeral.

This was the most difficult task I had ever had. Bo had been raised by his grandmother (his father's mother). I don't know why. His mother was, as far as I could tell, a very gracious lady and a Christian. He had listed his mother as his Next of Kin.

I stayed at his mother's house while I was there and was treated like royalty by her family and her Methodist pastor. There was obviously some friction between the mother and the grandmother and I had to avoid getting in the middle of it. While I didn't want to take sides in whatever their problem with each other was, I had to honor the mother as the next of kin.

The Life Of A Soldier

When the grandmother came to the funeral home and saw Bo in the casket with the uniform on, she demanded that the uniform be removed, alleging that the army had murdered him. I had to try to explain to her that Bo had listed his mother as the next of kin and the army policy was to honor that, therefore it was the mother's decision.

The big question of why Bo was driving the SPAT, was a question I couldn't honestly answer. I used the official explanation that all crew members were required to drive. I didn't dare tell them that Bo had never driven before, but they seemed to know that, or at least suspect it. I didn't ask any questions about that when I returned. I knew that whatever happened, there was no reason for Don Walker to expect that such a tragic accident could happen driving along a road.

Appendix "B"

Unforgettable Characters

1. Major General Wayne C. Smith............285

2. The Cussing Sailor............................287

3. Private Martin..................................288

4. Captain Riverbuck............................290

5. The Chief..296

6. Lieutenant Colonel Dufus....................299

The Life Of A Soldier

Major General Wayne C. Smith

In preparation for the move to Germany, the 11th Airborne Division went through some tough exercises at the hands of the commanding general, Major General Wayne C. Smith. General Smith established a program that required us to do certain things to become "qualified." It was never made clear what we were being qualified for. Some of the things he required of us made sense and were beneficial, such as the 25-mile march with full equipment. Some things , however made no sense at all.

At one point, the General required all noncommissioned officers to wear police whistles on their uniforms. This policy was changed after there was a lot of trouble with N.C.O.s getting intoxicated in the clubs and off-post establishments and all blowing their whistles at once. This interfered with the ability of the Military Police to use their whistles for their intended purposes.

During General Smith's tenure as commanding general, if an enlisted man received a ticket for traffic violation he lost a stripe---if he had any stripes. He required that any soldier who owned an automobile have it registered on the post. To enforce this he had the Military Police stopping traffic on highway U.S. 41-A which runs adjacent to Fort Campbell, and impound cars of civilians if they couldn't prove they were not in the Army.

If The GENERAL drove through a post housing area and saw a woman in shorts, he would take a stripe from her husband.

All junior commissioned officers were required to attend cook and bakers school and all noncommissioned officers had to attend a class on how to fire the coal furnaces to heat the barracks.

General Smith was extremely obese, yet he required any soldier who didn't meet the army's weight standards to attend a "fat man's school."

The division deployed in January-February 1956, and the General required that form letters be sent to the families of all soldiers who took leave during the Christmas 1955 holidays telling them the penalty for desertion or missing shipment. I was a Sergeant First Class and married, yet my Dad received such a letter.

These are only a few of the many things this general did. Fortunately, General Smith was relieved of the command of the division just before we left for Germany.

The Life Of A Soldier

The Cussing Sailor.

I learned on the trip to Germany aboard the U.S.S. Butner what is meant by the old saying, "Cussing like a sailor," through my dealings with a Navy Petty Officer the same pay grade as me. The Navy had issued badges, color-coded to designate where passengers were allowed to be on the ship. The badge I was issued only allowed me on the cabin class deck. As acting First Sergeant, however, I had to go down into the troop hold to see about the men and to assign work details. The first time I started down there I was confronted by a Petty Officer First Class who told me in very colorful language that I couldn't go down there because I didn't have the right colored badge. I learned through my experience with this man, to appreciate the old saying about someone "cussing like a sailor."

Finally, when I made him understand that he needed me to get my men to do the work he wanted done, he allowed me in. Every day, however, we went through the same drill. I also learned that the Navy, or at least this one Petty Officer, was very sensitive about Navy terminology. After learning this I purposely aggravated the Petty officer by calling things by their Army names. He would say he needed 4 men to swab the deck, and I would designate 4 men to mop the floor. Then he would say he needed six men to clean the heads, and I would designate 6 men to clean the latrines. He would say ladders, and I would say stairs. He would have a cursing fit each time I called things by their army name rather than the navy's.

Euell White

Private Martin

In the 76th Tank Battalion in Germany we had a Private Martin from West Virginia in the Supply and Transportation Platoon. Martin was barely literate and his job was driver of a 5-ton truck loaded with 5-gallon cans of gasoline for refueling of tanks in the field.

In our battalion tank park area, there was a little German snack shack where the German workers who did the building maintenance, etc. obtained their sandwiches and beer for lunch. There was a sign on the building, that read "OFF LIMITS TO U.S. PERSONNEL." Colonel Preer, the battalion commander, came along one day and found Private Martin standing there eating a sandwich and drinking a beer. The Colonel said, "Soldier can you read that sign?" to which Martin replied, "Yes sir." The colonel then told him to read it aloud. Martin read it very slowly and haltingly. Then the Colonel said, well what are you doing with the sandwich and beer? To this Martin replied, "Hell sir, I aint no US I'm an RA." Back then all enlisted men had a prefix for their serial numbers. For the draftee it was US . For the regular army volunteer it was RA and for the reservist, ER.

The Colonel came by the company orderly room where I was sitting in for the First Sergeant, and told us about the incident with instructions to do nothing to punish Martin, just explain to him the real meaning of the sign. He said he had a hard time restraining laughter when he was talking to Martin.

I had some doubts as to whether Martin was as dumb as he appeared. While we were on winter maneuvers, later on, The Supply and Transportation Platoon Leader

The Life Of A Soldier

positioned Martin near a town with a 5-ton truck load of fuel in 5-gallon cans and told him to wait there until he returned for him. Then after we were stopped from moving because of the damage we were doing to the forests due to heavy rains, the lieutenant didn't need the gas for the tanks and forgot to retrieve Martin until the exercise was over.

The result was that Martin was left without food and without any contact with the unit for about two weeks with a truckload of gasoline that in Germany was expensive at that time. When the lieutenant went to get Martin he found him in good health, and in good spirits, but with a lot of the gasoline missing.

The Lieutenant was planning to bring charges against him, but the company commander reminded him that if he did, he would have to explain why he left him there without supervision for so long, and suggested he just drop it.

Euell White

Captain Riverbuck.

At Fort Riley, Kansas, when Captain Woods left the company I assumed temporary command of Company E. One day the adjutant called and told me to come and pick up my company commander. The man that I met was a stranger to me. I will call him Captain Riverbuck (not his real name). I escorted captain Riverbuck back to the Company and began to brief him concerning the company.
I immediately noticed that the captain was very nervous. Within a few minutes he had cigarettes burning in all of the ashtrays in the room and was frantically taking notes on everything I said, trying to write down my every word.

As I talked with him and he asked me questions, it was obvious that he was overwhelmed with the thought of having the responsibility of commanding a company. He was a senior captain and I learned that he had never commanded even a platoon. Captain Riverbuck was a distinguished military graduate from ROTC in college and had been commissioned a regular army officer. In college he had begun shooting in marksmanship competitions and had made that his career in the army.

He arrived in the middle of the week, so I suggested we have a complete inspection of the Company on Saturday--troops, barracks, equipment, mess, motor pool, etc. It was customary to have some sort of inspection on Saturday mornings. The moment I mentioned the inspection Captain Riverbuck became more and more frantic. He inundated me with questions about how to conduct the inspection and asked me would he have to stand out in front of the troops and face them in formation.

The Life Of A Soldier

I said certainly but I will be with you and tell you what to do.

He worried over the inspection the remainder of the week. When Saturday came it was unbelievable. The beginning was the inspection of the troops in formation with their weapons. The First Sergeant called the Company to attention and received reports from the four platoon sergeants, then faced the Captain and reported to him. I stood beside the captain and led him through the inspection. He didn't inspect any of the weapons, but that is the inspector's prerogative.

After the troop inspection we went through the barracks, mess hall and motor pool. After the inspection, Captain Riverbuck didn't know any more about the company nor the condition of the equipment than he did before we began. He was in a dazed condition. I don't think the troops caught on, however.

The only other officer in the Company at the time was Lieutenant Wardell Caesar Smith, the weapons platoon leader. The First Sergeant caught on pretty quick that something was terribly wrong. You didn't get to be a first sergeant without being perceptive, but he and I never said anything about the captain's incompetence to one another. It was like an unspoken conspiracy. We were both professional soldiers and our duty was to make this the best company in the battle group. With the help of Lieutenant Smith and the platoon sergeants, we did just that. Lieutenant Smith and I did talk about the situation to each other, and agreed that we had to cover for the captain in order to fulfill our obligation to the unit.

Euell White

That summer Company E came out well in everything we did. We had the Army Training Test and the IG (Inspector General) inspection, both of which were competitive. We also ran a live fire demonstration for all of the ROTC cadets in 5th Army. In all of these things, E Company excelled and the captain was praised for it even though he didn't know what was going on most of the time.

While on a tactical exercise, Lieutenant Smith, as Weapons Platoon Leader, would accompany the captain to the Battle Group command Post (CP) to receive the orders. The Captain went through the motions, but he couldn't tell you anything about the order. On the way back to the company, they would stop and Lieutenant Smith would write out an order for the company.

When they returned I would assemble the platoon sergeants and Captain Riverbuck would read the order. If anyone asked a question, Smith would answer it. The platoon sergeants asked just enough questions to let us know that they knew what was going on. But they never mentioned it.

One day during the exercise, the Battle Group commander, Colonel Malone, dropped in by helicopter, landing near the captain's location. Before I could get there, the colonel flew away. I asked the captain what the colonel said and he replied, "I don't know." I asked if he gave him an order and he said, "I think so, but I don't know what it was." I told Lieutenant Smith to go to the Battle Group CP and find out what our tactical order was.

Soon after Smith left, a column of armored personnel carriers from the division transportation unit arrived. I asked the lieutenant in charge of them if he knew where he was to take us and he said, he was only told to

The Life Of A Soldier

report to the company. I had the platoon sergeants load the troops and we waited for Lieutenant Smith's return. I was careful to stay away from the troops for fear they would ask me where we were going.

When Caesar returned he told me we were to occupy the Combat Outpost Line by a certain hour. We made it on time. This is one example of the kind of things we did for the few months that Captain Riverbuck was in "command" of company E..

Dealing with Captain Riverbuck was a stressful situation for me. We covered for him and made his company the best in the Battle Group without any contribution from him except to get in the way. I became so frustrated at times that I would tell him how incompetent he was and try to make him angry enough to do something—fire me or bring charges against me. But he would only agree with me. At one point I decided if I could get him to do one simple task successfully that would make him feel confident and be a base to help him. Remember, Caesar Smith and I were second lieutenants and he was a senior captain, eligible for promotion to major. We were not trained to train a superior officer.

Once each month each company commander was required to conduct a session called something like Information and Education hour. This was supposed to be done by the commander and not delegated to someone else. The Department of the Army supplied a suggested topic with materials. Caesar Smith had been doing this for Captain Riverbuck, and we decided to make him do it.

Euell White

When I informed him that he was going to have to give the I & E lecture, the captain begged me to let Lieutenant Smith do it. I told him he must do it and if he didn't I would make sure the Battle Group Commander knew it. I also warned him that getting sick and going to the chaplain would not work. He had done this in the past to get out of things. He would either say he was sick and head for the dispensary, or say he had an appointment with the chaplain.

I arranged with an officer on the Battle Group training staff to inspect the class and tell him it was good no matter how bad it was. After that, he had the confidence to do that one thing, but nothing else.

In my frustration I would unload all of this on Euna when I came home at night. She told me that this man must surely resent me, and when he no longer needed me he would show it.

The Life Of A Soldier

About the time I was promoted to First Lieutenant, Captain Riverbuck was moved to fill a staff position for a new brigade headquarters that was being formed, and I assumed command of the company. Soon afterward the Battle Group had a "Hail and Farewell" party at the officers club for the newly arrived officers and those who were leaving as well as those who had recently left and were still on post. When we arrived at the club, the first person I saw was Captain Riverbuck. As soon as he saw us he made a beeline for us and told me how much he appreciated all of the help I had given him. He stuck to me like a leech for the entire evening. I never saw him again.

The Chief

Like any other profession, the military has its share of incompetents who somehow seem to slip through the cracks and hinder, rather then help. The battalion operations officer that was assigned to us when Major Ron Scharnberg was killed fit this category. I won't mention his name, but he nicknamed himself "Chief" and wanted to be called that. He was from one of the Pacific islands that was a U.S. territory or protectorate.

The army sometimes kept these incompetents while good officers fell victim to the so-called "up or out" policies and were separated because they failed to be promoted on schedule due to one efficiency resulting from a personality conflict with a vengeful superior. This happened to one of my best friends that I had served with and knew to be an outstanding officer.

I knew Major Chief from seeing him at brigade headquarters when I would go there for the daily commanders and staff briefing. He was a trouble-maker and a pain in the neck for me. The brigade operations officer one day called to coordinate with me concerning operations. When I asked why he was calling me instead of my operations officer he told me that Major Chief would not talk to him. I had to involve the battalion commander to get this straightened out.

Prior to Colonel Sutton's death I frequently had contact with the colonel who was Deputy Brigade Commander to Brigadier General Hill, of the 5th Mechanized Brigade. I got along well with him. Then, after Colonel Steverson took the battalion, that colonel seemed to be hostile toward me. I later learned after Colonel Steverson relieved major Chief, that the major was undermining me and sowing discord. He would tell that colonel that I was resentful because Colonel Steverson was

The Life Of A Soldier

given command of the battalion rather than me. This was, of course, a bald-faced lie. Even if I had felt that way, Major Chief would have been the last person I would have shared it with. I didn't learn of this in time to rectify the situation. I hated that this Colonel, and probably the General too, was left with the impression that I was disloyal to my battalion commander.

One day while I was at our forward base, a squad-sized patrol was inserted by helicopter and made contact immediately and had one man killed. The entire patrol was retrieved, for what reason I don't know. While the S-2 (intelligence officer), Captain Peale was debriefing the patrol and getting ready to send them back out, Major Chief walked up and took over from the captain. The captain came to me and asked me to come out and hear what was going on. Major Chief was telling this patrol, led by a young sergeant, that he disagreed with the battalion commanders tactics of using small unit patrols, saying it was suicidal. I couldn't believe what I was hearing and by the time he finished the entire squad, including the squad leader, had decided that they would refuse to go back out. I then took charge and privately told Major Chief to go back to his operations center and stay there.

Captain Peale and I talked with the patrol members one at a time and explained to them the seriousness of refusing to obey an order in combat. Ultimately they all changed their minds and were re-inserted.

When Colonel Steverson finally had all he could take of Major Chief, he relieved him. His replacement was Major Pierce who was senior to me by date of rank, but Colonel Steverson wanted me to remain as XO. Major Pierce was a good officer and did a good job as operations officer.Major Chief went to someone at division and objected to me being the rater for his efficiency report. Someone listened to him and Colonel Steverson had to do it. This illustrates how these misfits are able to manipulate the system. I saw the report that Colonel Steverson wrote.

In 1972 while at Fort Benning getting ready to retire, I received a call from Major Chief. He came on with the "old buddy" approach which is always a signal that a con man wants something from you. He told me that Colonel Severson ruined him with that efficiency report and he planned to protest it, because he would never be promoted if the report stood. He wanted me to write a letter to help him in his protest. I told him that I saw the report and I thought the Colonel was very generous. I reminded him that I was supposed to write the report but he objected. I also told him that I didn't think he should hold a commission in the army.

The Life Of A Soldier

Lieutenant Colonel Dufus

I wrote earlier about the Brigade Deputy Commander and the effort to cover-up the drug problem. Dufus is not his real name, but a good description of him. He was a pain in the neck and more of a hindrance than a help. My first conflict with him was about the power generators. All of the battalions except 3/187 were clustered around brigade headquarters and shared the power generated there.

The 3/187 was in a location remote from brigade and we even had our own flagpole. We had our own power generator, a 200 Kilowatt of which we could only use less than half even if everything was turned on at the same time.

Because the generators at brigade headquarters were being overloaded, Colonel Dufus ordered the PX to stop selling electric heaters. It was cold at Camp Evans when I arrived, so I sent our interpreter to Hue to buy me a heater. One night Colonel Dufus decided to inspect the bunker line guard and found a man from my battalion asleep at his post. He took his rifle and came to my quarters and barged in without knocking and awakened me. It was a rainy night and the rifle was wet and muddy. He tossed it on my bed and dirtied my sheets. I told him I didn't appreciate it and that he didn't have any right to enter my quarters without invitation. There was an officer of the guard and a sergeant of the guard who were responsible for the guards.

Colonel Dufus saw my heater and told me I wasn't supposed to have a heater. I explained to him that my heater did not take any power from his generators as we had our own. The next day a truck from the maintenance contractors arrived and unloaded a 100 KW generator and picked up the 200. This was supposed to bother me but I still had more power than I needed.

One evening after the Laos operation was over and with the battalion command post at Camp Evans, Colonel Dufus called me and told me to meet him and the other battalion XOs on the road above the amphitheater.

The amphitheater was near brigade headquarters and we never used it. He said there was a black power rally going on there and he wanted us to go and find out what the participant's problems were and see if we could solve them. This approach reminds me of the Liberal politicians ideas of how to deal with the Muslim terrorists.

I told him that I didn't believe that was a good idea and that if the rally was illegal we should have the Military police break it up, otherwise we should ignore it. He insisted however. I ordered a muster of the battalion to account for the whereabouts of every man. I was fairly certain that we had no one at the rally because it would be a pretty good walk to get there. A few minutes later the Sergeant Major reported that all of our men were in our camp. I called Colonel Dufus and told him that we didn't have any troops at the rally, but he still insisted that I meet them there at a certain time.

I went to Colonel Steverson and told him I was contemplating disobeying an order from the deputy brigade commander. He asked me to go ahead to the rally just to keep peace. My driver and I were the first ones there. The amphitheater was in a bowl. We looked down there from the road and watched what was happening. There were at least 100 men there and they were smoking dope. Soon, Colonel Dufus arrived with the other XOs following him in a convoy of jeeps. I attempted again to talk him out of it, but he wouldn't listen. He said to follow him and started down the hill toward the theater. I stopped short of the theater, but the colonel walked into the midst of them and made an ass of himself. He told them that we were there to find out what their complaints were, etc. They started making fun of him and jeering him.

It was so disgusting I couldn't stand it so I got in my jeep and left. Later on that night he called me and told me he was going to charge me with disobeying an order and I told him to go ahead. The next morning I was summoned to Brigade Headquarters and I figured this was it. I was told to report to Colonel Grange's office. When I arrived there Colonel Dufus was there. Colonel Grange said, "Euell I understand you went to a party last night." I said, "Yes sir." He then asked me what were my thoughts about it. I told him that I had told Colonel Dufus that if it was an illegal assembly we should send the MPs to break it up, and if not we should ignore it. He smiled and said, "I agree. We won't be doing that again." If looks could kill I would have been a dead duck from the glare I received from Colonel Dufus.

I learned later that the situation worsened after I left the amphitheater and the Colonel finally gave it up without accomplishing anything except to make an ass of himself and embarrass the other officers. I also learned that Colonel Grange was upset when he heard about it. He knew nothing about it until after the fact.

Appendix C

Unusual and Interesting Duties

1. The Television Play..........................303

2. Checkpoint Charlie………………………..305

3. The Courts-Martial………………………310

4. The Article 32 Hearing…………………….315

The Life Of A Soldier

The Television Play

One interesting experience I had in Germany was being in a television play. They were producing a series of plays for "Playhouse 90" about soldiers who were decorated for heroism in World War II in a certain division. The tank battalion I was assigned to was at a training center in 1957, and I was the Platoon Leader of the Headquarters Tank Platoon. The television production company asked for assistance and I was assigned to help, along with my platoon.

The story was about an infantry lieutenant and his fiancé was an army nurse. We were alongside some bombed out buildings. My four tanks were lined up in convoy and I was in front of them with a jeep. The only professional in the play was a German actress who played the part of the lieutenant's fiancee. The rest of the civilians in the play were American school teachers. The Lieutenant was played by an American soldier who had some acting experience.

If they gave you any words to say they had to pay you. I had a soldier named Segal from the Bronx who had studied drama in college. The convoy I was supposedly leading had stopped at that place where there was some kind of command post, and the army nurse had gone inside to ask about the outfit the lieutenant was assigned to. When they would shoot the scene we were in, I would have to be seated in the jeep and the tank crews in their tanks, appearing that we had just stopped there.. They went through this for days, and I started to understand why actors have addictions. I was so tired of hearing the command "Cut", over and over that I wanted to obey the command by cutting the throat of the director.

Segal's part was to go running into the headquarters and shout "The Krauts are coming, the Krauts are coming."

The crew that was doing the film was German, and the actress as well as the German crew objected to this characterization of the German Army. Segal had to re-learn his lines, and say "The Germans are coming, the Germans are coming." The rest of my men teased him about the difficulty of re-learning his lines.

In 1963 while stationed at Fort Riley Kansas, I was watching Television one Saturday afternoon and Playhouse 90 came on. As soon as it started, I realized it was the play I was in and called Euna to come and see it, but by the time she came into the room the scene was over. As it turned out the take they used was a scene where we were taking a break between shots, and I was leaning up against the jeep rather than seated in it as I was supposed to be. I still had to laugh when Segal, a short, pudgy little guy with the Bronx accent, came running in shouting "The Germans are coming."

The Life Of A Soldier

Checkpoint Charlie.

During our time in Berlin I had duty as Officer In Charge of the checkpoint between the U.S. and Soviet zone. The checkpoint was known as "Checkpoint Charlie." We monitored the traffic in and out of East Berlin which was the Soviet zone. There were always two U.S. military policemen on duty and a German police sergeant as interpreter. There were also two British military policemen and two French policemen as liaison. The French policemen never spoke to us the whole time I was there. They just sat in their little space in the guard shack and drank their wine.

Not too long before we were there, a young man named Peter Fechter had been shot and killed by the Communist East German police, trying to escape to the West through the checkpoint. I remembered seeing a television special about it. Our military policemen had helplessly watched this event and could do nothing to stop it because of the rules they were operating under. President John F. Kennedy had issued orders that this would not be repeated, and we were equipped to act should that ever again happen. We had machine guns mounted in a building adjacent to the checkpoint and flak jackets for all personnel. We also had classified written instructions on the rules of engagement.

Those of us who served as officers in charge, were accountable to the Berlin Command intelligence officer (G-2). There was a television camera mounted to monitor all of the traffic coming and going. We were required to report within a few minutes, on every official Soviet vehicle that came through the checkpoint. This was a pain in the neck because every time one came through, I would get a call from G-2 of the Berlin command before I had time to call in the report, asking why I hadn't reported. I think the officers on duty there were just bored and looking for something to do. We also were informed that if there was an incident like the Peter Fechtner incident, and we fouled up we would have to answer to the President himself.

An incident that I witnessed, and according to the Military Policemen, occurred every Sunday morning, was the appearance of two women. At the same time every Sunday, apparently by pre-arrangement a young woman showed up on the West Berlin side of the checkpoint, and on the East Berlin side, an older woman. They just stood there and looked at one another for a long time, weeping. They didn't wave or try to speak to one another for fear of reprisal by the VOPO (East German Communist Police). I learned from the Military police who worked at the checkpoint that they were mother and daughter.

I thought of this scene when I was confronted by a woman at the University of Alabama, Huntsville in 1969, about the reality of the communist threat. In 1969 while

The Life Of A Soldier

assigned as advisor to the Alabama Army National Guard's 20th Special Forces Group (Airborne) in Huntsville, I enrolled as a part-time student at the University of Alabama in Huntsville. I attended my morning classes in uniform, and a middle-aged woman in one of my classes tried to get a petition to stop me from wearing my uniform to class. When this failed because no one would sign it, she confronted me in the hallway after class one day and asked me, "Why do you wear that uniform to class?" I replied that it was the prescribed uniform for an officer in the U.S. Army. That didn't satisfy her, so she asked me if I was "waving" the uniform. I told her I had never heard of that, but if she was asking would I wave the flag, the answer was yes. Then she made the remark that the Vietnam War was wrong and that the "Domino Theory" which held that if we didn't stop communism, it would spread, was not valid, and that communism was not evil. When I asked her how many communist countries she had visited, she admitted she had never been to a communist country.

The news of the wall coming down a few years ago, had much more meaning to those of us who witnessed this. I can only imagine how much more it meant to those who were the victims of it on both sides of the wall.

A very good friend of mine that was in another company in the Battle Group, Lieutenant Tom Vaughn from Tennessee, had duty going on patrol through East Berlin. The stated purpose of this was to exercise our right to travel in the Soviet sector. There was also an intelligence-gathering mission associated with it. During the time we were there, the International Communist Party meeting took place in East Berlin. The Communist party of the U.S.A. was there and all the nations' flags were displayed. The place where the meeting was held, was along Tom's patrol route. I was really surprised one night when Tom showed me the flags he had hidden under his bed. He had, at the risk of being shot if caught, removed several of the communist flags. I don't know what he ultimately did with them. Tom was an infantry officer candidate school graduate with a few years enlisted service. He eventually applied for and received a regular army appointment. He retired as a full colonel in 1988 and is now in his hometown of McMinnville Tennessee where he is a songwriter and teaches political science in a university.

I went into East Berlin once on a sightseeing tour. It was part of the program of exercising our right to be there. I went in a military sedan and we had to follow the designated route. The driver, who did this all the time, pointed out to me, store fronts that displayed attractive merchandise, but the buildings they belonged to were non-existent. The communists had these phony displays to show to the Westerners who came how prosperous the people were under communism. It was early on a Sunday morning and we saw some young couples walking. They would wave to us, but if they saw a police vehicle they would quickly turn their faces away from us.

On the evening before the Russians' annual ceremony at their unknown soldiers tomb, a courier brought a classified message from the Berlin Command G-2, instructing me to not allow any Soviet vehicles to enter through our checkpoint if they were on their way to the tomb. The shortest route for them was through the American sector and the year before the Russians had used combat vehicles to transport troops to the tomb which was in violation of the four powers agreement.. I was instructed to stop every Soviet vehicle and ask them if that was their destination and if they said it was to inform them they could not enter.

All night I wondered how I was to communicate in the event a Soviet vehicle came and there was no one in it who spoke English nor German. The only interpreter I had was a German police sergeant but he didn't speak Russian,

The Life Of A Soldier

only English and German. I needn't have worried. At dawn a bevy of officials both civilian and military descended upon the checkpoint. When I went off duty at 0800 hours there had been no Soviet vehicles attempting to enter.

The diplomacy game is interesting and at times seems childish. When General Eisenhower was the Supreme Commander there, his Information Officer was escorting Mamie on a sightseeing tour, and the Soviets stopped them at the check point and delayed them for a long time. Ever since then, the Soviet counterpart of that Information Officer was barred from entering through the checkpoint. We kept up-to-date photographs of the current one so that we could recognize him should he attempt to come through.

The Courts Martial.

While on Okinawa I was appointed as defense counsel for a special courts martial. There are three levels of courts in addition to non-judicial punishment by the commander under Article 15, which the Navy calls Captain's Mast. This non-judicial punishment does not become a matter of permanent record.

The three levels of courts martial are the General, Special and Summary. The General is for the more serious crimes and the maximum sentence can be death for certain crimes. For the General Courts Martial, lawyers were required and there was a military judge present to advise the court. The next level is the Special Courts Martial. The maximum sentence under the Special is reduction to the lowest grade, confinement for six months, and forfeiture of all pay and allowances for six months. The lowest court is the Summary Court. This court was comprised of one officer who had to be at least a major. I don't remember what the maximum sentence of this court was, but it was less than for the special.

The soldier I was appointed to defend on Okinawa was a specialist 5 who was charged with three counts of forgery and three counts of larceny. He was assigned to the psychological operations battalion and manager of a bowling alley on his off-duty time. The bowling alleys were operated by the Special Services, a non-appropriated fund activity. The bowling alleys, and clubs for officers, noncommissioned officers and enlisted men had slot machines. The small jackpots paid off by spitting out coins, but when someone won the big jackpot, the manager had to verify the win and have two witnesses verify it. The jackpot winner, the manager and the two witnesses signed a form verifying the win, then the manager paid the winner in cash from the cash register. Once someone pulled the

The Life Of A Soldier

handle again, there was no evidence that the machine had paid off.

My client had made up names for winners and witnesses and made phony payoffs to himself. I don't know how many he did in all. Someone who worked at the bowling alley had anonymously reported him giving the Criminal Investigators (CID) three dates and the phony names for payoffs. The CID obtained handwriting specimens from my client and sent them to the crime lab in Japan. The crime lab confirmed that all of the signatures were my client's handwriting. The crime lab report was the only evidence against the accused. The person who reported him never came forward and identified herself.

A few days before the trial, the wife and children of the accused all came down with Diphtheria, and he told me he could not afford to go to jail. He wasn't concerned about whether he was found guilty, only that he didn't go to jail. I knew that the only way to insure that he didn't go to jail was to get a not guilty verdict. The pre-trial agreements, or "deals" as the TV shows portray them today, were not so common in such cases.

I learned that the trial counsel (prosecutor), a captain, was not planning to subpoena any witnesses from the crime lab in Japan to corroborate their report. My plan was to object to the introduction of the crime lab report. The only way for the trial counsel to use this report would be for the trial to be delayed until a witness was brought from Japan. My backup plan, in case they did bring the expert witness from Japan, was to challenge the charge sheet which alleged that my client defrauded and stole from the United States of America. The official position of the government, I understood, was that it did not own any slot machines. They were the property of a non-appropriated fund activity. Euna worked for special services and in fact, her job was counting all the monies from the clubs and depositing them in the bank. She was not considered a government employee. I planned to contend that if the military didn't own them they couldn't charge my client with stealing from the United States government. I still don't know whether that defense had any merit, but that was my plan. My third alternative, which I always gave a lot of attention to as defense counsel, was a good presentation for extenuation and mitigation to minimize the sentence in the event there was a guilty finding.

My client had agreed to this line of defense until the day of the trial. The trial was to begin at 1300 hours. I went to the mess hall to have lunch with my client and go over the trial procedures with him. He told me then that he had decided to plead guilty to the larceny and not guilty to the forgery. I asked why and he said he had been assured that if he pled guilty he would not go to jail. I asked who gave him the assurance and he would not tell me. The only person who could give such an assurance was the convening authority, which in this case was the 1st Special Forces Group Commander, and it would have to be communicated to the accused through the defense counsel. I knew therefore that there was some illegal dealings going on and to this day I don't know who had an interest in his pleading guilty, nor what that interest was. I could have pressed this issue and he would have been forced to identify the person that was interfering with the process, but I decided it would not be in his best interest.

I expected that when the guilty plea was entered, the trial counsel would drop the forgery charges and there would be no need to go though the trial, but he insisted on presenting the case for both the larceny and forgery charges. My commanding officer, Lieutenant Colonel Hiebert, was the president of the court.

The trial counsel began by trying to introduce the crime lab report and I objected on the grounds that it was inadmissible without a witness to corroborate it. Colonel Hiebert wouldn't rule on the objection without a legal opinion. The court was recessed while the trail counsel and I went to a room where there was a phone with an extension and called the Judge Advocate General (JAG) office. Two lawyers, one for the trial and one for defense, sustained my objection, and we went back to court and told the president. This set the tone for the trial. The trial counsel would open his mouth and I would object. The president would instruct us to get a legal opinion, and we would call the JAG officers again. A friend of mine who was a spectator told me that he kept count and there were 18 objections by me and all of them were sustained.

When the court finally went into closed session they found my client guilty on all counts, based on his guilty plea. They reasoned that if he committed the larceny, he had to have committed the forgery because that was the only way he could have committed the larceny. I don't know what the military Court of Appeals would have said about that.

After a guilty finding in the special court, there is a recess then the defense gets to present matters of extenuation and mitigation to mitigate the sentence. I told the court about my client's family being ill with diphtheria and stressed the need for his presence at home. I couldn't mention confinement, but they knew what I was driving at. Then I had three character witnesses, his company commander, first sergeant and the captain he worked for in the battalion supply. I thought I had sufficiently coached all of the character witnesses so that they would understand that if they were called the accused would have already been found guilty and our purpose was to mitigate his sentence. The company commander and first sergeant did just fine. Both said he had been a good soldier and they would like to keep him in their unit. The supply officer, however, didn't understand what he was there for. After identifying him and his relationship with the accused, I asked him to tell the court in his own words, what he thought of the accused. I intended for him to focus on my client's work as a supply specialist and say that he wanted to keep him in that job. However, his response was immediate and enthusiastic. He said: "He is as honest as the day is long. He wouldn't steal a thing." The courtroom erupted in laughter, including the members of the court. The trial had gone on into evening, way past suppertime, because of the time taken up by the eighteen recesses for consultation with the JAG. I said, "Thank you Captain, you are excused." I believe this witness helped more than the others. Everyone was worn out and the laughter provided some relief of tension.

    The court could have reduced my client to the lowest grade, Private 1, and sentenced him to six months confinement with a forfeiture of two-thirds of his pay and allowances for that six months. Instead, they reduced him one grade and fined him a few hundred dollars. I believe it was three hundred dollars. One of my friends who was either a spectator or a a member of the court, named me the "Poor man's Perry Mason."

    This was not my first courts martial experience. I had served as both trial counsel and defense counsel while in the 1st infantry division, at Fort Riley Kansas and in Germany. This was one of those extra duties that many officers tried their best to avoid, but I purely enjoyed. I seriously considered becoming a lawyer when I retired from the army, but God had other plans for me.

Article 32 Hearing

The Article 32 is equivalent to the Grand jury hearings in the civilian system. The Article 32 required a field grade officer (Major or above). I did several of them during my year tour. The last Article 32 hearing that I presided over, involved a soldier in one of the other battalions of the division. Who went AWOL from his unit and missed his rotation date.

He left his infantry unit and went to Phu Bai Airfield and made friends with the Military policemen who provided security for the airfield. He actually became one of them. They gave him the equipment for a military policemen and he was performing military police duties. He was discovered when a new Colonel took command of the airfield and started accounting for all of the personnel there. The Colonel discovered that there was no record of this man and his investigation revealed that the man didn't belong there.

He was returned to his unit to await court martial. His First Sergeant, Company Commander and Battalion Commander had already returned to the States, and there was no one in the unit that was there when he went AWOL. The length of time he was gone made it possible for him to charged with desertion, but the fact that he never changed his name or did anything to hide his identity eliminated that possibility.

My job was to hold a hearing and make findings and recommendations as to what should be done. He apparently did a good job as a military policeman. The First sergeant and Company Commander of his unit that hadn't known him before he went AWOL testified on his behalf that he was a model soldier. This was a bit perplexing for me, but when I thought it through I came to the conclusion that it really didn't matter how well he performed as a military policeman. He let his unit down by going AWOL. He was assigned as an infantryman. Not a military policeman. No doubt there were many infantrymen who would have preferred to have a job that was less demanding and dangerous than serving in the infantry. I recommended to the convening authority that this man be tried by a special courts martial.

Appendix D

Guerilla Warfare Exercises

1. Korea 1964.............................318

2. Taiwan 1965............................324

3. Korea 1966..............................340

Euell White

Korea 1964

In October 1964, I participated in a guerilla warfare exercise with the Republic of Korea (ROK) Army Speical Forces. I was at that time a first lieutenant and executive officer (XO) of a special forces "A" team consisting of two officers (Captain Allen and myself) and 10 noncommissioned officers. We also had a Second Lieutenant Savage from the psychological operations unit on Okinawa.

After about a week of what is aptly called the isolation phase we parachuted into a river valley near the city of Kuyre. The isolation phase is where you are in a secure compound with no contact with the outside, to be briefed and to prepare for the infiltration behind enemy lines to train and equip guerilla forces.

Pusan, Korea, chuting up for night jump into the river valley near Kuyre

The Life Of A Soldier

This was my first time in Korea and I learned a lot about the discipline in the ROK Army. We had to go to another building from our sleeping quarters to the latrine. Every morning I awoke about daybreak and walked to the latrine. At this time every morning a Korean Sergeant was having reveille formation with his platoon. The sergeant would walk down the ranks and hit each man with something he held in his hand, knocking the soldier to the ground, uttering something. The soldier would then get up and resume his attention stance, uttering something, I suppose in response to what the sergeant said. If the soldier was quick to recover, the sergeant would then move on to the next man. If not he would knock him down again and again until he was satisfied with the response. He did this with every man in the formation.

We jumped near midnight. Lieutenant Ho Hwap Yong of the R.O.K. Special Forces had joined us in isolation and jumped with us. Lieutenant Ho played the part of guerrilla chief and had recruited 55 Korean War veterans to play the part of guerillas.

For this exercise all of South Korea below the demilitarized zone was divided into 11 Guerilla Warfare Operational Areas (G.W.O.A.s). Each G.W.O.A. had 55 civilians hired to play the role of guerillas. Some of the teams were all Americans, some were all Koreans, and some were combined.

Some of our men landed in the river and lost most of their equipment. We were met on the drop zone by our guerrillas and we moved partly up the mountain that night. The following night I went into the city of Kurye with two of our guerrillas to make contact with an intelligence asset. We spent the night in a Korean home and leftbefore dawn to avoid being spotted.. There was a R.O.K. regiment against us as well as the National Police. On the way down the two Koreans laughed at me because I wasn't moving as fast as they wanted to move. They took turns carrying my rucksack. The next morning they tried to get the lady in whose home we stayed to make breakfast for them but she refused. She apparently wanted to be rid of us for fear of the police.

About an hour up the mountain, the guerillas gave me my rucksack back to me, and the situation was reversed from the night before. I constantly had to stop and wait for them to catch up. With their rice diet they can't miss a meal and maintain their strength.

After I rejoined the team we headed up the mountain. We didn't quite make it to the top that day. That night I slept beside the trail with my sleeping bag tied to a tree to keep from falling hundreds of feet. When we arrived at the top of the mountain the next day it was covered with snow. There were two buildings, and two large army tents. It was a way station for the R.O.K. Army engineer survey teams. There was an elderly couple living in one of the buildings. They were caretakers. The "A" team occupied the other building and the guerillas occupied the two tents.

We were out of food when we arrived. The men who landed in the river had lost all of theirs and we had shared with them. The Korean couple offered us food but it was filthy rice and some kind of greens that had a foul odor. Only one of our men could eat the food. At first he would bring the food into the warm building to eat, but it was so sickening to the rest of us, we made him eat it outside.

The U.S. Air Force was supposed to drop supplies to us the following night after our arrival on the mountain top, but they couldn't find us, although they were supposed to have flown over all of the drop zones that were used in the exercise. They tried to find us for several nights. We could see them way off. The next day after our arrival on the mountain, a unit from the Korean Regiment that was

The Life Of A Soldier

against us came up the mountain to capture us but with the binoculars we could see them hours before they arrived. We sanitized the area, doing away with all evidence that we were there and paid the old Korean couple to tell them we were long gone. We then went to the reverse slope of the mountain, removing our tracks as we went, and waited for them to leave. They always left in time to get back down the mountain for a hot supper. This was repeated for several days. We were completely without food and I ultimately lost 43 pounds from it.

We sent two of our guerillas to a town in the valley on the opposite side from the valley where we jumped, to buy same food for us. We gave them a lot of Korean money and two rucksacks that they were to fill with canned meat. We reasoned that the canned meat would be safe. After a few days we decided they had taken our money and gone home. One day we awoke to find a dense fog. You couldn't see your hand in front of your face, and neither could we see the Korean regiment with the binoculars. We foolishly reasoned that they would stay put until the fog lifted, but they attacked us that afternoon.

Just before they arrived, our two guerillas returned with their rucksacks full. After Lieutenant Ho finished reprimanding them for being so late, we found that the rucksacks were filled with canned whale blubber. The odor of that when we opened one of the cans, was more nauseating than the Korean lady's greens. There was some good news though. On the way up the mountain, they had killed a mule deer. Lieutenant Savage claimed he knew how to dress and cook the deer, so he went out with the Koreans to do that.

Immediately after he left the house, the attack came. There was shooting (with blank ammunition of course), except for Lieutenant Ho and we captured two of their officers. We were to learn later that the reason he was able to do this was that he had live ammunition in his pistol and fired near enough to them to cause them to give up.

At that time the Korean Special forces were considered the palace guard. They were the unit that the president counted on to protect him from a military coup. They carried live ammunition and were exempt from curfew regulations. We never knew what happened to the deer. When our attackers withdrew we couldn't find it. Our feet were wet from running around in the snow and we were in our sock feet, letting our socks dry–the Koreans heat under the floors so that the floors are warm.

Captain Allen was of the opinion that because it was so late they wouldn't come back that day. I was of the opinion that because of the face they had lost by having two of their officers captured, they would come back in spite of the fog and darkness. I urged him that we should pack up and leave the mountain. Sergeant Card, the Team Sergeant, agreed with me.

While we were discussing this, they attacked again. When we went outside they had our guerillas and were beating them. They had broken the leg of one of them in two places. The Captain, the team sergeant and myself went in amongst them and got between them and the guerrillas and demanded they stop. They did but insisted that we acknowledge they had captured us fair and square or they would resume the beating and take all of them away. We agreed and they marched us down the mountain that night. They took us to the national police station and locked us up.

While we were in the police station, our guerillas quit on us. We learned that the national police had obtained a list of them and was harassing their families. Early the next morning an American officer who was an exercise controller came and took us to a Buddhist monastery where we stayed for the remainder of the exercise. The only thing we did for those few days was receive the air re-supplies from the Air Force that they didn't deliver to us when we really needed them.

The guerillas came back to pose for the picture taken on the steps of the Buddhist Monastery. The front row is our team The one with the black face was our team leader, Captain Allen.

Taiwan, 1965.

In 1965 before going to Vietnam, I participated in a guerilla warfare exercise in Taiwan with the Special Forces of The Republic of China (R.O.C.) Army. I had 60 hours of the Mandarin Chinese language just before going to Taiwan. When I started speaking to the Chinese soldiers however, they started laughing. When I asked why they laughed, I was told that I spoke like a woman. My teacher was the wife of a Republic of China diplomat on Okinawa.

This exercise with the Republic of China Army Special Forces was very educational. There is an expression that I had often heard to describe any event that was disorganized or chaotic, "It was as fouled up as a Chinese fire drill." I came to understand and appreciate that expression during this exercise.

I was the executive officer of an "A" team but they split up some of the teams and cross attached. With four Noncommissioned officers and one Private First Class I was attached to a Chinese team commanded by a Captain Lo. Half of his team was attached to our team commanded by Captain Drenzeck.

Captain Lo, the ROC Team leader. PFC Childs in the background.

During the isolation phase, we lived with the Chinese. They had habits that became pretty irritating to us after a few days. Everyone was eager for the infiltration phase to come. In fact, I have often said, I was so eager to get out of the confinement with them, I would have been almost willing to jump without a parachute.

The radio communications between the teams and the Special Forces Operational Base (S.F.O.B.) was to be through scheduled contacts. In our signal instructions each team was given a time or a window of time each day for both transmitting and receiving. This meant that when it was your time to transmit the S.F.O.B. would be tuned to your frequency, but at any other time they would not. And when it was time for you to receive, you had to have your antenna up and be tuned to that frequency.

My radio man, Sergeant Carter, accompanied the two Chinese radio operators to training each day during isolation and assured me that they understood the system. It turned out however, that they didn't understand, nor could I make Captain Lo and the Lieutenant Colonel who was playing the role of Guerilla Chief understand it. They continually tried to send messages to the S.F.O.B. when there was nobody there monitoring the frequency. Then they thought something was wrong with their radio and wanted Sergeant Carter to fix it. When he didn't fix it because there was nothing wrong they would appeal to me. I explained the system in detail several times to the interpreter and he supposedly explained it to them, but it did no good.

I remember when we had an air re-supply scheduled and they decided to change the drop zone after the time had passed for our transmitting the day of the drop. They sent the message, but there was no one to receive the message because it was not the time for our contact. We went out that night to the new drop zone, knowing that the plane was going to fly over the original drop zone. It was amusing to watch the Chinese when they saw the plane flying miles away looking for the signal to drop. They became excited and pointed to the plane and had a lot of conversation about it.

The Life Of A Soldier

Another foul up with the communications concerned the final phase of the guerilla warfare exercise--the linkup with conventional forces. At the time the linkup took place, we were required to change frequencies. These were crystal sets and the two Chinese operators were issued the crystals for the change of frequencies for the linkup. Sergeant Carter saw them receive the crystals, but when the time came to change frequencies, they not only didn't have the crystals, but didn't remember anything about them. Therefore, we were out of communications. We were able to salvage the situation by having a controller notify the S.F.O.B. of our plight.

The day of the scheduled infiltration certainly justified the label "Chinese fire drill." The atmosphere at the airport was nothing short of chaotic . Because of bad weather some of the teams that should have been gone were still there and the conditions were crowded.

Captain Lo asked me to be the jumpmaster for the jump. We were jumping from a C-46 cargo plane flown by a Republic of China Air Force pilot. The operation order for the exercise was written in English and Chinese. Our designated heading or track to approach the drop zone was 15 degrees. In the operation order they made the mistake of writing 15 followed by the symbol for degrees, then the abbreviation deg. The Chinese pilot interpreted this as 150 degrees. I tried to explain that it was not 150 but 15 degrees but I couldn't get through. We had an interpreter, Lieutenant Wang, but he was not a parachutist and had gone to the drop zone by train.

Although it was clear where we were going, near Tai Chung, about 250 miles from the Airport near Taipei, as I remember, it was raining hard and there were no shelters for us to don our parachutes. We had to do it in the plane and that was more chaos because it was so crowded and there was no light except flashlights. When we started putting on our parachutes someone observed that there were no extensions for the static lines. Because of some incidents of parachutes getting caught on the tail of the C-46, we had a safety requirement to use an extension for the static lines when jumping the C-46. Apparently the Chinese had no such regulations and I wasn't about to cancel this jump. I told my men that if anyone got hung up on the tail they could activate the quick releases to the risers and fall free then open their reserve parachute. Private First Class Childs said he didn't have a quick release. It turned out that two of the parachutes, his and mine, were the older model and didn't have quick releases. I said, just use your knife and cut the risers, to which he replied, "I don't have a knife with me." One of the sergeants handed him a knife and I saw fear in his eyes.

    Childs was a good man. Five years later, in 1970, as a major, I attended the Infantry Officers Advance Course at Fort Benning and discovered that Captain Childs was one of my classmates. He had attended Officer Candidate School soon after our adventure together in Taiwan.

    The drop zones for night jumps were marked with lights forming a designated letter with the long axis in the direction of the heading or track. I knew that we would be on a heading of 150 degrees rather than the 15 degrees the marker was set up for. The pilot couldn't figure out what was wrong. He kept circling around and I would see the marker off at a distance occasionally, then it would be out of sight. Finally I turned and told Sergeant Reinburger, who was in the other door, "The next time we see the marker, no matter how far it is, we will jump." Just then, he said, "I see it" and jumped. I jumped immediately and everyone followed us. None of us hit the drop zone which was a fairly smooth field. We landed in the rice paddies. It took most of what was left of the darkness to get everyone assembled and link up with the guerillas.

Some of the terrain we traversed in Taiwan.

For several days during the exercise, we stayed at a Buddhist convent. This particular order of Buddhist nuns wore uniforms similar to catholic nuns, black and white. They were vegetarians and no male was allowed to enter their quarters. They had a special little annex, however, that was used by the monks who visited there. This was made available to the American part of the team while the Chinese officers stayed in homes nearby.

Euell White

P.F.C. Childs, the junior man on our team.

**Master Sergeant Fenton,
WWII Ranger, Team Sergeant**

The Life Of A Soldier

There was one bed in the monks' quarters and I took it. It was a bit short for me but it beat sleeping on the floor where my men slept. There was a Buddha and altar in this room and an old lady who I understood was the mother of the head nun, brought food for Buddha every day. We were getting tired of eating our own cooking and these fresh vegetables smelled awfully good. I made a joking remark one day while the old Lady was placing the food before Buddha, that I wondered if we ate Buddha's food would she think Buddha ate it. I don't think she understood English but I think she caught on to what I was saying, because she came back with food for all of us, and gave us one meal a day for the remainder of the time we were there. We Americans would joke with one another and the .interpreter would report to his superiors and tell them everything we said. I learned to use this to my advantage. If I couldn't get them to do anything I would talk about it within earshot of the interpreter and say that if they didn't get with it I was going to notify headquarters that they weren't doing a good job. They would buck up for awhile trying to make me happy. I couldn't confront them directly. That would have made them lose face.

    The Chinese liked to have staff meetings. We were supposed to be Conducting guerilla warfare training, doing ambushes, raids, etc., but they seemed to be satisfied to just have staff meetings and talk about it. We would begin fairly early in the morning with our meetings and stop at noon for lunch and a siesta. Then start again in the late afternoon and go into the night. We drank gallons of hot water—they rarely served tea. The Lieutenant Colonel who was supposed to be playing the part of Guerilla Chief simply took command. The soldiers playing the part of guerillas were in his command. He designated me to be chief of staff, and I quickly learned that my primary function was to take the blame for anything that went wrong.

In our army, we have primary staff and special staff. At the battalion level, for example, the primary staff are the Personnel,(S-1), Intelligence(S-2), Operations and Training(S-3), Logistics (S-4) and Civil Affairs(S-5). The surgeon and chaplain are considered special staff and would not have anything to say about combat operations. On this staff, however, the medical officer had opinions about everything which he freely expressed.

I learned that they always had a plan "A' and a plan "B." They discussed the merits and demerits of both plans endlessly and often after all that did not make a decision. They had a saying that was so frustrating to me. If you pushed for a decision, the commander would say, "Let us lay this matter aside" and that was usually the end of it even if we had spent a whole day discussing it. I learned to submit one plan that was sound and another that was absolutely unworkable to reduce the time spent discussing it.

One thing I learned about the Chinese was the way they mask their emotions. Sergeant Carter, my communications specialist, was blind in one eye and had a glass eye. Somehow he had managed for years to hide this fact. It would have disqualified him from special forces. We discovered it when we were walking narrow mountain trails at night in the darkness and he kept falling down. One night he fell and almost went over the side of the mountain which would have meant death for him. The reaction of the Chinese was to laugh and chatter. I became angry because one of my men almost fell to his death and they seemed to think it was funny. Later when I approached the subject with Lt. Wang, the interpreter, he explained that laughter is the way they respond when they are really nervous or frightened and concerned about something.

My Interpreter, Lieutenant Wang

  This illustrates the importance of knowing something about the culture you are working in before making too many judgments.

  The weather was very hot and as we walked the endless mountain trails we would joke with each other about what we would like to have. One would say that a good steak would be good and another would talk about cheeseburgers and fries. I would talk about how good some ice cream would be. Lieutenant Wang, of course, told the Chinese officers what we were saying. One day while we were staying outside a home, Captain Lo disappeared early in the morning and was gone all day. Nobody seemed to want to tell me where he was. Just before nightfall he appeared with what looked like a bucket, but it was their

The Life Of A Soldier

version of a thermos container. In it was Chinese ice cream. He apparently thought that I was really unhappy because I didn't have any ice cream and had walked some distance to catch a bus into Tai Chung to get the ice cream.

Dairy products were at the very top of the list of foods to avoid because of the danger of contracting hepatitis. Besides that the ice cream tasted terrible. I thought of the account of King David who longed for a drink of water from the well of Bethlehem, and three of his mighty men broke through the camp of the Philistines and drew water from the well of Bethlehem and brought it to David. David wouldn't drink the water, but poured it on the ground because the men put their lives in jeopardy to get it for him. I considered doing this with the ice cream and reading the passage from 2 Samuel to Captain Lo, but I was afraid it wouldn't work, so I ate the ice cream.

In some of the mountain villages we visited the children had never seen a white man. The children would run from us as we approached. Then there was always at least one who would approach us gradually until finally he was close enough to touch one of us. The child would touch one of us then run away. Later he would come back and one of the guys would give him candy. Then he would go back to the other children and soon they would be swarming all over us. The adults in these villages tried to communicate with us in Japanese. Taiwan was Japanese territory until after World War II.

Taking a break along a mountain trail

When we went into one village, a Black Sergeant who was one of the exercise controllers, was with us. They had never seen a black man before and all of the children had to touch him. One of my sergeants told them that the black sergeant was a god and they believed him. I Had the interpreter to tell them that he was only joking.

The school children gathered every morning in formation in front of Generalissimo Chiang Kai-Shek's picture and sang their national anthem. In this photo they had just finished.

Euell White

I received a Letter of appreciation from Generalissimo Chiang Kai-Shek for my participation in the combined exercise.

We had a lot of fun during our training as a team before going to Taiwan for the combined exercise with the Nationalist Chinese Army Special Forces. We went to the North Training Area on Okinawa for a few days. The most interesting and fun part of the training was with boats. The First Special Forces Group had a boat named "The Green Beret." I suppose it was in the tugboat class, but it could transport about 200 troops and their equipment. We spent several days in boat training. We practiced capsize drills with the rubber life boats and learned how to work as a team with the boats.

The final phase of this boat training was a night infiltration onto the island from the Green Beret in the life boats. There were several teams and each team was to have a boat. The Green Beret anchored about a mile from shore. Our team commander was Captain Drenzek and he was the type that wanted to do everything himself rather than delegate. During the training, each of had a turn as coxswain (the one who gives the commands). Some of the sergeants had experience at this, but the Captain insisted that he would be the coxswain. When we started loading, the master sergeant who was the Master of the Green Beret told us that one of the lifeboats was defective and we would have to tow a rope so that he could winch the boat back for another team to use. We got in the boat and the Captain gave the command, "Make way together." Everyone started rowing but I saw that we weren't' moving. I was in the back of the boat and the Captain was near the front. It was very dark and the diesel engines form the Green beret were making so much noise you couldn't hear anything. I felt the rope and discovered it was taut, the winch was locked. I could not get the attention of anyone on the Green Beret. Everyone in our boat was facing the beach and didn't know that we were not moving. I yelled to the captain that the winch was locked and I couldn't get the attention of the Green Beret crew. He told me to cut the rope.

When we arrived at the beach, the Captain told me to take one man and row the boat back to the Green Beret where we took on another 12-man team with their equipment. The boat was overloaded with just one 12-man team with equipment. I thought surely we would sink on the trip back to the beach but we made it.

Euell White

Korea 1966.

In the summer of 1966, I went to Korea again, this time as part of the planning group for the annual combined guerilla warfare exercise with The R.O.K. Republic of Korea) Special forces. About a dozen officers from Okinawa went to Seoul for the planning. We were billeted in Yong Son Compound where the 8th Army was headquartered. There was an American High School there for the dependents of those privileged to bring their dependents to Korea. We were billeted in the High School dormitory. The American Officers were on the ground floor and the Korean officers on the second floor. We worked in an underground bunker. During this planning phase I learned that if you work in close quarters with Koreans you must eat some Kimchi or you won't be able to stand it. Kimchi is fermented fruits and vegetables that has a strong odor. I remember when I was a kid, we would have community ice cream suppers. Every family would bring milk and other ingredients. Back then we got our milk directly from the cow without a dairy as go-between. Inevitably someone would bring milk from a cow that had eaten wild onions, giving the ice cream an onion flavor. My mother taught me that if you ate some onion before you ate the ice cream you wouldn't taste the onion in the ice cream. This also worked with Kimchi. If you ate some, you didn't smell it on others.

We learned the hard way about how important saving face is to the Koreans. It was our practice to play volleyball every afternoon on Okinawa. This was usually our daily exercise. We didn't have a rule book, but played according to what we called "combat rules." This meant there was no limit to the size of the teams and you could do just about anything. If you got near the net you were likely to get pounded on the head by the opposing team.

The Life Of A Soldier

Someone came up with the bright idea of inviting the Korean officers to play against us. They accepted, but they knew the rules and didn't know how to play any other way. We beat them because we were playing a different game. They lost face and it looked like we needed to get the State Department to solve an international crisis. Our commander, however, came up with a solution. He decided we would have a re-match and play by the rules. He made sure we understood that we were not to throw the game, but play the best we could. I never had any doubt about the outcome. Our team, fouled over and over because we didn't know the rules, and the Koreans beat us fair and square.

After a few days in the bunker I was given an assignment to go out and reconnoiter a large area of South Korea. I was provided a jeep, a sack full of Korean currency and accompanied by a R.O.K. Special Forces sergeant. The jeep was the model that was used in WW II and the Korean War.

Once as I was crossing a bridge going into a town, my brakes went out. I managed to get to a repair shop by gearing down. I was surprised when the man running the shop, opened up a big federal parts catalog to find the stock number of a wheel cylinder repair kit and had the parts arranged in bins by federal stock number. I learned that he had worked for the Americans. Although I knew he had stolen those parts, I was thankful that he had the parts he needed to fix the jeep.

Euell White

Chang Hung Korea, June 1966

The sergeant didn't know any more English than I knew Korean which was very little. I still have a little phrase book that we used to communicate by looking up the word in our own respective language and pointing to the definition beside it in the other's language.

During those days of driving around the countryside of Korea, I enjoyed learning about their culture. One thing that I saw every day and admired was their respect for elders. The old men wore stove-top hats that identified them as elders. As they walked about the younger people bowed to them and talked with them They equated age with wisdom. I hope this hasn't changed in the four decades since I was there.

The Life Of A Soldier

Our mission was to locate and photograph potential guerilla targets such as factories, bridges, etc., and locate parachute drop zones and landing zones for small aircraft. It was an interesting experience. Sometimes we slept on the ground and sometimes the best hotel in whatever town we were in. We ate the best Korean food money could buy.

The President of the Republic of Korea was on vacation in the area and we followed him for a few days. We would arrive at the hotel where he stayed the night before, and I would tell the waiters that we wanted the same food that the President ate when he was there. The sergeant never had it so good. One day we were stopped by a military police patrol and they warned us that there had been an assassination attempt on the President by guerillas from the North and they knew there were guerillas in the area. They cautioned us to be on the lookout.

One day as I was driving through a village, the people were lined up on either side of the narrow street to see the American. A little girl, about 3 or 4 years old, broke loose from her sister who was holding her hand and started to run across the street where she saw her mother and ran into the bumper of the jeep. I was driving very slow, in second gear. Immediately, the crowd closed in on us and I thought we had really had it. I later realized that they were mainly curious and wanted to see how badly the child was hurt.

The sergeant took charge and found out there was a medical clinic in a nearby town, but the parents wouldn't let us take them to the clinic. The Sergeant took a bar of soap, and two boxes of combat rations and gave them to the parents. He also gave them the forms they could use to file a claim, but if they ever filed a claim I didn't hear about it. We had no communication with the headquarters in Seoul, but a couple of days later we arrived at Kurye and went to the national police station, where I had spent a night in jail during the 1964 exercise when my team was captured. I had managed to get the message across to the sergeant that I needed to get to a telephone.

When we parked outside the station, the sergeant ordered a military police private that was at the police station, to guard our jeep while we were inside. I spent about 30 minutes trying to get a call through to Seoul to report the accident with the little girl, but couldn't get through. When we started to leave and got in the jeep, I opened the glove box to make sure my camera was there, and it was gone. The Sergeant turned white, then red, and he went back inside. I didn't have anyone to guard our stuff so I stayed in the jeep. In a little while I heard the soldier screaming and I assume begging for mercy and the noise of

The Life Of A Soldier

a scuffle going on inside. I was afraid that the sergeant was going to kill the man. About that time a plain clothes policemen who remembered me from when I was a guest in their jail, came by and he spoke good English. I asked him to watch the jeep and I went inside the station to stop the sergeant from killing the man. As I went in the front door, the sergeant and the Military policemen went out the back. I thought he was taking him out of my sight to kill him, but in a few minutes they returned with my camera.

I didn't know the details until a few days later when we were in an American Military Assistance Group compound and had an interpreter. The M.P. had walked away from the jeep for a moment to see what we were doing in the police station and when he returned to the jeep a bunch of kids were around it. He ran them off not realizing that they had already taken the camera. That is where the two of them went, to find the kids and get the camera back.

I could tell the sergeant was really down about it. Every time I would take the camera out of the glove box, he would hang his head in shame. I knew that if his officers were to learn about that incident he would probably be punished. When we talked with an interpreter, a few days later, I told him that when we returned to Seoul we would not mention about the camera to anyone. At that time he regained his smile.

Saving face, is a big deal with the Koreans. When we visited the American compound the first time a KATUSA drove the jeep to the motor pool, and apparently chided the sergeant for not driving the jeep. KATUSA stands for Korean Augmentation to the United States Army. These were Korean soldiers who spoke English and were selected to work with the Americans. The following morning when I finished breakfast, I found the jeep already parked in front of the house where I spent the night, with all my gear loaded. The sergeant was behind the wheel. He had never driven a vehicle before and we jumped and jerked til we were out the gate and out of sight of the compound, then I took over. I knew that he was saving face. We came back there several times and each time I would have to stop before we got there and let him drive so that no one saw me driving.

I became quite fond of this man. He was a Tae Kwando expert. I don't remember which belt he held, but a black belt was required before they could even join special forces. They practiced every day. When we were out on this mission that was the first thing he did every day. The special forces in the R.O.K. Army at that time, had a lot of authority. I was told the president trusted them more than any other unit, and they were considered the palace guard to protect him from a military coup. I do know that the officers carried weapons loaded with live ammunition at all times. One day on a narrow road we came upon a big bus that was stopped in the middle of the road, blocking us from passing, while someone was selling tea to the passengers. The sergeant, got out of the jeep and jumped up as high as his head and kicked the side of the bus right under the drivers window and yelled something to the driver. Immediately, the driver moved the bus out of the way so we could pass.

The Sergeant invited me to jump with him after we returned to Seoul. I accepted the invitation and we jumped on the Hahn River beach with steerable parachutes and he was the jumpmaster. I made my first and last standing landing and someone took a picture of it and gave it to me. Had the 1st Special Forces Group Commander seen me I would have had to pay a fine. It was against the rules. I didn't do it intentionally, the parachute slowed down so slow that I didn't have enough momentum to fall.

The Life Of A Soldier

Euell White

The Life Of A Soldier

Hahn River Beach, 1966

When the planning staff returned to Okinawa, I stayed in Korea as the C-4 (Combined Logistics Officer) to make preparations for the exercise. We were provided buildings for the staff offices and billeting for the staff and the teams on an engineer unit's compound. I had to obtain the materials for securing the area for the isolation phase– barbed wire, concertina wire, etc.-- and establish a mess hall to serve both Americans and Koreans.

All I had to begin with was one jeep, a handful of computer punch cards that were requisitions for the items I needed, and a letter from the G-4 of 8th U.S. Army directing all support depots to give me what I needed from them. At first I started getting nothing but the runaround, especially when I asked for several jeeps for the staff. I made one phone call to the 8th Army G-4, and had no more trouble after that except when the computer went down at the depot that had the barrier materials.

The depot relied on the computer to tell them where everything was located, and although I could see the items I needed on pallets as I drove along the road adjacent to the fence, they said they couldn't issue anything until the computer was up to tell them where the things were located. This went on for several days, but they finally came through.

I became somewhat anxious about this delay because the time was closing up on my opportunity to go back to Okinawa and see my family before the exercise actually began. I did however, have a few days on Okinawa between the planning and the exercise. I heard about an incident that happened during that same period I was having trouble getting materials from the supply depot. A major general who was commanding a division on the Demilitarize Zone, was having difficulty getting pierced steel planking which they used for floors in their Quonset huts. Finally, on a Sunday, he came to Seoul with a convoy of trucks, drove in the gate drew his pistol and disarmed the gate guard, then loaded up his trucks with what he needed and drove away. I would have given a lot to have witnessed that operation. As far as I know, the general was never punished for that. An effective leader must not be a bureaucrat and should never allow bureaucracy to take precedence over the welfare of his troops.

When the exercise actually began, we were pretty busy. We had 11 teams in all counting the Korean teams, and each team linked up with 55 civilians who played the part of guerillas for the exercise. The exercise was a combined one. The Korean commander of the Special Forces Operational Base was a Colonel whose name I can't remember, and the American commander was a Major Rung. Major Rung was so intent on having every aspect of the exercise combined, that he even decided that they would all eat the same food during the isolation phase, and that would be American food. I tried to talk him out of this, but he didn't want to hear that it wouldn't work.

One of the "B" team commanders was a Major Hayes, who was fluent in Korean. After a couple of days in isolation, he sent word that he needed to see me. I went to see him and he told me the Koreans were getting sick from the American food, or rather from the lack of rice and kimchi. The solution that we came up with was to add rice and kimchi to the line in the mess hall. This was not really pleasing to the Americans because of the odor of the Kimchi but they were, after all, Green Berets, and trained to endure such inconveniences.

We had one team that was to be infiltrated into its G.W.O.A. (Guerilla Warfare Operational Area) by locking out of a submarine. Another team, which was commanded by my friend, Captain Luke Johnson, infiltrated by HALO (High Altitude Low Opening) parachutes. They actually jumped from near 50,000 feet if my memory serves me correctly, and landed in a small space. They had spent months training together for this drop. The SCUBA team that was to lock out of the submarine was commanded by a Captain whose name I will omit—I will call him Captain Kenley, who was also one of my friends. The remaining nine teams infiltrated by conventional parachute. All of the infiltrations took place at night. There were some humorous incidents as well as some frustrations. Some of the frustrating ones are humorous looking back on them.

Captain Kenley's team forgot an essential item of their equipment when they boarded the submarine. I didn't then and still don't know anything about scuba diving. They didn't bother to tell the submarine captain about their oversight until it was near time for them to do their thing. This situation was illuminated by the fact that several VIPs came out to observe this joint operation of the Army and Navy. What really happened was that the submarine surfaced and they swam to shore on the surface. I could have done that without any training.

When Kenley was asked by one of the VIPs why they did this, he replied that the Submarine captain had decided it was unsafe to lock out. This was half truth. Really it was impossible for them to do what they were supposed to because they didn't have the needed equipment.

On orders from our commander, I dropped a Lieutenant Frye in by parachute to replace Kenley, with a message for him to return to the base as soon as possible. After months of training the team didn't get to do it. I don't think Kenley realized that there would be people on the beach watching and thought he could cover up his oversight. The HALO jump went well.

We re-supplied the teams by parachute. One night we would have a C-130 from the U.S. Air Force and the next night a C-46 from the R.O.K. Air Force. I flew with the resupply missions almost every night once the resupply schedule started. The U.S. Air Force had a safety regulation that they must fly at least 1,000 feet above the highest terrain feature within a certain radius. In order to have the parachutes open at a low altitude and reduce the drifting, my parachute riggers devised a system using demolition time fuse, so that the parachute opening was delayed. This system required them to know exactly at what altitude the plane would be flying because they had to cut the time fuze to the appropriate length when they rigged the bundles. This system worked very well. We might be flying at 5,000 feet but the parachute would open at 500 feet.

The R.O.K. Air Force had no such safety rule. They flew at whatever altitude we wanted to drop from. One

The Life Of A Soldier

evening when the R.O.K. Air force was flying for us, the pilot had heard about the delayed opening system, and decided he wanted to do this. I was very wary of it, but he insisted. I explained very carefully through an interpreter, that he must decide in advance what his altitude would be and stick to it and that we wouldn't be able to change once we rigged for the drop. He said he understood. One of my riggers and I went on the mission. When we were approaching the drop zone I thought that we were much lower than we were supposed to be. When the green light and the bell came on, I pushed the bundles out of the door I was in and the rigger pushed his bundles. Then the plane went into a steep climb. I ran to the front of the cargo compartment. There is an altimeter at the front of the cargo compartment in the C-46. I saw that we were so low, that the parachutes would hit the ground long before the time fuse burned up. When we returned to the base, the pilot was smiling and made a comment that it was a "number one" meaning "good" drop. I said "no, number 10, the parachutes didn't open." He was puzzled by my comment.

The next morning at our daily combined briefing, the Korean Colonel was upset because those parachutes didn't open. The team we were re-supplying was an all Korean team and the drop included M-1 rifles for the guerillas, rice and other food items for the Koreans and medical supplies. Of course, the rice and medical supplies were all mixed together and the rifles were damaged beyond repair. This illustrates, as does the incident I wrote about in the Taiwan exercise, how difficult it is to communicate with people of another culture. It is more than language. It is a way of thinking and reasoning.

The day I returned to Korea for the exercise, after my brief time with my family back on Okinawa, there was a message for me from Captain Ho Hwap Yong, the officer I had befriended in 1964 when he played the part of the

Guerilla Chief for our team. I learned that he had been in Vietnam with one of the Korean Divisions when I was there in 1965 and tried to locate me. He came to Nha Trang to look for me and arrived there the day after I was evacuated to Okinawa. I called the number he had left and found that he was assigned as Aid de Camp to a General who was their equivalent to our Army Deputy Chief of Staff. We agreed to meet at a hotel dining room in Seoul for dinner on a certain evening. Dan Biggs was the C-1 for the exercise and I asked him to go with me. .

    Ho arrived at the hotel in a staff car and told us that we were going to a party instead of eating at the hotel. Dan and I sat in the back of the car and Ho sat in front with the driver. I sensed that something was wrong with Ho. He wasn't talking and he had this expression that I had seen before when he was upset about something. He told us this was a party that would be attended by the very highest ranking military officers of all their services.

    When we arrived, he asked us to wait in the car, then he got out and went inside. I told Dan that something was wrong and my guess was that we weren't invited to the party and he was trying to get us invited. When he came out, Ho was really sad looking. He sat in the car saying nothing for awhile. I broke the silence and told him I thought I knew what was wrong and it was okay. That we understood and we could get together again later on. He was so embarrassed. He had lost a lot of face. He had his car take us back to the hotel where our jeep was parked.

    That "later on" never came. Once the exercise got underway we were so busy we didn't get around to it. Then one day, a helicopter with stars indicating a three star general, landed right in front of the building that we were using for a warehouse. Ho, got out of the helicopter and told me that he was leaving Seoul. His boss had been reassigned as a corps commander. He regained some face by demonstrating that he could use the general's helicopter.

The Life Of A Soldier

I regret that I lost contact with this man. He was one of the most honest and moral men I have ever met. In 1968 while in Vietnam for my second tour, my handbag was stolen at Ton Son Nhute airbase and all my addresses, including his, were in the bag.

My Korean Counterpart, for the 1966 exercise, a captain whose name I can't remember. We had a very good working relationship.

One memorable incident that the Captain in the photo above shared with me was a flight in a typhoon. We had been unable to supply one of the guerilla teams by parachute, so we decided to fly their needed supplies to Taegu, which was near them, and let the exercise controllers deliver them by truck. The Captain and I both decided to go on the flight which was a C-46 flown by a Korean Air Force Pilot.

The weather was beautiful as we left Kimpo on that Saturday afternoon, but about half way to Taegu we ran into a storm. There was a typhoon and we were in some very strong winds. I had a parachute on and gave some thought to jumping, but I figured I might end up in North Korea even if I survived the jump.

When we arrived at Taegu the pilot made several approaches but the plane was swaying back and forth. Finally he touched down and we bounced up and down from the runway several times, then just fell down on it and stopped. The wind was so strong we had to remove our berets to keep them from being blown away and had to push hard against the wind to walk to the operations building. When we got inside, the pilot said to me. "I think maybe we don't fly back today," to which I replied, "I know maybe I won't fly back today." The Captain and I stayed overnight and rode the UN train back to Seoul the next day.

The Korean Colonel who was the commander for the exercise wanted everything given to him in his own language, but I knew that he could understand everything said in English. Often he would forget to wait for the interpreter and ask me a question through the interpreter when I was doing the briefing.

When we were leaving Okinawa to come home, we stayed at the Fort Buckner Officer's club for the last couple of days. One evening while we were dining there, that colonel, who had since been promoted to Brigadier General, was visiting Okinawa and was in the club with his entourage of Korean officers, seated at a table next to ours. I saw him and as we got up from our table, I said "Good evening general,' and he replied, "Good evening Captain White" then proceeded to converse with me in flawless English.

The 1966 exercise in Korea was the last significant thing I was involved in with the 1st Special Forces group. We returned to Okinawa in November, then we came back to the United states in January 1967.

The Life Of A Soldier

Appendix E

Vietnam 1965

I deployed from Okinawa to Vietnam in August 1965 as a First Lieutenant and executive officer (XO) of a special forces "A" team, commanded by Captain James Walker. We had trained to work with a specific Montagnard (Mountain) tribe, but our mission was changed when we arrived at the Special Forces base at Nha Trang. Our team was assigned to Project Delta. This was an elite unit within the elite.

Project Delta was commanded by Major Charlie Beckwith, commonly referred to as "Charging Charlie Beckwith." As his nickname implies, he was a colorful character. Project Delta consisted of reconnaissance teams and an airborne ranger battalion. The reconnaissance teams were made up of Vietnamese Special Forces L.L.D.B. (Luoc Luong Dac Biet) and/or Chinese mercenaries (Nungs).

The teams were led by U.S. Special Forces noncommissioned officers. The 91st Airborne Ranger Battalion, the only airborne ranger battalion in the South Vietnamese Army, had four companies. American Special Forces officers and NCOs were advisors to the ranger battalion.

Project Delta would go into an area where they were requested by the local commanders. The reconnaissance teams would be inserted clandestinely by helicopter or by parachute and they would locate the enemy. Then, depending upon the size of the enemy force, the ranger battalion would attack or be part of a larger attack force. I don't know whether any of the teams were ever inserted by parachute, but Delta had smoke jumpers equipment sufficient to equip the ranger battalion to jump into jungle terrain.

The Life Of A Soldier

Charging Charlie was not in Nha Trang when we arrived, but he came in like a whirlwind a few days later and sent for Jim Walker, Master Sergeant Lloyd Fisher (our team sergeant), and me. He gave us a brief description of the mission of Project Delta and promised each of us a medal or a body bag or both. As it turned out, I got two medals--a purple heart and bronze star for valor-- and came very near to getting the body bag. Jim Walker got the purple heart but I don't know what else. One of the NCOs on our Okinawa Team, Sergeant George Hoagland, was killed after I was evacuated. He was on one of the reconnaissance teams.

The major said that he would not hesitate to volunteer for any mission if he believed we could accomplish it, no matter what the cost. . He was letting us know that we were expendable. During his briefing of us, he made reference to some of the off duty activities of the troops, and made the remark "I am a puritan myself." When he said that I laughed, and he said "Lieutenant what do you find so funny?" I replied that his language, which was colorful to put it mildly, would never give him away as a puritan. When he finished his briefing, he told us to get our team together and load onto the C-47 cargo plane.

Beckwith had served with the British SAS (Special Air Service) years before on an officer exchange program, and had seen combat with them. Ever since his tour with the Brits he had been trying to convince the pentagon that we needed a commando-type unit such as the SAS where the commander would have direct command and control of all his assets for any mission. I learned of this later by reading his books.

During Jimmy Carter's presidency, Colonel Beckwith organized and trained the first sky marshals, and he was the commander of the joint task force that attempted the rescue of the hostages in Iran. Ironically, according to the reports I read, that mission's failure was primarily due to the very weakness that Beckwith sought to overcome. The helicopters collided during refueling killing several and the mission was aborted. The President had insisted that this be a joint operation and that Navy and Marine helicopters be used.

In Project Delta, Beckwith had a little of what he was trying to sell to the Pentagon. He had two C-47 cargo planes and four H-34 helicopters that were under his direct control. I had the impression that Beckwith paid the Vietnamese pilots, or at least supplemented their pay from CIA funds, although they wore the uniform of the Vietnamese Air Force. These aircraft were obsolete, but the pilots were skilled and would go anywhere, anytime that Beckwith ordered them regardless of the danger involved.

We flew in to Bien Hoa air base after Major Beckwith's briefing in one of the C-47s and our team went on a three day operation in the Tay Ninh Province. It was a post-strike analysis for a B-52 strike, and was led by Captain Len Boulas . We were told that we were only observers. It was educational to see the effect of the B-52 bombing. We had a map overlay that showed the area they were supposed to bomb. It was truly amazing. They bombed from maybe 50,000 feet, yet the area that was on our overlay was completely pulverized and there was very little damage outside that.

I don't know what was supposed to be there, but nearby we found medical supplies like a hospital had been there, and Russian typewriters which we assumed was for propaganda production. There was so much stuff that we called in a Chinook cargo helicopter to take this stuff out.

We walked for two more days and had some minor contacts, ending up at Tay Ninh then were flown back to Bien Hoa. I think the main purpose of that operation was to get us acclimated. On the last day of that trek, we ran out of water and all of us, I suppose, were near dehydration. I drank some water from a rice paddy that was filthy beyond description, to avoid dehydration. Amazingly, I didn't get sick from it and when I was tested for parasites I was clear.

At the helicopter pad at Tay Ninh immediately after arriving there from the three day operation. There was a sign there reading "Tay Ninh International Airport" and telling how many miles to San Francisco.

Euell White

At Tay Ninh after a night's sleep

While at Bien Hoa, I met Captain Tom Pusser who was the senior advisor to the 91st Airborne Ranger Battalion. I was assigned as his assistant and was to replace him when he went home, but we both became casualties at Plei Me on 22 October.

While we were at Bien Hoa we had our meals at a mess hall in a MACV (Military Assistance Command

The Life Of A Soldier

Vietnam) compound. The people there were afflicted with the anti-elite virus. Captains Jim Walker, Tom Pusser, the infamous Bo Gritz and myself would go together.

Bo Gritz is a retired Lieutenant Colonel who has been in the news a lot. He was one of our instructors when I attended the Special Forces Officer course in 1964 at Fort Bragg. Bo was working with the recon teams. The MACV people didn't want us to take our weapons inside their compound. I don't know why unless they were afraid we would shoot the place up. They showed a movie in the mess hall each night and required that everyone attending the movie have a weapon with them in case the compound was attacked. This put us in a bind, but we worked around it by taking pistols and concealing them until we got through the gate. They charged us about four times as much as their officers paid for our meals. They assumed we were all drawing temporary duty pay. Actually Jim Walker and I were, but the others were not. The food was excellent so we didn't mind paying for it.

We wore what we called tiger suits which was unique to special operations, and we wore no insignia of rank when we were operational. This bothered the MACV people. One day the four of us, three captains and one 1st Lieutenant, were stopped by a 2d Lieutenant who chewed us out for not saluting him. We all stood at attention and took the chewing out, then saluted him. I was promoted to Captain in September.

The anti-elite attitude was not so uncommon in those days and exists at some levels today. I believe this was a factor in the stupid attempt a few years ago to discredit the Green Beret and the Airborne Beret.

After the shakedown in Tay Ninh Province, Jim Walker and half of our Okinawa team was assigned to the training camp at Dong Ba Thin, a few miles south of Nha Trang. I was never clear on what their specific mission was.

The other NCOs were assigned to reconnaissance teams. I was assigned as advisor to the 91st Airborne Ranger Battalion and was to replace Captain Tom Pusser who was due to go home soon. I visited Jim Walker once at the training camp, then I never saw him again until I ran into him the day I landed at Bien Hoa on my second tour in Vietnam, on 11 December 1967.

In October 1965 Major Beckwith took two of the ranger companies and Delta headquarters staff to a training center at Qui Nhon for training. The other two companies were providing security for Special Forces camps. I Never saw Qui Nhon except from the air. I dropped the 5th Group deputy commander, a Lieutenant Colonel Bennet, by parachute from one of the C-47s for a visit with Delta there. I think he went there to deliver the order for Project delta to relieve the Plei Me camp that was under siege.

Beckwith left me at Nha Trang to work with the ranger battalion staff in preparation for what was for them a change in the supply system. They had not been under the supply system of their army, but had been supplied by Delta. This meant they never had a shortage of anything they needed. They knew this would not be the case if it changed and they were not eagerly anticipating such a change. In fact, they didn't seem to believe it would ever happen and I don't know whether it did or not.

The Life Of A Soldier

At the SFOB Nha-Trang 1965

Euell White

In mid October, 1965, the Special Forces camp at Plei Me in the Central highlands came under attack by troops of the 32nd, 33rd, and 66th Regiments of the North Vietnamese Army (NVA). This action, which was described as a siege, went on for days and was the prelude to a long drawn out operation in the Ia Drang Valley. But for good weather and the U.S. Air Force, the camp would have been overrun. This was hot news at the 5th Group base at Nha Trang. Everyone was listening to the radio traffic and concerned about the "A" Team at Plei Me commanded by a Captain Moore.

On the evening of 20 October, Major Beckwith called me on the secure radio and told me that Project Delta was moving to Pleiku to stage for a mission to relieve the camp at Plei Me. He said to me, "If you are making any money, stay there, but if not, meet us at Pleiku." I checked on transportation and found that the next opportunity would be the following morning. The Commanding General of the L.L.D.B. (Vietnamese Special Forces) was flying to Pleiku in one of the C-47s.

I didn't sleep well that night. It would have been easier if Beckwith had simply ordered me to meet him at Pleiku and I have always wondered if he did it that way to test me. One of the NCOs, Sergeant First Class Leone, who was a part of our Okinawa team, overheard the radio conversation and urged me not to go, predicting that I would be killed.

I cannot describe what it was like that evening lying on my bunk, knowing that the following day I was going into that situation that I had been monitoring on the radio and knew that it would be terrible. When I see a World War II movie of the troops on the ships on the way to the

The Life Of A Soldier

Normandy invasion, I can identify with their feelings. Beckwith left me with the option of staying put or joining them, but, I knew immediately that I would go, even if I had been "making money."

On 21 October I flew to Pleiku and found that Delta had just landed by helicopter about five miles from Plei Me. They were unable to land at Plei Me because of the anti-aircraft fire of the NVA.(North Vietnamese Army). I began trying to get a ride into the Camp and was told the first thing going in would be a medevac flight. I found the commander of the medevac unit, a major, and he told me to move into his tent and he would get me there as soon as he had clearance to fly into Plei Me.

While I was seeking a ride I met Sergeant Jimmie McBynum. He was a Special Forces medic with the C team at Pleiku who was going to Plei Me to help out because some of the medics there had become casualties. Later on in the day Project Delta called for a medevac while enroute to the camp. The medevac commander told me he was going to take the mission himself and get me out to my unit. I found Sergeant McBynum and told him he could go with us but he had his focus on getting to the camp where he was needed. He was afraid this would be a delay.

I joined Delta on the ground in the late afternoon. When nightfall came we were near the camp but not there yet. Major Beckwith called the camp on the radio and gave them our location. The camp commander said he would send out a patrol to meet us and guide us into the camp. A few minutes later we heard the automatic weapons fire as the patrol was ambushed just outside the gate. The patrol withdrew into the camp. Then Beckwith gave the camp commander our grid coordinates to draw a circle around us and told him to go ahead and employ air strikes everywhere except that circle.

We formed the troops in a tight perimeter for the night. There were four journalists with us. I don't know what news agencies they represented. I was standing right next to Beckwith when one of the journalists came up to him and said, "Major I want to know what you are doing to provide for our security." Beckwith's reply is not appropriate for printing but the essence of it was to lie down, be still and be quiet.

The Air Force bombed all around us nearly all night. The bombs were so close at times that the concussion would lift us off the ground. The next morning, 22 October, we went into the camp through the main gate. On the way, one of our journalists, a cameraman, was shot through the camera lens in the eye. Joe Galloway, co-author of the book, "We Were Soldiers Once...and Young," recently told me that the journalist died from that wound. One of the American Special Forces NCOs with Project Delta was carrying his rifle with the muzzle pointed downward and his finger on the trigger. . A sniper shot him in the shoulder and he involuntarily pulled the trigger and shot another NCO in the foot. Fortunately the bullet just went into his boot and didn't' hurt him.

As far as I know those were the only American casualties we had on the way to the camp but there were some Vietnamese casualties. When we arrived at the camp there was a sense of chaos. I don't mean this as criticism. War itself is chaos. The Montagnard troops that the "A" team trained and led, had their families living just outside the gate. When the siege began they moved inside. The NVA had been attacking with mortar and recoilless rifles as well as storming the fence trying to penetrate the camp. The building they called the team house where the "A" team lived had been hit and it was in somewhat of a shambles. There were bodies of the NVA on the perimeter fence, and the stench of death permeated the camp. When I looked around I thought that if we got a mortar attack there were not enough trenches and holes for everyone to take cover.

Around noon, soon after we arrived, I was watching as one of our H-34 helicopters came in on Beckwith's orders to bring something he needed. Someone got off the helicopter—I can't remember who—and told me that Jimmie McBynum didn't make it. I found out that Sergeant McBynum was hit and killed before the helicopter landed.

A few days later, while I was in the 8th Field Hospital at Nha Trang, a friend of Sergeant McBynum visited me and told me that when Jimmy found out he could get to Plei Me on the H-34, he started desperately searching for a chaplain. He told his friend that he knew he was going to die that day. His friend told him that if he felt that way, maybe he shouldn't go since the H-34 flight was an unauthorized flight. But Jimmy said he had to go because it was his duty. His friend said that he saw McBynum again just before he boarded the helicopter and was told that he found a chaplain, and he seemed to have peace.

Jimmy McBynum was a Black man. I mention his race only because it occurred to me that at that time in history, he could not have joined me in a restaurant for a meal or cup of coffee in his home town in North Carolina, nor in my hometown for that matter.

In the afternoon of 22 October Major Beckwith alerted Tom Pusser and me that we were to take the two ranger companies and one company of the Montagnards and conduct a sweep of the high ground adjacent to the camp. Our mission as I understood it, was to clear any remaining resistance, count bodies, and recover documents and weapons from the dead. We didn't know that we were up against two regiments plus, with about 200 Vietnamese soldiers and less than a hundred Montagnards. It didn't matter. We would have gone anyway.

As Tom was assembling all of the U.S. advisors for briefing, he told me to locate the journalists and invite them. I found the three surviving journalists hunkered down in the corner of the team house. I told them what we were going to do and said, "If you want to see the action this is where it is." I had no idea how prophetic this was. All three of the journalists declined my invitation.

We went out the gate and passed the Montagnard family housing, to the high ground without seeing anyone or meeting any resistance. Tom was with one of the ranger companies and I with the other. I don't remember who was with the CIDG company, but I suppose it was one of the NCOs from Captain Moore's team.

After we had swept along the long axis of the plateau, we were to turn around and go back in the direction from which we had come to cover ground we hadn't covered. Tom's company was to swing around so that he would still be on the right side of me. During the turning maneuver, Tom came by where we were searching the body of a Chinese officer and told me his radio was out. He asked me to call the camp and tell them they could communicate with him through his Vietnamese counterpart's radio.

That was the last time I saw Tom. A few minutes later we started receiving automatic weapons fire from the direction we had come. At first I thought it was Tom's company firing at us. We got the company turned around and the company commander ordered an assault. We had by-passed the NVA machine gun positions. I later learned that some of the NVA soldiers were chained to their machine guns.

I can never fault the company commander. He was aggressive. He would wave his swagger stick and yell something and the troops would charge. I saw one of the ranger platoon leaders shot in the crotch. One of the Special Forces NCO's ran to him and was there almost by the time he hit the ground, but he was already dead. We were taking a lot of casualties and getting nowhere.

An Air Force observer came over and contacted me on the radio. He said he had some napalm for me and wanted to know if we were at a safe distance. I asked the company commander his opinion and he said we were too close and immediately ordered a withdrawal.

The withdrawal turned into a rout and I understand they never stopped til they were back inside the camp. I have heard some criticism of this, but anyone who has studied military tactics and history of warfare, knows that any retrograde maneuver requires a lot of control measures or control will be lost. The initial stages of the Korean War provides some good examples of this.

I was at a disadvantage in that I had not worked with this company commander before. We didn't know each other. Neither did I know the Special Forces NCOs who were with me. I must have taken no more than three steps after we turned around when a bullet struck me in the back missing my spine and right kidney by only a hair. The bullet exited my right side and went through my right forearm. The bullet didn't knock me down but I sat down. Immediately I was alone. The Rangers were so focused on getting out of there they either didn't see me or didn't bother. None of my NCO's were near me at that time and apparently none of them saw that I was hit.

I continued to communicate with the Air Force and continued with the napalm strike. The fact that I was not hit by the napalm was proof that the withdrawal wasn't necessary. I can appreciate, however the caution of that company commander since he was depending on me, a complete stranger to him, to communicate with the Air Force. As far as I know from reading later accounts of the action, the napalm strike was ineffective. I know that the

NVA kept firing at me and the bullets were kicking up dirt all around me as they conducted the napalm strike..

I called the Camp and told them I was wounded and they told me they couldn't help me at the moment. My thoughts as I continued to communicate with the Air Force observer, and saw the dirt being kicked up around me as the North Vietnamese soldiers continued to fire at me, was for my wife Euna and daughter Sherry Lynn who were on Okinawa. I knew that if I didn't get out, the enemy would eventually come for me. Considering this I realized that there was no way I could prevail in a fight with them and decided that if they came I would not resist so that they would capture me. I remember recounting this to some of my friends after returning to Okinawa and one of them said he would fight until they killed him. But he had not ever been in that predicament. It is easy to say what you woul have done if you have never been in a situation. I hear political candidates say what they would have done in certain situations if they had been president.

I was in shock and thought I was hurt worse than I was. Eventually Sergeant First Class Holloway whom I had only met that day, came back for me. He found a hole which was like a foxhole but designed for a small man, and got me into the hole. He was in the prone position beside the hole as he called in a mortar smoke screen from the camp. Holloway was a heavy weapons NCO and knew all about all mortars. He told me that when the screen was in place, we would have to move immediately and fast.

I intended to recommend Holloway for a medal. While I was in hospital later on, I received from the Project Delta adjutant a citation that was already written with the instructions that if I wanted Holloway to get the medal I should just sign off on what they had written. I felt it was inadequate but I signed it and never learned what medal he received. I have tried for years to contact Holloway.

The Life Of A Soldier

When the smokescreen was in place, Sergeant Holloway, grabbed me by my good arm and pulled me up from the hole. We started running but there was only a brief lull in the NVA fire. We had to do the low crawl for quite a distance until we were out of their line of fire. Then we pretty much ran the rest of the way til we were on the back side of the camp perimeter fence, and went in through a hole that was made for the rangers to come in earlier.

As we went through the fence one of Delta's s staff NCOs, Sergeant Shaw, was there and I said, "Tom Pusser is dead, isn't he?" He acknowledged that he was. I had no way of knowing this. It was premonition, a phenomenon I have experienced many times.

Although I hadn't known Tom for very long, I felt close to him. A few weeks earlier we had gone to Saigon together and I had helped him shop for Christmas presents for his 13-year-old sister, Betsy. He was to be home before Christmas. Tom was from South Carolina and a West Point graduate. He was not married. Tom was truly a professional soldier.

While I was out there that day, wounded and alone I was certain that the North Vietnamese would eventually come and get me and that I would be killed or captured. A few years ago when I read the book, "We Were Soldiers Once...and Young" by Joe Galloway and General Hal Moore, about the battle at LZ Xray, only 13 miles in distance and a few days away in time from Plei Me, where then Lieutenant Colonel Moore's 1st Battalion, 7th Cavalry confronted the same enemy that we were up against--then saw a TV interview of the North Vietnamese Officer who was in command of that force--- I realized that if I had remained there until dark, I would have been killed. When the NVA general was asked why his troops killed Moore's wounded men during the night, he replied that it was their policy in the Ia Drang Valley campaign to take no wounded prisoners.

> **From a letter to my brother, Almon while in 8th field Hospital**
> I really came out lucky on my wounds. The bullet that came in my back barely missed my kidney. If it had hit my kidney I probably wouldn't have made it because I would have fainted. If I hadn't been able to walk, run and crawl the Viet Cong would have captured me and they were so desperate that I am sure they would have just shot me where they found me...As glad as I am to be going to Okinawa, I feel a little bad that I am leaving with the others still out there fighting....There have been two more Americans wounded out there that were with me. One of them, a sergeant major, hovered over me like a mother hen that night while I was lying in a bunker in the camp wounded. The next day he went out with the same mission and they shot up his arm so badly he will probably lose it. They didn't bring him to this hospital, so I haven't seen him.

I spent the night of 22 October in an underground bunker that was being used as a hospital. There was a Special

The Life Of A Soldier

Forces doctor there, a Captain Hunter. I recently read a book by Dr. Lanny Hunter and learned that he was awarded the Distinguished Service Cross (DSC), the Silver Star, The Bronze Star and the Purple Heart. When he was caring for me through the night of 22-23 October, he had been wounded himself but refused evacuation because he was needed there. I was in pain all night, mainly because I couldn't urinate. The muscle that allows you to do that was shocked.

I was never in a position in either of my three Vietnam tours where I had to actually fire my weapon. I am grateful for that. I killed enemy soldiers by directing artillery and air strikes, but never fired at an enemy soldier with my weapon. Ironically, Lanny Hunter, a Medical Doctor who was supposed to be a non-combatant, had to kill with a rifle at Plei Me because they were about to be overrun. This happened before the arrival of Project delta.

If Major Beckwith ever came in to see me that night I wasn't aware of it, but his new Operations Officer, Captain Bo Baker, came in and out all night. Bo had just joined Delta and I had never met him until I joined up with them on the afternoon of the 21st. That night Bo and I slept under the same poncho and huddled together because it was so cold. Bo was soon to be promoted to major and I believe he succeeded Beckwith when he was critically wounded in 1966. Colonel Bo Baker died on active duty as commander of the Special forces Group at Bad Tolz Germany a few years ago.

According to Lanny Hunter, Joe Galloway, co-author of "We were Soldiers Once and Young." Came in on the medevac chopper that took me out. The medevac chopper took me to Camp Holloway at Pleiku where they checked me over, then on to the 8th Field Hospital at Nha Trang adjacent to the 5th Group base. While I was in the dispensary at Pleiku, the pilot of the medevac chopper came in to see me, and I was surprised to see who he was. I can no longer remember his name, but he was one of my classmates in the Infantry Officer Basic Course at Fort Benning in 1962. He was an R.O.T.C. graduate and I had done some one-on-one tutoring of him on leadership while we were in school. In our class most of the lieutenants were right out of college. There were about a half-dozen like me who were commissioned from the ranks. Most of the R.O.T.C. guys recognized that we knew some things that would help them when they became platoon leaders, and relied on us for guidance. Some, of course, thought their college degrees automatically made them smarter than us.

The medevac pilot asked me if I remembered him and admired my boots. The medics had taken them off. At that time, only the Special Forces had the jungle boots that later became standard issue for all troops in Vietnam. I gave him the boots because I could get more at no cost. I never saw him again, but a few days after I returned to Okinawa, my boots arrived. I suppose he felt guilty for taking them, but I wanted him to have them.

In his book, *My Soul To Keep,"* Doctor Hunter describes the medevac: *"The Dust Off came in...braving anti-aircraft fire. As it flared and touched down, Joe Galloway, a reporter for United Press International, leaped off...We piled on Shea, Moore, Sloan and White, KTLA-TV's Burnett, and a couple of Yards and Rangers. The Dust Off pilot revved the Lycombing prior to lift off. I heard someone bellowing behind me, 'There's an airstrike laid on!' Someone yelled, "Get him out!' Someone else, "hold him !' I shouted at the crew chief, and the pilot throttled back on the Huey. In the confusion, Berry got in touch with Tac Air. The strike was held for a moment. Everyone was yelling at the chopper. "Go! Get out! Now! Now!' We watched tensely as the chopper lifted off and pounded toward the east, skimming the ground. Moments later a*

The Life Of A Soldier

flight of F-105s screamed in on the deck and discharged their ordnance. The Dust off cleared the ridge safely.

Shea was one of the team medics of the team based at Plei Me. Moore was Captain Moore, the team leader there. Sloan was Sergeant Sloane, one of the weapons specialists of the team. He was in the ward with me at 8th Field Hospital.

At 8th field hospital the surgeons did surgery on me. I had never before had surgery and the only time I had been hospitalized was when I fractured my ankle on a parachute jump at Fort Benning in 1952. There was no visit from the surgeon nor from the anesthesiologist to tell me what was going to happen. A heavy-set, jovial female major came in with a needle and rubbed alcohol on my arm, then as she injected the needle, said "I am the gas passer." That was the last thing I was aware of until I awoke after the surgery. Just as I awoke, I understood the pun and began laughing.

I can't remember what they called the surgery but it involved connecting the entry and exit wounds, determining the extent of the damage and cleaning it. When Euna saw me a few days later she said it looked as though they had cut me half in two.

When I awoke I was in the recovery ward. This was a long concrete block building with a lot of beds, probably about 30 or 40. The ward was air conditioned and had hospital beds. I was told I could remain in that ward as long as they had enough beds if I could endure all of the activity there. The alternative was a hot tent without the comforts. I opted for the noisy air conditioning and stayed there until I was evacuated to Okinawa.

I was hospitalized on Saturday 23 October 1965. The following day, I was told that I had to put on a pajama shirt because General Westmoreland was coming to pin the purple heart medal on me. I learned that this was his practice, to go to the nearest field hospital on Sunday, visit the wounded and pin purple hearts.

The surgeon had just finished cleaning out my wounds and applying fresh gauze–which became his daily routine–and had given me a shot of Demarol which gave me a feeling of euphoria and dulled my natural shyness and inhibitions. The General recognized me. He had a gift for remembering faces and names. I had met him at Fort Campbell when I was a sergeant and he was commanding general of the 101st Airborne Division, under circumstances that were memorable. He said, "Captain, we have met before but you were not an officer then." After acknowledging this and telling him I was in the 502nd in 1958-60, he asked me about the enemy we were up against at Plei Me. I told him they were uniformed NVA soldiers, apparently well-trained, well-equipped, and well disciplined, and that they were either led or advised by Chinese officers.

This conclusion on my part was based on the Chinese officer that we had found just a few minutes before I was wounded. I didn't get a chance to tell the general this, because a colonel who was with him and standing behind him looked at me, frowned and shook his head, giving me the message that the subject was off limits. The general smiled and changed the subject.

Later, while still in hospital at Nha Trang, one of the NCOs who was with me at Plei Me came by for a visit and told me that intelligence had confirmed that the man we found was indeed a Chinese officer. In 1966, while in Korea, I read in the Pacific Stars and Stripes newspaper that although there had been reports of Chinese in South Vietnam, there were no Chinese Soldiers in South Vietnam. This was an official government statement. Then when I read the book, We Were Soldiers Once...and Young, I learned that the 1st battalion, 7th Cavalry, fighting the same NVA force at LZ XRAY that we fought at Plei Me, also found the body of what they presumed to be a Chinese officer and told General Westmoreland about it. His reaction to that report, however, was not as subtle as his reaction to mine.

According To General Hal Moore, General Westmoreland went to Pleiku on 18 November 1965 to be briefed on the battle at LZ XRAY. During the briefing, Captain Matt Dillon mentioned a report that the body of an enemy soldier had been seen that they suspected was Chinese. He was large and dressed in a uniform different from the NVA. According to Moore, Westmoreland reacted angrily and forcefully, saying: "You will never mention anything about Chinese soldiers in South Vietnam! Never!" General Moore thought that Westmoreland's sensitivity to this issue may have been provoked by an article by Charles Mohr in the November 17, 1965 issue of the New York Times about some prisoners captured near the Plei Me camp appearing in a Saigon news conference and telling reporters that each People's Army regiment had one Chinese Communist adviser. Moore thought that Westmoreland was reacting this way because of President Johnson's fear of Chinese intervention in Vietnam, remembering what happened in Korea.

On Monday, two days after the surgery, I awakened hungry and smelled food. I saw a food cart at the other end of the ward working its way toward me. I was all set to receive my food, but the cart passed by my bed without stopping. I said, "Hey what about me?" The soldier with the cart looked at my chart and said you can have only clear liquids. When I asked what that meant, he said I could have water, black coffee or apple juice, but he quickly added that they were out of apple juice. I could see that the trays had scrambled eggs, bacon and toast. I had him bring me water and black coffee, but my stomach was complaining.

Later on that morning, Captain Posey, a Medical Service Corps officer who was one of my classmates at the Special Warfare School and jumpmaster for my 52nd parachute jump, and was in charge of medical supplies at the 5th Special Forces Group, came to visit me. After he asked how I was doing, I said, "Lets do the last thing first then we can visit. You know the part where you ask me if there is anything you can do for me. I need some apple juice." Posey left and came back in a few minutes with a case of 46 ounce cans of apple juice. Each can had a strip of masking tape with my name on it. The following day they allowed me to start eating real food so I donated the apple juice to the other patients. That was the old army. It didn't occur to me to complain to my congressman nor to the media that they didn't have enough apple juice.

I was supposed to be a bed pan patient, but that was too humiliating for me. I managed to get up and walk or shuffle to the latrine, though it was painful and slow. The surgeon, a Captain Moore, would come through the ward on his way to breakfast and speak to his patients, then return after breakfast to examine and treat us. He would give me a shot of demerol, pull away gauze he had inserted the day before, clean out the wound then insert fresh gauze and bandage. His method was to not suture the wound until it healed from the inside out.

The care I received from Dr. Moore and the nurses in the ward was excellent and professional. I did, however, have some problems with two of their enlisted medics, both Specialist 4s. At first I couldn't urinate and had to have a catheter. One day the nurse told these two medics to do the catheter. I had dozed off and was awakened by their voices as they were preparing for it. I kept my eyes closed and heard one of them say he would like to just punch me in the face. The other one made a similar remark about me and about officers in general. I opened my eyes and told them to get away from my bed and get the nurse. When the nurse

The Life Of A Soldier

came I told her I didn't want either of them doing anything for me.

There was a Korean marine in the bed next to Sergeant Sloane, from the "A" team at Plei Me. The Korean marine had serious internal injuries and occasionally became delirious. They would send for a Korean marine officer to talk to him and calm him down. One of these medics slapped the Korean one day and SGT Sloane told me about it. I reported the incident along with what they had said about me and both of them were removed., I was told they were sent to infantry units. I hoped they were not sent out to be medics.

One night while I was sitting on the side of my bed writing a letter I dropped my pencil. Momentarily forgetting about my condition, I reached for it. I felt the sharp pain that I would have expected for a moment, then I felt this liquid-like warmth going through my body, and had instant knowledge that someone was praying for me and that God was healing my body as a result. I cannot describe the euphoric feeling that I had. The buzz from the daily shot of Demerol didn't come near it.

It was past lights out and everyone in the ward was apparently sleeping. I walked normally, not shuffling as I had been since the surgery, to the nurses station. When the nurse, a young second lieutenant, saw me, she looked frightened. I was so excited I couldn't think of the right thing to say but I felt like I had to tell someone. I started doing the exercise where you bend at the waist and touch your toes and saying over and over, "Someone is praying for me." This only seemed to increase the nurse's anxiety and she kept telling me I should be in bed. Finally, she spoke very authoritatively and insisted that I return to my bed.

I didn't sleep at all that night. I was too excited. As I lay there thinking about what had happened and realized the doctor would be around the next morning, I thought that if I told him what had happened he might refer me to a psychiatrist and my evacuation to Okinawa where Euna and Sherry were, would be delayed. I decided to say nothing.

When the Dr. came in and started to give me the Demerol, I told him I didn't need it. When he pulled away the gauze, he murmured that the infection was gone. A couple of days later he came in with two other surgeons and he told them about the infection disappearing overnight. They asked him to what did he attribute this, and he said that my chart showed that I had never had any antibiotics in my system before and I was responding well to the penicillin. They didn't ask my opinion and I was glad. By this time I was walking outside on the the hospital grounds every day trying to stay in shape.

After this I began to really pester the head nurse about getting on a medevac plane for Okinawa. She was a major and very compassionate with a good sense of humor. She cautioned me not to be too hopeful because the old colonel who was the hospital commander was strange. She told me that he was obsessed with a bump in the road on the way to the airfield, and had delayed the evacuation of some men who really needed to go because he was afraid they would be injured. She also told me she had evacuated some when he wasn't around or wasn't looking. Then she told me about getting the colonel's jeep driver to take her out to see the bump. She said they were driving along and he said, "There it was" but she didn't feel it so she had him to back up and hit it again. It was a hilarious story the way she told it and I had a good laugh, but I didn't take it too seriously. I assumed that like most funny stories, there was an element of exaggeration in it.

A few days later the nurse came in with a sad face and told me she had me on the list for a medevac that would be flying the following day, but the colonel had scratched me because of the bump. Colonel McKean, the commander of the 5th Special Forces group had been by to see me several times, and frankly I was surprised that he found the time. I think I found the answer to that puzzle recently in a book written by Charlie Beckwith, but that is a story for a later chapter. Colonel McKean had told me that if there was anything he could do to let him know and he seemed sincere. I called him after the nurse gave me that bad news and told him that I needed him to get the hospital commander to let me go to Okinawa. He took care of it and I left the next day on the medevac plane.

After I returned to Okinawa, I learned that Euna and Sherry were very close to being told that I was killed instead of wounded. The 1st Special Forces Group had a boat, the Green Beret, which was used for training. It would take about 200 passengers. Some of our teams in Vietnam had taken HAM radio sets with them and they would use them to call their wives on Okinawa by calling the Green Beret and having it patched in to the phone system.

Lieutenant Keller was in charge of the scuba team that was on the boat the next day after I was wounded. One of the teams had heard a report on the radio in Vietnam that Captain Tom Pusser was killed and I was wounded. They got it backwards and reported to the Green Beret that I was killed. Lieutenant Keller ordered the boat to the dock and was planning to go home, get his wife and visit Euna and Sherry. The Kellers were not close friends but they were our neighbors in the housing area. Fortunately he thought to double check his information by calling group headquarters and learned that I was wounded and not killed. My commanding officer and another officer did visit Euna and Sherry to tell them I was wounded.

In Dr. Hunter's book, *My Soul to Keep* he tells of returning to Vietnam in 1997 to check on his Montagnard assistant. He visited the Cathedral Notre Dame Church in

Saigon and lit a candle "for old comrades who died in the bloody jungled mountains of II Corps." He listed the names, "Bailey, Pusser, McBynum, White." Bailey was one of the NCOs on The "A" team at Plei Me who was killed before we arrived. Later in the book, Dr. Hunter tells of visiting the Vietnam War Memorial and finding the names of Bailey, Pusser and McBynum. I guess by then he had realized that I hadn't died. He had many Vietnamese casualties to care for that night at Plei Me.

My category as a patient was based on my chart, not my true condition and I was on a litter for the entire trip. I would have been more comfortable sitting in a seat, but they wouldn't allow it. I stayed two nights at Clark Air Force Base Hospital in the Philippines. I called Euna and told her I was on my way to Okinawa, and told her about my healing experience. She really prophesied in response to that news, although neither of us thought of it as that. She said that God must have some special plan for my life. I am sorry to say that it was several years before I really committed my life to God's will.

The second night at Clark Air Force Base Hospital I sneaked out and walked around the hospital grounds. When we landed at Kadena Air Base on Okinawa, there was a bus-type ambulance there to transport us to the hospital. When we arrived at the Hospital the surgeon that would be taking care of me, a major, met the bus. He looked at my chart and chatted with me. I let him know that my family was there and that I intended to go home. He chuckled and said it would be awhile before I could leave the hospital.

As the medic rolled me through the hospital corridor to take me to a room, I saw a telephone and asked him to stop. I called Euna at Special Services where she worked. She got excited and was going to come to the hospital right away, but I told her to first go home and get me some civilian clothes. I didn't have anything to wear except hospital pajamas. They put me in a room with two lieutenants; one army and one marine. The doctor's office was across the hall from the room. He came into the room and looked me over. Again I brought up the subject of going home and told him I was in good shape. He asked if I could walk to his office and I said certainly. He told me to come to his office in about five minutes. I walked normally into his office and immediately gave him the same demonstration that I gave to the nurse at 8th Field Hospital, bending down and touching my toes.

After looking me over and poking around for awhile, the doctor told his nurse to call my wife and tell her to bring me some clothes. I told her not to bother, that I had already done that. The doctor laughed and said, "You were pretty sure of yourself, weren't you." I said nothing, but the truth was I had made up my mind I was going home that night with or without permission. He gave Euna some instructions about taking care of me, and also told her about some restrictions of my activity which no young man who has been away from his wife for months would welcome.

After a few days in hospital on Okinawa I was released on convalescent leave. I ran into Sergeant Hubbard in the hospital. He went to Vietnam on the same plane with me, but was on a different "A" team. He was evacuated because of hepatitis. Hubbard was also going on convalescent leave. We had been fishing buddies there on Okinawa. He was married to an Okinawan woman and his brother-in-law owned a fishing boat. We could hire him and his boat and he furnished all the bait, for about $10 a day. He knew where the fish were and we could catch them until we were tired. Our maid, Ukiko was happy to clean my fish for half of them.

During our convalescence Sergeant Hubbard taught me how to play handball, a sport which I continued to play for years until I changed to racquetball.

I was discharged from the hospital in December and the surgeon gave me permission to make a parachute jump, even though it was less than two months since I was wounded, with the condition that I would jump in the South China Sea rather than on the coral rock field we called a drop zone. This was nothing new to me since I had made two water jumps while we were being familiarized with the steerable parachute. In fact I had become acquainted with Bryan Sutton, my battalion commander who was killed in action in 1971, on the boat, "Green Beret" during a two-hour ride back to port after one of the water jumps.

When I returned to duty I was assigned to the "C" Detachment staff as the S-4 (Supply Officer). Near Christmas time we had a formal Christmas banquet at the officers club. When Euna and I were dressed and ready to go, with me in my mess white uniform and Euna in a long formal gown, we stepped out the front door of our quarters to find all the neighborhood kids lined up on either side of the walk to see us. Sherry had run through the neighborhood and told the kids to come and see her mom and dad, all dressed up.

I was again to be surprised by becoming the focus of attention that evening, when the group commander Colonel Francis J. Kelly announced to about 200 officers and their wives that I was a hero and had been recommended for the silver star by Colonel "Bulldog" McKean, commander of the 5th Special forces Group in Vietnam. I never got the Silver Star but I was awarded the bronze star with "V" for valor. The award was presented at a parade by Major General Bruce E. Kendall, Deputy Commanding General of US Army Ryukyu.

Left to Right: Colonel Ladd, CO, 1st SFG, LTG Kendall, Captain White

Colonel McKean was a puzzlement to me. I was surprised that he took the time to give me so much attention while I was in 8th Field Hospital and called Colonel Kelly about the Silver Star recommendation. Then later in 1969-

70, I was advisor to the 20th Special Forces Group, Alabama National Guard. We made parachute jumps and had other training at Fort McClellan. Colonel McKean was the post commander there and the first time I went by to see him, he treated me like a long lost son. He let me know that anything I needed from Fort McClellan would be provided, and he instructed his operations officer concerning that.

For the entire time I had that assignment, all I had to do was call the operations officer and he would send a helicopter, ambulance and safety officer to the drop zone when we wanted to make a parachute jump. I had NCOs in Huntsville, Birmingham, Montgomery and Pell City. We would have our monthly meetings at McClellan and the Sergeants from Birmingham would bring a trailer load of parachutes and they would jump as many times as they liked. I didn't always jump with them.

I think I found the answer to the mystery when I recently read a book written by Colonel Charlie Beckwith. In the book, in his account of Plei Me, Beckwith wrote that the decision to send the three companies out against the dug in North Vietnamese, was Colonel McKean's decision. Beckwith said he advised against it but Colonel McKean ordered him to do it. If that happened, and I have no reason to doubt it, Colonel McKean was probably dealing with guilt. Tom Pusser was killed and I was wounded.

One day in 1967 I was having coffee with some other officers in the snack bar of Infantry Hall at Fort Benning when Charging Charlie Beckwith entered the room. He came straight to me and said, "I need you. I have taken charge of the Ranger training at Eglin Florida and I need you to help me." I replied, "Major I didn't attend Ranger School." He replied, "I don't give a ____ about that. You are a _____ (using a name that he used to describe those he approved of) and I need you." I am certain that

The Life Of A Soldier

had I agreed to go with him he could have arranged it, but I declined.

> While in the hospital on Okinawa, a letter caught up with me from my Sister, Eddie, that she had written in the early morning hours that coincided with the afternoon of 22 October when I was wounded and for awhile abandoned outside the Plei Me Special Forces Camp. She had awakened with a feeling that I was in trouble. She woke her husband and they prayed for me. Her husband went back to bed and she wrote a letter to me that very night. I have always believed that because of their prayers, angels were dispatched to protect me from further harm. I never knew who was praying for me when I was supernaturally healed in 8th Field Hospital, Vietnam, but by that time my family both on Okinawa and back in Alabama had been notified and they were all praying for me.

Appendix F

Significant Battles, Vietnam 1967-68

1. The Attack on 9th Company..........................391

2. Pete Egan's Cavalry Troop............................394

3. The VC in our Blocking Position......................397

4. The Battle at Bung School.............................403

5. The High ranking Hoi Chan...........................413

6. The Battle in the Rubber Plantation...................417

The Life Of A Soldier

The Attack on 9th Company

At 2100 hours on 29 December I received a call that the 3rd battalion, 8th regiment was under heavy attack. They were somewhere to the north of us. When they called, the VC were already coming over the walls. Artillery and air support was rushed to the area and the last I heard they were holding their own. A few minutes later a Popular force outpost just outside our area to the northwest came under attack and requested illumination support from us which we furnished with our 81 mm mortars. About 2300 hours the 4th Battalion of our regiment at Phu Hoa Dong, across the Saigon River and the district headquarters of the Phu Hoa District were attacked. I became convinced that we would be attacked before the night was over. I told the battalion commander and he agreed. I was already in my PJs and shower shoes, but I got dressed and moved to the command bunker with my carbine and gear. My men followed suit and the Dai-uy also got dressed. I stayed up listening to the other battles on the radio until about 0045 hours. The Battalion commander kept calling his companies and reminding them to remain alert. At about 0045 hours I decide to lie down and try to get some rest. at 0130 hours I heard firing nearby so I ran to the command post bunker. Our 9th Company was attacked by what was estimated to be a company size VC force with automatic weapons, mortars and rockets. The company commander and several soldiers were wounded in the initial assault according to the first reports. I called for every kind of support available but received none. It seems there were priorities everywhere that trumped our needs. After expending all of our 81mm mortar illumination rounds, I

391

finally got some artillery support from the First U.S. Division Artillery.

One of my NCOs, Platoon Sergeant Morales, fell apart when the attack came. Before I realized how panicked he was, he got on the radio to division and told them the camp was being overrun. I took the microphone from him and told the division tactical operations center to disregard. Then I ordered him not to touch the radio microphone again. To get him calmed down, I told him to go and make a pot of coffee. I was already worried about him. A day or two after I arrived we were ordered to monitor some of the night ambush patrols and report on them. I scheduled the three sergeants to take turns. When it became Morales' turn he tried to con me into taking his place. He said the senior advisor should set an example. I laughed and told him I had my turn on my previous tour in Vietnam. Then he said Sergeant Czap didn't have children and he did. I very emphatically told him that the life of a man with no children is every bit as valuable as the one with children. The next day after the attack, I overheard Morales telling someone that I had ice water in my veins. He said that with the camp about to be overrun, I calmly told him to make a pot of coffee.

I tried desperately to get a medevac helicopter to evacuate the wounded but to no avail. If I had a wounded American, they would have come immediately. The only wounded man we had that was really critical was the 9th Company commander. He died in the ambulance on the way to the hospital. He could have been saved, I believe, had we received the medevac. The theory was that the VNAF (Vietnamese Air Force) would do the medevac but they didn't show until late the next day.

The battalion commander ordered the other two companies to link up with 9th company and reinforce them. The battle actually only lasted a few minutes with sporadic firing until about 0400 hours. At daybreak the

The Life Of A Soldier

battalion commander and I moved to the area to assess the situation and reorganize the units. Bodies were still being found when we arrived. Two houses were destroyed by the VC rockets and three civilians were killed--a man, a woman and a child. The company reported five VC bodies were found, but the report was never confirmed. At about 0930 hours the regimental recon platoon arrived for reinforcement. We sent the survivors of 9th company back to the battalion command post. They seemed to be in a state of shock.

    At 1130 hours we returned to the C.P. to find the Corps Commander, Major General Tin, his advisor, Colonel Woelfer, the Division commander, Brigadier General Thuan , his advisor, Colonel Sonstielle and the regimental advisor, along with all of the aides, reporters, etc that accompany the generals, waiting for us at the C.P.

    The American Colonels wanted a briefing from me. I told them that while I appreciated their interest in us after the fact, I would have appreciated some help from the division advisory staff while the action was going on. I told them that I couldn't get artillery nor a medevac helicopter when I needed it. And that the wounded company commander died while being evacuated by ambulance. After they left, the division staff people started calling me trying to do the thing abbreviated CYA, Cover Your……posterior. Our final casualty count was 18 Killed and 9 wounded.

Euell White

Pete Egan's Cavalry Troop.

On 13 February our battalion participated in an operation with the Cavalry troop that Captain Pete Egan was advisor for and it was unusual in that we were very close to the action but couldn't fire a round.on my team at the Infantry school made me proud.

Since we were assigned a blocking mission, I thought it would be another day of boredom but didn't turn out that way. The operation started at 0800 hrs. We were in a blocking position from west to east along the road. Captain Pete Egan and his Cavalry troop was in a blocking position to the east of us from south to north. Another Calvary troop and the third Battalion of the 9th Regiment started search and clear operations from about 6 km north of us working to the south. It was a picnic until about 1215 while we were eating lunch when the VC opened up on Egan's troop from about 200 meters in front of us. I guess they had been there the whole time and could have fired at us anytime but apparently were waiting for bigger target.

It was the craziest affair I have ever seen. Even though they were right in front of us we couldn't fire at them because the vegetation was so thick and we couldn't see where they were. We couldn't close in on them because the east-west road was the fire coordination line and we had to stay south of it. A few rounds went over our heads but they could just as well have been from the tanks. When it started I thought it was our company on the right flank in contact. Egan was ordered to close in on the enemy and he did, while the infantry battalion and the other cavalry troop moved in from the north.

The Life Of A Soldier

One platoon of the enemy escaped to the woods where we had conducted operations the day before. I estimated their strength was at least one company and they were well dug in. They had 51 caliber machine guns and rockets. Pete lost two of his tanks. The entire crew was killed on one of them and he had one killed and three wounded from the other. There were also some infantry wounded. All of the casualties were ARVN. The other cavalry troop advisor temporarily lost his hearing from concussion. Egan went in with his tank to recover the wounded and protected them while an observer aircraft called in artillery within 50 meters of him. Then the Cobra helicopter gunships came and fired all sorts of stuff into the area. While they were doing this a flight of A1E Skyraiders flown by VNAF (Vietnamese Air Force) showed up Nobody knows where they came from and nobody could communicate with them. The Cobras moved out of the way and we marked all friendly positions with smoke.

The VNAF did an excellent job. They were so close we had bomb fragments flying into where we were but none of us were injured. We were in a cemetery and ducked behind tombs when they made their bomb runs. When the fighters spent all of their ordnance, the Cobras continued. When they finished theirs the artillery came back in and by that time it was 1600 hours and we were ordered to return for our night mission of securing highway 13. The firing in that area and adjacent areas was continuous for several hours.

I was really proud of Captain Pete Egan. He was one of the instructors on my team in the platoon tactics committee at the Infantry School. He was the instructor for the reinforced rifle platoon in the attack. He is of course, an armor officer.

Euell White

On 16 February I went by the Armored Cavalry compound to see Pete Egan, but he wasn't there. One of his NCOs showed me the final report of the operation. They killed 87 VC, captured 12 and a whole pile of weapons. Their casualties were 5 killed and 11 wounded. I took pictures of the tanks and armored personnel carriers that were destroyed. The enemy were NVA regulars who stopped over on their way to Saigon from I don't know where.

What the rockets do to armor.

The Life Of A Soldier

The VC In Our Blocking Position

We received an order to block for the Cavalry Squadron and the 3rd Battalion of the 9th Infantry Regiment, along a road running Northwest to Southeast about two kilometers Southeast of our location.

The maneuver forces were to start about two kilometers Northeast of us and sweep Southwest. My battalion Commander, Captain Hoang Kim Ninh, took the usual precautions of moving the two companies plus headquarters to a point about two kilometers behind or to the southwest of the blocking position and started to clear the area from there to the blocking position. The decision to do this saved us from being wiped out because we fought from 0800 hours until 1800 hours and never reached the blocking position. It turned out that the units we were supposed to block for blocked for us instead because the enemy was occupying our blocking position. I will attempt to describe the events in chronological order.

We arrived at our starting point along Highway 13 at about 0745 and started moving toward our blocking position. I had my one Noncommissioned Officer, Sergeant Czap, who was the only American with me then, with one of the rifle companies and I stayed with the battalion headquarters following up behind the companies. At exactly 0800 hours one of the companies spotted an enemy rocket gunner aiming at them They killed the gunner and captured the rocket launcher and one rocket. Two other VC (Viet Cong) who were with the rocket launcher ran behind a building then turned and ran right in front of the other rifle company and were killed.

At about 0900 the company which Sergeant Czap was with, started receiving automatic weapons fire about 500 meters from our assigned blocking position. They captured a prisoner and he told the location of what he said was a battalion. The remainder of the day was spent moving up and maneuvering to the flank of the VC. Then calling in support and moving again. We had two ARVN artillery units and one U.S. unit firing for us at the same time. We had helicopter gun ships three different times. We had two U.S. air strikes with jet fighter planes and one Vietnamese Air Force (VNAF) air strike with A-1E Sky Raiders.

Three of our soldiers were wounded but none of them critically. One of the wounded soldiers was hit in the arm shattering the upper arm bone but he killed two VC with his M-1 rifle after he was wounded. I recommended him for a U.S. medal.

After the last air strike at about 1630 hours, Captain Ninh decided it was time to quit. I told him we must go in and search the areas where the artillery and air strikes were fired, or at least regain contact so that we could get a team of Cobra helicopter gun ships which were on standby but wouldn't come until we had contact. Captain Ninh expressed his concern about taking too many casualties. I told him I didn't like casualties either but it was our duty to go in there. This was the first time I ever got him mad at me. He said "What about Sergeant Czap?, He may be wounded or killed." I replied, "He is willing to go because he knows it is his duty." Then Ninh thought he had me. He said "I will call 10th Company Commander and have him ask Sergeant Czap if he wants to go, and if he says yes I will order the companies to move." I heard him call and all the Vietnamese soldiers near enough to hear what was going on laughed. I understood what Captain Ninh said, but

The Life Of A Soldier

my interpreter, Sergeant Tu told me anyway. He told the Company Commander to ask Sergeant Czap if he wanted to go. (I didn't call Sergeant Czap to tell him what was going on because I knew what he would say). Sergeant Czap told the Company Commander essentially the same thing I told the Battalion Commander. Both companies were moving within five minutes.

The companies moved past the area where they had their last contact, finding nothing but empty bunkers. Then they started receiving automatic weapons fire and the companies started maneuvering like professionals. Then the VC circled behind them and it looked like they really had them. At this time, I must admit, I had some misgivings when Sergeant Czap reported he had contact to the front and to the rear, but about that time the Cobra fire team arrived and we already had an observation aircraft which we called ALOFT, on station.

I told the battalion commander to have both companies mark their flanks with smoke and told Sergeant Czap to direct the ALOFT who was controlling the Cobra team. They really tore them up. We had been using the UH-1 which we call the Huey and it did a great job, but the COBRA is so superior to the Huey it is beyond description. I am sure more VC were killed in that last action than were killed all day with all the air strikes and artillery because they were caught out of their fortifications.

We pulled out at 1800 hours while the Cobra strike was still in progress, to return to our primary mission of securing a portion of Highway 13. As we left, the ALOFT called in 8-inch artillery.

An incident that happened that day is humorous but also illustrates the vast gap between the staff people and those who were with the battalions. After we briefly interrogated the prisoner we captured and learned from him the designation of his unit, I requested a helicopter to evacuate him to division. Someone on the intelligence staff at division wanted a reliability rating on the information we obtained from the prisoner, who had told us that it was a particular battalion we were up against. My reply to him was that if he would wait awhile I would ask the VC Sergeant Major to hold a muster formation so that we could determine exactly the strength of his unit. I didn't hear anymore about the reliability rating.

This operation tended to prove my opinion that a good ARVN battalion properly supported, could be as effective as a US unit the same size. Although I had the battalion commander mad at me for awhile, he was really in good spirits the following day.

Another incident that afternoon while I had both US and VNAF fighters on station and was trying to get it straightened out as to which would make the first strike and at the same time get a checkfire on the artillery so they wouldn't hit the planes, involved the TOC (tactical Operations Center) duty officer at division. He started bugging me for petty details. The division senior advisor, Colonel Sonstielle, was flying around in his chopper and apparently had just tuned to our frequency. He said: "Who is the senior advisor to the unit in contact?" I replied, "Painful Grips 46" (which was my call sign). Then the colonel said, "Everyone else stay the hell off the air so he can do his job." Needless to say that silenced the idle chatter on the radio.

Another item worthy of note was the apparent stupidity of the regimental commander. Although we were working under the operational control of the commander of the armored cavalry regiment for the operation, our regimental commander, Colonel Chong, ordered the battalion commander to use trucks and go down the road where we were supposed to block. If we had done that I probably wouldn't be writing this today. We would have been ambushed and slaughtered on the trucks because the enemy was there.

The battalion commander ignored his order and we went on foot, clearing the area from highway 13 to that position. In spite of these facts, the battalion commander had to go to regiment after the operation to be punished for disobeying an order. He was given a suspended sentence of 15 days in jail. This was only a paper exercise, but it could have hurt his chances for promotion. It didn't seem to bother him. It was more of a nuisance than anything else. He would always find a way to avoid doing something stupid that unnecessarily endangers his men.

From My journal on 26 February 1968

I went to sleep at about 2330 hours last night and slept like a baby until about five minutes ago when I awakened like I had a full night's sleep and it was time to get up. Now that my body and mind is rested some, I want to fill in some of the gaps I left last night. First of all, I want to say that both of the company commanders were like tigers all day. Neither of them hesitated to close with the enemy. The 9th Company commander joined the battalion only a few days ago. He was kicked out of Division Reconnaissance Company, but probably only because of a personality clash. The 10th Company commander (Lieutenant Tien) is the Battalion Commander's son-in-law. He has always been eager to mix it up with the VC. The conventional opinion of Americans in the American units is that the ARVN are cowardly and can't be depended on to fight. The ARVN commanders have their own unique problems that American commanders don't have, which I won't go into at this time. I pushed Captain Ninh into taking what he considered a big gamble with the lives of his troops and with his own standing as a commander. He came out of it "smelling like a rose" as the old saying goes. No other battalion in this task force since this thing began has been exposed to so much combat without having anyone killed. I think he realizes that the NCOs I have assisting me(at least two of the three) are valuable to him. Before I came here the NCOs stayed right with the senior advisor and were more or less flunkies for him. I have given them a job to support the mission and they like it better…....I am proud of this battalion and I don't want to ever again hear anyone make a statement that the Vietnamese soldier will not fight…I am recommending Sergeant Czap for a medal.

The Life Of A Soldier

Battle at Bung School.

In the late afternoon or early evening of 4 march we moved our command post to the Bung school. It is just north of the town of Bung on Highway 13. We had a good defense organized except for fortifications. We had open fields for at least 300 meters for about 250 degrees around us which gave us good observation and fields of fire. We had the troops dig foxholes and selected two bunkers across the highway from the school behind a house for our fighting command post. I really wanted to have that as our command post from the beginning but Captain Ninh decided to stay in the school. I had no choice because I needed to be near him to provide the air and artillery support should we have a contact. We had learned the lesson about sleeping in buildings in December when one of our company commanders had set up in a house and it cost him his life as well as the others that were in the house with him.

Bung School

Euell White

The only American with me was Sergeant Ludwig. I also had with me my interpreter, Sergeant Tu, and my two houseboys. Sergeant Ludwig and the others were in one of the School rooms. My Vietnamese jeep driver Louie had brought my folding cot and I set it up on the porch. I recommended against sleeping in the room to Sergeant Ludwig and the others but I didn't order them.

At 0050 hours on 5 March just as I lay down on my cot after writing a report that was due to Division, the VC initiated their attack. I heard one rifle shot then a rocket came in the window of the room where Sergeant Ludwig and the others were. I don't know for sure how many rockets were fired into the building, but they initiated a ground assault from the opposite direction also. Immediately we were receiving fire from automatic weapons as well as rockets. The first rocket wounded Sergeant Ludwig and my houseboy who had been with us only a few days, and me.

The Life Of A Soldier

Sergeant Ludwig died a few minutes later. The rocket fragments had made a big hole in his head and small holes were all over his body. I was hit in the right arm in two places. The wounds were small but deep. When I was hit the concussion stunned me for an instant, but I regained my senses and got on the radio to call for help. While I was on the radio, hunkered down behind the masonry wall of the porch my dog Lady was jumping all over me trying to get in my lap. Then I felt someone tugging at my pants leg. I first thought it was Lady then turned around and saw one of my houseboys, the cook, who is like a mother to us. He said Dai-uy, Dai-uy, Trung-si Ludwig bi-thuong. (Captain, Captain, Sergeant Ludwig is wounded). Then I saw Sergeant Ludwig lying there a few feet away from me on his back with a big pool of blood beside him. I had a medical kit on my pistol belt with several bandages, morphine, etc. I moved over to where he was, opened the kit and laid it out beside him. Then I started looking for his wounds. It was dark and in the confusion I couldn't find my flashlight. While I was feeling all over him trying to find the wounds, another rocket hit right above me and the blast from it blew away all my medical supplies.

Sergeant Ludwig

The Life Of A Soldier

About that time our Vietnamese Medical officer arrived and took over and I returned to the radio. Captain Ninh, the battalion commander, was sleeping in a room three doors from where I was. Since I hadn't heard from him I assumed he was either dead or badly wounded, but he came crawling up to me with his radio operator and body guard. He said, "we move to bunkers." He was wounded, but not seriously. We had to crawl and drag our radios across the school yard under grazing automatic weapons fire. (Grazing fire is fire that is low enough if you stand up you will be hit). My interpreter, houseboy/cook, the operations officer and Heavy Weapons officer followed behind us. While this was going on the troops were fighting off the attack.

When I was about half way across the schoolyard, crawling as low as a snake to stay below the grazing fire, dragging my radio by the handset cord, the radio operator at the division TOC (Tactical Operations Center), called me and requested an 11- line spot report. This is a report that answers eleven questions, such as the time of the contact, the direction, the size of the enemy force, etc. My reply was that I didn't have time to give the report at the moment because my priority was to stay alive and I would give it later. The radio operator replied that he needed the report now because he was going off duty in a few minutes and he would be chewed out if he didn't have it.

Later on that day when I went back to division for medical treatment for my wounds, I tried to find the Duty Officer that was on duty. I didn't blame the radio operator but the Duty Officer should have known better. Apparently someone else had heard this conversation and expected me to react to it. No one would tell me who that officer was.

Euell White

This again illustrates the vast gap between those of us out with the troops and those at division trying to tell us what to do. They didn't know what it is like except for a few that have been out there themselves.

This turned out to be a pretty significant battle. The enemy had a battalion but only committed two companies against us. I had good support all night until daylight. It seems impossible for one man to coordinate and control so many things at one time, but we had no foul-ups. I had continuous support from the observation plane which we call ALOFT. This is a single engine plane and very maneuverable. The pilot serves as the go-between for the other air support and for the artillery. We had Helicopter gun ships, U.S. artillery support and two SPOOKIES. The SPOOKY is a C-47 cargo plane specially rigged with all kinds of guns, rockets, etc. that provides its own battlefield illumination. They have enough ordnance to last for two hours or more. We also had two U.S. medevacs for the wounded. Probably we wouldn't have had the medevacs if Sergeant Ludwig and I hadn't been wounded. I didn't get on the helicopters nor did I put Sergeant Ludwig on one since he was already dead by the time they arrived.

The companies fought well. The contact stopped about 0300 hours. The enemy was trying to withdraw, but I pretended we still had contact until daylight because the rules of engagement say that you can only have the SPOOKIES when you are in contact. About an hour before daylight I had the SPOOKY and everything else to stop firing but keep the area illuminated. Then we started searching for weapons and bodies.

At daylight, the Armored Cavalry and another Infantry Battalion were committed to search the area of the enemy's withdrawal route where I had directed a great deal of artillery fire and fire from the spookies. The final results were: Friendly casualties: Killed: 1 American, and 6 ARVN. Wounded: 1 American, 11 ARVN. (Many more of

The Life Of A Soldier

the ARVN were lightly wounded. They didn't report them unless they were evacuated). Enemy casualties: Killed: 38 (bodies actually found). Captured: 5. It is assumed there were many more killed that they evacuated as well as many wounded. Weapons and equipment captured: 19 machine guns, 5 Rocket launchers, various rifles, etc., 60 mortar rounds, 60 hand grenades, 13 rockets, 2 bangalore torpedoes, various items of military clothing and equipment. We killed both company commanders.

At about 7 A.M. on 5 March the Regimental Advisor, Major Steffaniw (my boss), came and brought one of His Sergeants who was with me before, to stay with the Battalion while I went to Division at Lam Son for medical treatment. I also went to Phu Loi (the U.S. First Division compound) to graves registration with the doctor to identify SGT Ludwig's body and make a death certificate. He had been evacuated by ambulance. After seeing how badly he was hit I realized that he was already beyond saving when I got to him.

The doctor at Lam Son tried to remove a fragment from my arm after x-raying and finding it. I am not sure he got it out. He gave me a shot of penicillin and some penicillin pills to take. I cleaned up at Lam Son and tried to eat lunch, but couldn't, then came back to the battalion.

I had an unpleasant incident to deal with that morning after the battle was over and the bodies of the NVA soldiers were laid out so that the locals could reclaim any from their families. A young captain, whose name I can't remember, who was the pilot of the ALOFT which is a single engine fixed wing observation plane, came down in a jeep and was planning to run over the bodies of the enemy dead with the jeep. When I was told I went out and stopped him. He was like a mad man, yelling and screaming with a hatred I had not seen demonstrated. I warned him that he would end up in prison if he did this.

Finally when I got him calmed down I told him it is not necessary nor healthy to build up a personal hatred against the enemy soldiers. I warned him that I was making a record of this and if I ever heard of him attempting anything like that again I would press the issue.

Weapons Captured during battle at Bung School

The VC attempted to attack us again the night of 5 march, but because of good intelligence from an old man who was a lieutenant in the local regional force, we were warned of the attack and were able to stop them with artillery before they could initiate an assault. I didn't sleep that night. By 7 March my arm was extremely swollen from the shoulder to the fingertips and I hadn't slept a wink since the evening of 3 March. I had been unable to remember to take the pills.

I went back to the dispensary at division. The doctor wasn't in and his NCO assistant, a Master Sergeant, recommended that I go to the 1st US Division at Phu Loi and see a real doctor. I didn't need to ask him to explain

The Life Of A Soldier

what he meant by the words "real doctor." I followed his advice and went to the Phu Loi Dispensary. As soon as the doctor there saw me he wanted to put me on a chopper for the hospital at Long Binh, but I told him I couldn't go until I arranged for someone to look after the battalion. The doctor asked me if I had anyone who could administer injections and I told him my Vietnamese medic could do it. He gave me a bag full of disposable syrettes of penicillin and made me promise to return early the following morning to be flown to Long Binh.

I called Major Steffaniw and told him the situation. He told me to go to division and sleep in a bed that night, and assured me he would take care of the battalion. I Told him to leave Sergeant Czap with the battalion and Sergeant Morales with the company at Anson, I didn't trust Morales enough to leave him with the battalion. I went to the medics at division and they gave me the shots, then went to the officers quarters—-the same building that I stayed in for the few days of my processing when I arrived.

There was an elderly Vietnamese lady who cleaned the barracks, and did washing and ironing for the officers. All of the officers called her "Mama San" which was a carry-over from the occupation of Japan. I addressed her politely as "Ba" and conversed with her in Vietnamese. I treated her as I would have wanted my own mother treated. I always thanked her for what she did and paid her well. Even after I went out to the battalion, I often took my laundry to her.

When I entered the barracks on 7 March, she was there and when she saw my arm she began weeping. This caught me by surprise and I had difficulty restraining my own tears. I didn't get any sleep that night because the pain was too intense. I kept my word the next morning and reported to the Phu Loi dispensary for transport to Long Binh.

When I arrived at Long Binh the surgeon there asked me when this happened and what treatment I had received for it. When I told him he asked me who was this idiot that tried to remove the fragments and gave me pills to take for the infection? I told him but wished later that I hadn't. He called that idiot doctor and chewed him out. The doctor called on the phone every day to check on me and always wanted to talk to me.

The diagnosis was Cellulitis (infection under the skin), and the surgeon said that had I waited one more day to get treatment, I would have lost my right arm. He immediately started giving me antibiotics intravenously. They put me in a maxillofacial ward because that was where they had a vacant bed. This is where they reconstruct faces that have been blown away. I was glad to get out of there, and if I had any inclination toward self-pity that would have cured it. I have seen movies of previous wars where the wounded were crying and moaning, but I didn't hear any of that from these men who had their faces blown away.

On 14 March Major Steffaniw showed up in a helicopter to visit me as I was checking out. I went with him to visit the 4th battalion across the Saigon River, then back to regimental headquarters where my jeep came to pick me up.

The Life Of A Soldier

The High -Ranking Hoi Chan.

On 19 April we kicked off a big operation which would have really amounted to something had it not been called off just as it was a getting started good. My battalion had one company blocking and the other two companies were to land by boat. One company each from the popular forces and the division reconnaissance company also landed by boat. The 4th battalion was blocking and one company of the 1st battalion was flying around in helicopters as a mobile reserve. The operation started at 0730 hours with an artillery preparation followed by three flights of fighter planes. The first wave landed by boat at about 1000 hrs right after the last air strike. The first wave consisted of one of our companies, the popular force company and the recon company. There were not enough boats for all of us in one trip.

My lieutenant, Lieutenant Matt., went with the company in the first wave with the battalion XO and one company. The popular force Company made contact very shortly after landing. Our company was waiting on the beach for us to land. Just as we were unloading the boat with our other rifle company and headquarters, and I was already on the ramp to exit the boat, Captain Ninh took hold of my flak jacket and pulled me back into the boat. The boat raised the ramp, backed off to the middle of the river and stopped. Captain Ninh said "operation fini" then he started talking on the radio again. I called Major Steffaniw on the radio and asked him what was going on. He told me our orders were to withdraw all elements and return to the starting point. He said he could not tell me more than that. The popular force company which was in contact had a hard time disengaging and evacuating their wounded, and it was about 1500 by the time we got everyone back to where we loaded the boat.

I tried to think of reasons why they would pull us out of an operation like that. I decided that either Johnson had called a cease-fire or there was something big going on some place else where we were needed. I didn't find out what it was until I returned to the regimental command post.

A VC lieutenant colonel turned himself in to division as a hoi chan on the Chieu Hoi (open arms) program and gave them the location of a regimental headquarters near Paris Tan Quy and division wanted us to take it that day. Those people on the division staff didn't realize that you can't just turn around and leave a battle when you are in contact with the enemy. It was too late to do it that day by the time we got everyone out and back to base, so it was scheduled for the next day.

My battalion was in a blocking position for the operation. Although the operation on the 19th was cut short the results were not bad. The popular force company suffered 5 wounded and one killed. They killed 4 VC and captured one as well as a few weapons. Our 9th company which was to block, accompanied by Sergeant Czap, ran into a large cache on the way and spent the day digging out weapons and ammunition. They captured 23, 122mm rockets, a whole pile of B-40 rockets ,some Chinese rifles, mortar ammunition, etc. A Chinook helicopter had to make 2 trips to haul it all out. The division recon company found a cache containing 1,000, one-pound blocks of C-4 plastic explosives and 200 Kilos of TNT. They had 2 wounded by friendly fire from a chopper. The Hoi Chan also told division that an attack on Saigon was planned for 22 April by a regiment with a strength of over 1,000.

The operation which we started on 20 April to wipe out a VC Regimental command post lasted until 1800 hrs 23 April. for my battalion. We were in a blocking

The Life Of A Soldier

position to the west and a battalion of the US 25th Division was blocking to the south. The Cavalry of this division blocked to the north. The 4th battalion of the 9th regiment landed by boat from the Saigon River to the east, and was supposed to search the objective area. The objective area was a road which junctioned Highway 8-A with streams running in from the Saigon River all-around. According to the Hoi Chan there was a regimental headquarters there with tunnels in under the road and bunkers throughout the area. I predicted that we would end up doing the 4th of the 9th's job for them and we did. They stumbled around and made contact with three VC and let them get away.

About two hours prior to darkness division ordered our battalion into the area and withdrew everyone else. To get there from where we were we had to cross two streams, one of which we had to swim. We were all completely wet by the time we arrived at the objective area. We were ordered to defend there that night and search the area the following day. When we first got there I was convinced that the Hoi Chan had given us a complete bum steer. The tunnels under the road idea was ridiculous. Water was up to the shoulders of the road on both sides and the surrounding area was wet rice paddies. However there was a big headquarters there before.

One of our ambushes made contact that night, killing one VC and captured one weapon. The VC was a platoon leader according to his papers. We also had one soldier killed. The next day we searched the same area which the 4th of the 9th supposedly searched. We found the headquarters in a house. They had a large flag about 8 by 4 feet on the wall, and 2 brand-new Chinese made AM/FM radio sets. We also found various uniforms and other military equipment in the house. We burned the house after removing everything. Then we flushed three more VC out of the thickets and killed them. We stayed there again that night and searched again on the 22nd but found nothing else.

The documents we found in the house indicated it was a sector headquarters rather than a regimental one. I think that when the Lieutenant Colonel disappeared they moved out assuming he had turned himself in, and left the platoon leader and a few men behind.

I mentioned that we found a cache which included 122mm rockets. On April 20 an ARVN lieutenant from division G2, along with six soldiers came and picked up the captured material and took it back to division. While they were unloading it a soldier dropped one of the VC grenades. It went off and set off the whole mess. They were all killed and other people nearby were wounded. The battalion commander and I agreed that from now on we would destroy captured grenades in place rather than turn them in. They were too unpredictable and unstable, especially the homemade ones.

The Life Of A Soldier

The Battle in the Rubber Plantation.

On 5 May the 1st and 4th battalions had a big battle. That morning a Chieu Hoi turned himself in to the 1st Battalion at Tan Than Dong. They sent a jeep to take him to regiment and the Jeep was ambushed on the way. It turned out that there was a VC or NVA battalion in the rubber plantation about 800 meters from the regimental headquarters at Paris Tan Quy, about 5 km south of Phu Hoa Dong, where we were located. The 1st and 4th battalions, supported by several air strikes, light fire teams (2 Huey gunships), and artillery, fought them until dark that night. . I talked to Captain Rickman the 4th battalion advisor on the radio and got the casualty count. The 1st Battalion had three wounded, and the 4th had three killed and 17 wounded including the battalion commander. The pilots estimated the enemy dead at least 100. They kept artillery in the area all night and searched the following day.

> I noted in my journal on 5 May: *I'm happy for Rickman. This is the nearest thing to the victory his Battalion has had. He had just had this battalion commander a few days. The regimental XO took over the Battalion this morning when the commander was wounded.*

On 6 May my battalion went out to Paris Tan Quy to help with the mop up and I was filled in on all the details. The Regimental base camp was located right at the edge of a rubber plantation. Highway 15 going from Paris Tan Quy to Tan Than Dong where the 1st Battalion base was located runs right through the center of the rubber plantation.

At 0500 hrs on 5 May the VC started a heavy mortar bombardment on regimental headquarters killing 5 and wounding 20. The mortar fire also destroyed a brand new jeep that was supposed to be mine. While the regimental CP was distracted by the mortar attack and evacuating the wounded afterwards, a North Vietnamese battalion moved into the rubber plantation and started digging in. Apparently their intent was to launch a ground attack and the holes they were digging were to fall back to.

Regiment had no idea that they were there and had no plans to search that area yesterday. Most of the NVA soldiers were dressed in uniforms the same color as US and ARVN fatigues. At about 0700 a jeep from 1st battalion at Tan Than Dong was bringing a Hoi Chan to regiment. The driver noticed soldiers in the rubber plantation but he thought they were soldiers from the regiment.

The NVA could have had the element of surprise and would have had a good chance of success had it not been for one of the NVA soldiers who couldn't resist firing his AK machine rifle at the jeep. The driver ducked down, floor-boarded the jeep and made it to regiment. Neither he nor the Hoi Chan were injured although two other men in the jeep were. The 4th battalion, located with regiment, moved out immediately and engaged the NVA.

The 1st battalion at Tan Than Dong engaged them from the opposite direction. The battle lasted all day long with tactical air, artillery and light fire teams. Both the 1st and 4th battalions withdrew by dark and artillery was fired into the plantation periodically through the night. The aircraft pilots estimated at least 100 VC killed, judging from the bodies they could see from the air.

At about 0500 hours on 6 May the VC fired about 100 rounds of 82mm mortar into the 1st Battalion base camp. The senior advisor, Captain Bedford, from New Bedford Massachusetts, who by the way has had 2 lieutenants and 1 Sergeant killed since I have been here, was seriously wounded in the head. He didn't have a lieutenant so they sent a helicopter to take my lieutenant (Lieutenant Matt) to replace Captain Bedford. I knew Matt would do a good job.

The 1st battalion blocked one end of the plantation while my battalion and the 4th searched and cleared out the plantation. My battalion killed 2 VC and captured one. Between my battalion and the 4th we found 26 VC bodies of VC who were killed the day before. Only a few weapons were found. Apparently the survivors got away with most of the bodies and weapons. We had one soldier killed and one wounded.

On 7 may a battalion of VC (or NVA) moved back into rubber plantation next to regimental headquarters. Regiment had the 4th battalion with them for security and I couldn't understand how they let a battalion move in that close to them. The 1st and 4th battalions supported by armored personnel carriers fought them all day.

The VC just wouldn't give up on the rubber plantation between Paris Tan Quy and Tan Than Dong. After being defeated there from 5-7 May, they moved back in there the evening of 13 May and mortared the 1st battalion again. Our regiment started another operation in the rubber plantation They had the 1st and 4th battalions and an armored Cavalry troop from the US 25th Division. Together they came up with a body count of 69, captured several prisoners, two 82mm mortars, 2 rocket launchers, 125 mortar shells, and several rockets.

Euell White

www.ingramcontent.com/pod-product-compliance
Lightning Source LLC
Chambersburg PA
CBHW020729160426
43192CB00006B/158